International Criminal Justice Series

Volume 37

The *International Criminal Justice Series* aims to create a platform for publications covering the entire field of international criminal justice. It, therefore, deals with issues relating, among others, to:

- the work of international criminal courts and tribunals;
- transitional justice approaches in different countries;
- international anti-corruption and anti-money laundering initiatives;
- the history of international criminal law.

It is peer-reviewed and seeks to publish high-quality works emanating from excellent scholars.

Editorial Office

Prof. Dr. Moritz Vormbaum
University of Münster
Faculty of Law
Bispinghof 24-25
48143 Münster, Germany
vormbaum@uni-muenster.de

Melville Ludwig Jacobs

The Consequences of Non-cooperation with the International Criminal Court

An Analysis Through the Lens of General International Law

ASSER PRESS

Springer

Melville Ludwig Jacobs
Faculty of Law
Palacký University Olomouc
Olomouc, Czech Republic

ISSN 2352-6718 ISSN 2352-6726 (electronic)
International Criminal Justice Series
ISBN 978-94-6265-674-1 ISBN 978-94-6265-675-8 (eBook)
https://doi.org/10.1007/978-94-6265-675-8

Published by T.M.C. ASSER PRESS, The Hague, The Netherlands www.asserpress.nl
Produced and distributed for T.M.C. ASSER PRESS by Springer-Verlag Berlin Heidelberg

This research was supported by the Palacký University Young Researcher Grant (Grant No. JG_2023_043).

This T.M.C. ASSER PRESS imprint is published by the registered company Springer-Verlag GmbH, DE part of Springer Nature
The registered company address is: Heidelberger Platz 3, 14197 Berlin, Germany

Foreword

At its core, the motivation for this book by Melville Jacobs, *The Consequences of Non-cooperation with the ICC: An Analysis of Frameworks under General International Law*, is, to borrow from the famous words of the UN Charter, "to save succeeding generations from the [inhumanity and] scourge" of conflict.

I know this, not only because I have read the book, but also because I was there at its conception. The initial version of this book was written as a Ph.D. thesis under my supervision and I can confirm that every step of the way, Melville was motivated by a desire to ensure that those that commit serious international crimes such as war crimes, crimes against humanity, genocide and aggression face the consequences of their actions, and a desire to remove obstacles in the path of accountability.

The importance of this noble goal can hardly be overstated given the horrendous mass sufferings on display on a daily basis reminding us that our generation has not been saved from the scourge of inhumanity arising from conflict. In most of these conflicts, accountability remains, at best an exception, and at worst, a hollow promise. The cooperation committed by States to promote accountability is often sacrificed at the altar of political considerations—and I would add, political considerations include double standards.

Against this background of impunity, Melville Jacobs' book focuses its attention on the promotion of accountability in those situations covered by the International Criminal Court. In particular, it seeks to clarify the consequences for States Parties that fail to cooperate with the International Criminal Court in breach of their obligation under the Statute (or possibly under the UN Charter). But it does so in particular through the lens of the Responsibility to Protect, as part of the fabric of general international law, as well as the traditional framework for State responsibility. The book is, of course, not oblivious to the, let's say, ambiguous legal character and status of the Responsibility to Protect and addresses this head on.

The doctrine of the Responsibility to Protect places a responsibility upon States and the larger international community to protect populations from genocide, war crimes, crimes against humanity and ethnic cleansing. The doctrine sits comfortably within the discussion of the Rome Statute in part because of the large overlap between

Rome Statute crimes and atrocities against which the Responsibility to Protect is intended to protect.

Placing the statutory duty to cooperate under the Rome Statute within the context of the Responsibility to Protect, the book attempts to construct consequences for non-cooperation with the International Criminal Court.

Despite his deep desire for a world without conflict—a world in which the commission of atrocities is met by immediate accountability—I am well aware that Dr. Jacobs is not blind to the political realities on the ground. He is fully aware that, as we have recently seen, States that have called on cooperation with the Court can suddenly change their tune when it is they that are called upon to cooperate with the Court. I hope this will not dampen his deep desire but lead him, as he moves into the second part of his academic life, to find even more novel ways of securing cooperation in a divided world.

The Hague, The Netherlands
May 2025

Dire Tladi
Judge of the International Court
of Justice (ICJ)

Acknowledgments

There are several groups of people who I would like to thank for their support and assistance while developing this text.

Firstly, I would like to thank my LL.D. (Ph.D.) supervisor, Prof. (now ICJ Judge) Dire Tladi, for the countless hours spent guiding me to writing the best thesis I could. I am thankful for his kindness and his broad knowledge of international law.

Secondly, I would like to thank my family for supporting me on my academic journey. Especially my mother: Elizabeth, and my father: Ludwig, for always being there for me and encouraging me to pursue further education. I would also like to thank my siblings, Gisela and Joshke, for their moral support and staying up with me while I wrote. (I also appreciate the countless cups of tea.)

An incredibly special mention goes to my grandmother, Lorraine van Der Spuy. I would not have started my studies if it weren't for her. She encouraged me to study law when I had no idea what I wanted to study. She has been present throughout my academic career and I appreciate her continued support.

I would also like to thank T.M.C. Asser Press for agreeing to take on my monograph. I hope that this book will contribute to the further development of international law.

Finally, I would like to thank Palacký University Olomouc for assisting me with resources during the final stages of writing this book.

Contents

1 Introduction—The ICC's Failure to Effectively Address Non-cooperation 1
1.1 Background and Scope of Book 2
1.1.1 Frameworks for Non-cooperation and their Ineffectiveness 3
1.1.2 The Search for More Effective Responses to Non-cooperation 4
1.1.3 The Responsibility to Protect and General International Law 5
1.2 Objectives and Structure of this Book 6
1.3 Significance of this Book 7
1.3.1 Narrow Approaches to Non-cooperation 8
1.3.2 The Relationship between the ICC and R2P 8
1.3.3 Individual State Responses to Non-cooperation 9
1.4 Delimitations 9
1.4.1 Specific Aspects of Cooperation 9
1.4.2 Head of State Immunity and Claims of African Bias 10
1.4.3 Amendment of the Rome Statute 11
1.4.4 Regional Tools for Enhancing the ICC's Cooperation Frameworks 12
1.4.5 The Use of Force as a Remedy for Addressing Non-cooperation 14
1.5 Chapter Outline 14
References 15

2 Frameworks for Cooperation under the Rome Statute 17
2.1 Introduction 18
2.2 Cooperation 18
2.2.1 The Obligation to Cooperate 19
2.2.2 Forms of Cooperation 20

2.2.3 Non-cooperation ... 21
2.3 Case Law on Non-cooperation ... 23
2.3.1 The Situation in Sudan: The Failure to Arrest Al-Bashir ... 24
2.3.2 Upcoming Non-cooperation Responses: The Situation in Ukraine ... 34
2.3.3 Case Law on the Discretionary Powers of the Court ... 38
2.4 Analysing the Content of Current Non-cooperation Case Law ... 41
2.4.1 The Court's Exercise of Discretion ... 42
2.4.2 The Standard of a Failure to Cooperate ... 42
2.5 Conclusion ... 44
References ... 44

3 The Role of the Assembly of States Parties and the UN Security Council in Responding to Instances of Non-cooperation ... 47
3.1 Introduction ... 48
3.2 The Assembly of States Parties ... 48
3.2.1 The Assembly Procedures Relating to Non-cooperation ... 49
3.2.2 The Bureau Toolkit ... 51
3.2.3 Analysing the Assembly's Responses to Non-cooperation ... 54
3.2.4 Highlighting the Need to Strengthen Assembly Responses to Non-cooperation ... 56
3.2.5 Analysing the Effectiveness of the Assembly's Responses to Non-cooperation ... 59
3.3 The UN Security Council ... 60
3.3.1 The Security Council's Mandate Towards the ICC ... 61
3.3.2 Analysing the Security Council's Responses to Non-cooperation ... 66
3.3.3 Enhancing Security Council Responses to Non-cooperation ... 71
3.4 Conclusion ... 74
References ... 76

4 Enhancing Responses to Non-cooperation Through the Responsibility to Protect ... 79
4.1 Introduction ... 80
4.2 The Origins of R2P ... 81
4.2.1 Origins: Humanitarian Intervention ... 81
4.2.2 Origins: The International Commission on Intervention and State Sovereignty ... 83
4.2.3 Origins: Reports of the Secretary General ... 85
4.2.4 The Recognition and Development of R2P ... 86
4.3 The Pillars of R2P ... 89
4.3.1 Pillar One ... 90
4.3.2 Pillar Two ... 90

4.3.3 Pillar Three ... 91
4.3.4 Assessing the Implementation of the Three Pillars of R2P ... 92
4.4 R2P and the ICC ... 93
4.4.1 The ICC in R2P Texts ... 93
4.4.2 Overlaps and Differences Between the ICC and R2P ... 94
4.4.3 The ICC Analysed through the Lens of the Three Pillars of R2P ... 98
4.4.4 The Role of R2P in Strengthening the ICC ... 102
4.5 R2P and the UN System ... 104
4.5.1 The Security Council and R2P ... 104
4.5.2 The General Assembly and R2P ... 107
4.6 Conclusion ... 118
References ... 119

5 General International Law as a Tool for Strengthening ICC Responses to Non-cooperation Through the Lens of R2P ... 125
5.1 Introduction ... 126
5.2 Non-cooperation and R2P Analysed Through the Lens of State Responsibility ... 127
5.2.1 Identifying an Internationally Wrongful Act ... 127
5.2.2 The Consequences of a Breach of an International Obligation ... 128
5.2.3 Recipients of the Obligations of Cessation, Non-repetition, and Reparation ... 130
5.2.4 Non-cooperation with the ICC as an Internationally Wrongful Act ... 130
5.3 Non-cooperation as a Breach of a Peremptory Norm of General International Law ... 131
5.3.1 Identifying Peremptory Norms ... 132
5.3.2 Obligations Under Peremptory Norms ... 135
5.4 Individual State Obligations to Protect Peremptory Norms ... 141
5.4.1 Legal Bases for Individual Responses to Breaches of Peremptory Norms ... 141
5.4.2 Specific Individual Responses to Breaches of Peremptory Norms ... 142
5.4.3 Analysing the use of Individual Responses to Non-cooperation ... 149
5.5 Conclusion ... 150
References ... 151

6 The Responsibility to Protect and General International Law as Tools for Strengthening the Assembly of States Parties ... 153
6.1 Introduction ... 154
6.2 Pillar Two of R2P as a Tool for Enhancing the Assembly of States Parties' Cooperation Frameworks ... 155

6.2.1 Complementarity as a Tool under the Second Pillar of R2P ... 155
6.2.2 Promoting Positive Complementarity ... 158
6.2.3 Strengthening Complementarity Activities through the Secretariat of the Assembly ... 162
6.3 Pillar Three of R2P as a Tool for Strengthening the Assembly's Responses to Non-cooperation ... 166
6.4 Developing Remedies for Strengthening the Assembly's Responses to Non-cooperation ... 168
6.4.1 Approaching the ICJ ... 169
6.4.2 Warnings ... 172
6.4.3 Administrative Fines ... 173
6.4.4 Loss of Participation Rights in Assembly Decisions ... 174
6.4.5 Analysing the Adoption of Additional Remedies for Addressing Non-cooperation ... 178
6.5 Conclusion ... 179
References ... 180

7 Strengthening the Security Council's Responses to Non-cooperation Through the Lens of R2P and General International Law ... 183
7.1 Introduction ... 184
7.2 The Security Council's Role in Protecting Peremptory Norms ... 185
7.2.1 The Duty to Protect Peremptory Norms ... 185
7.2.2 The Responsibility Not to Veto ... 187
7.3 Peacekeeping Operations as a Tool under R2P for Strengthening the Security Council's Role in Following up on ICC Situations ... 192
7.3.1 Peacekeeping Operations as Tools under the Pillars of R2P ... 192
7.3.2 Peacekeeping Operations and the ICC ... 193
7.3.3 Obstacles to Cooperation between the ICC and Peacekeeping Operations ... 194
7.4 Analysing the Role of the General Assembly in Strengthening the Security Council's ICC Mandate ... 197
7.4.1 Analysing the Application of the Uniting for Peace Resolution in the Scope of the Security Council's ICC Mandate ... 197
7.4.2 Analysing General Assembly Action in Reforming the Veto Powers of the Security Council ... 198
7.4.3 What Role for the General Assembly for Addressing Security Council Inaction? ... 200
7.5 Conclusion ... 201
References ... 202

8 Conclusions and Recommendations 205
8.1 Conclusions 206
8.1.1 Enforcing the Obligation to Cooperate 206
8.1.2 R2P and General International Law as Additional Tools for Strengthening Responses to Non-cooperation 208
8.1.3 The Role of R2P and General International Law in Strengthening Responses to Non-cooperation 209
8.2 Recommendations 212
8.2.1 Strengthening the ICC's Responses to Non-cooperation 213
8.3 Final Recommendations and Conclusions 214
References 216

Index 217

Abbreviations

ASP	Assembly of States Parties
AU	African Union
DRC	Democratic Republic of the Congo
EU	European Union
ICC	International Criminal Court
ICISS	International Commission for Intervention and State Sovereignty
ICJ	International Court of Justice
ICTR	International Criminal Tribunal for Rwanda
ICTY	International Criminal Tribunal for the Former Yugoslavia
ILC	International Law Commission
R2P	Responsibility to Protect
UN	United Nations
UNGA	United Nations General Assembly
UNSC	United Nations Security Council
WHO	World Health Organization
WSOD	World Summit Outcome Document

Chapter 1
Introduction—The ICC's Failure to Effectively Address Non-cooperation

Contents

1.1 Background and Scope of Book 2
1.1.1 Frameworks for Non-cooperation and their Ineffectiveness 3
1.1.2 The Search for More Effective Responses to Non-cooperation 4
1.1.3 The Responsibility to Protect and General International Law 5
1.2 Objectives and Structure of this Book 6
1.3 Significance of this Book 7
1.3.1 Narrow Approaches to Non-cooperation 8
1.3.2 The Relationship between the ICC and R2P 8
1.3.3 Individual State Responses to Non-cooperation 9
1.4 Delimitations 9
1.4.1 Specific Aspects of Cooperation 9
1.4.2 Head of State Immunity and Claims of African Bias 10
1.4.3 Amendment of the Rome Statute 11
1.4.4 Regional Tools for Enhancing the ICC's Cooperation Frameworks 12
1.4.5 The Use of Force as a Remedy for Addressing Non-cooperation 14
1.5 Chapter Outline 14
References 15

Abstract This chapter introduces the research framework and rationale underpinning the study for this monograph: whether the Responsibility to Protect (R2P) and General International Law can assist in enhancing the International Criminal Court's (ICC) mechanisms for addressing non-cooperation. This chapter highlights the shortcomings in the Rome Statute's current cooperation regime, as well as the challenges posed by instances of non-compliance by States. The chapter outlines the primary research questions, which address whether R2P can serve as a prism for reforming the ICC's responses to non-cooperation and whether it provides frameworks and tools not integrated into the Rome Statute. In addition, this chapter poses the question whether general international law offers additional mechanisms that may strengthen or complement existing responses to non-cooperation.

This chapter also sets out the objectives of the study, including the identification of obligations tied to the failure to cooperate under general international law, and the potential role of R2P in enhancing the Court's cooperation frameworks. Finally, it introduces the potential for institutional reform within the ICC and the UN Security

M. L. Jacobs, *The Consequences of Non-cooperation with the International Criminal Court*, International Criminal Justice Series 37,
https://doi.org/10.1007/978-94-6265-675-8_1

Council to assist in more effective responses and remedies for responding to non-cooperation.

Keywords International Criminal Court · Rome Statute · Non-cooperation · Responsibility to Protect · Remedies · General International Law

1.1 Background and Scope of Book

The Rome Statute of the International Criminal Court (hereinafter the "Rome Statute" or the "Statute") was adopted in July 1998 and came into force in July 2002.[1] The purpose of the Statute was to create the International Criminal Court (hereinafter the "ICC" or the "Court"), a permanent international court tasked with prosecuting individuals for war crimes, crimes against humanity, genocide, and the crime of aggression.[2] As the Court does not have an internal police force or enforcement body, it is reliant on States, as well as international and regional organisations to assist in the investigation of situations and the arrest and surrender of suspects.[3] The implications of such a cooperation model is that the failure or refusal to cooperate on the part of a State, results in the Court being unable to function properly.[4]

In the more than twenty years that the Court has been in operation, it has opened up several investigations into situations where atrocity crimes have occurred and has successfully prosecuted suspects involved in the commission of such crimes. However, the Court has also had to contend with several instances where States have failed to comply with their cooperation obligations towards the Court. These instances of non-cooperation have been addressed through the institution of legal remedies against these States by the Court and its associated bodies. However, as will be shown below, instances of non-cooperation have not been addressed effectively, with little to no consequences being faced by the non-cooperating State.[5] With the recent failure of Mongolia to arrest Russian President, Vladimir Putin,[6] the remedies available to the Court and its associated bodies in this regard will be put under the spotlight.

This book therefore seeks to investigate the following aspects of the ICC's cooperation regime.

---

[1] The Rome Statute of the International Criminal Court. (17 July 1998, 2187, UNTS 3, Entry into Force, 1 July 2002) [hereinafter Rome Statute/RS].

[2] Ibid. Article 5.

[3] Turlan 2016, pp. 59–60.

[4] Cassese 1998, p. 13.

[5] Kress and Prost 2022, pp. 2240–2441.

[6] ICC, Situation in Ukraine, Findings under Article 87(7) of the Rome Statute on the Non-compliance by Mongolia with the request by the Court to cooperate in the arrest and surrender of Vladimir Vladimirovich Putin and Referral to the Assembly of States Parties, (24 October 2024) ICC-01/22-90.

1.1.1 *Frameworks for Non-cooperation and their Ineffectiveness*

Under the Rome Statute, States are under a general obligation to cooperate with the Court.[7] Such cooperation ranges from the arrest and surrender of suspects,[8] to assistance with investigations and prosecutions.[9] Where a State fails to respond to such non-cooperation, a judicial finding of non-cooperation is made by a chamber of the Court, followed by a decision to refer the matter to the Assembly of States Parties (hereinafter "the Assembly",) or the UN Security Council (hereinafter "the Security Council",) where it has referred a situation to the Court.[10] The Assembly and the Security Council, as political bodies, are therefore required to apply measures that they have developed in order to determine an appropriate remedy in response to such non-cooperation.

However, these frameworks have been less than effective in their goal of addressing and remedying instances of non-cooperation.[11] The ineffectiveness of these frameworks can be attributed to the lack of concrete action taken by the entities empowered to react to instances of non-cooperation, and the limited remedies available to these entities for addressing non-cooperation.[12] The inability to appropriately address non-cooperation can also be attributed to a lack of political will from all bodies involved in these procedures.[13]

The ineffectiveness of the ICC's frameworks for addressing non-cooperation has been recognised by the Court itself. In the 2017 decision on South Africa's failure to cooperate in the arrest and surrender of Sudan's Omar Al-Bashir, the Pre-Trial Chamber determined that referring the matter to the Assembly of States Parties and the Security Council would be of no consequence as a mechanism for the Court to obtain cooperation.[14] One of the reasons presented was that previous referrals of non-cooperation had not resulted in any consequences for the offending States.[15]

This case has had the effect of allowing some dangerous precedent with regards to the ICC's responses to non-cooperation and has had an influence on the outcomes of the decision on Jordan's non-cooperation in December 2017. In this decision, a finding of non-cooperation was made by the pre-trial Chamber, and the matter was

[7] RS, above n. 1, Article 86.

[8] Ibid. Article 89.

[9] Ibid. Article 93.

[10] Ibid. Article 87(7).

[11] Kress and Prost 2022, p. 2441.

[12] Tladi 2014, p. 398.

[13] Sluiter and Talontsi 2016, p. 109.

[14] ICC, Prosecutor v Omar Hassan Ahmad Al Bashir [Decision Under Article 87(7) of the Rome Statute on the non-compliance by South Africa with the request by the Court for the arrest and surrender of Omar Al-Bashir] (6 July 2017) ICC-02/05-01/09-302 para 137.

[15] Ibid. para 138.

referred to the Assembly and the Security Council.[16] The decision was appealed by Jordan based on various errors of law relating to Head-of-State immunity, and that the Pre-Trial Chamber had abused its discretion in its decision to refer the matter further,[17] claiming that the distinction between its case and South Africa's was unfair and unreasonable.[18] The Appeals Chamber has since upheld the decision that Jordan failed to cooperate with the Court, but found it appropriate to reverse the decision to refer Jordan to the Assembly and the Security Council.[19]

The failure of the Court to effectively respond to multiple instances of non-cooperation, and the claim by the Pre-Trial Chamber that previous referrals of non-cooperation had no consequences for States, illustrate the importance of cooperation for the ICC and highlights some weaknesses in the armour of the Court. Firstly, the ICC cannot function effectively without the cooperation of States, and secondly, the ICC and its associated bodies do not have effective remedies in place to address the failure of States in complying with cooperation obligations. While non-cooperation is rare among States,[20] its occurrence and the failure of the Court to effectively respond to such non-cooperation has a negative impact on the image and reputation of the Court amongst States, victims and the international community.[21]

1.1.2 The Search for More Effective Responses to Non-cooperation

Considering the above, this book aims to investigate whether existing frameworks under the Rome Statute can be strengthened to address instances of non-cooperation by States Parties in a more effective manner. Looking outward, this book also aims to determine whether international law frameworks outside the black letter of the Rome Statute can be applied to further complement and strengthen the ICC's non-cooperation responses. In analysing the potential for additional frameworks to be applied in this context, consideration should be made as to the non-mandatory nature of the remedies available to the Court.

Some non-cooperation cases have highlighted that the use of Article 87(7) measures was not a mandatory action, but instead one of many tools available in

---

[16] ICC, Prosecutor v Omar Hassan Ahmad Al Bashir [Decision under Article 87(7) of the Rome Statute on the non-compliance by Jordan with the request by the Court for the arrest and surrender or Omar Al-Bashir] (11 December 2017) ICC-02/05-01/09-309 paras 50 & 55.

[17] ICC, Prosecutor v Omar Hassan Ahmad Al Bashir [The Hashemite Kingdom of Jordan's appeal against the "Decision under Article 87(7) of the Rome Statute on the non-compliance by Jordan with the request by the Court for the arrest and surrender of Omar Al-Bashir] (12 March 2018) ICC-02/05-01/09-326 para 3.

[18] Ibid. para 98.

[19] ICC, Prosecutor v Omar Hassan Ahmad Al Bashir [Judgment in the Jordan Referral re Al-Bashir Appeal] (6 May 2019) ICC-02/05-01/09 OA2 para 216.

[20] Hillebrecht and Straus 2017, p. 174.

[21] Jones 2016, p. 190.

the arsenal of the Court to be used as a measure of last resort, or part of a strategy at promoting cooperation.[22] In addition, this provision was not designed to punish or criticise a State for non-cooperation, but instead make provision for additional tools to assist in eliminating obstacles to non-cooperation.[23] This therefore suggests the availability of remedies, other than those within the framework of the Rome Statute, that could be implemented to assist in improving responses to non-cooperation. In searching for more effective responses to non-cooperation, consideration should be given to the application of the Responsibility to Protect and its potential role in strengthening and complementing the Rome Statute's frameworks for addressing non-cooperation through the lens of principles entrenched in general international law.

1.1.3 The Responsibility to Protect and General International Law

The Responsibility to Protect, otherwise known as R2P, is a global political doctrine which places States under a primary responsibility to protect its populations from serious international crimes, namely genocide, war crimes, crimes against humanity and ethnic cleansing. This doctrine also places a collective duty upon the international community to assist States, in accordance with the UN Charter, to ensure that this responsibility is met.[24] In identifying the link between the ICC and R2P, these two bodies share the same origins. Both of them were developed in response to the failure of the international community to address serious international crimes. They rely on the cooperation of States to function effectively, and they share a similar mandate to respond to situations where serious international crimes have been committed.[25] However, they also exhibit some key differences that may influence their relationship. The most notable difference is that while R2P is a political norm designed to strengthen State capacities to prevent or halt the commission of atrocity crimes, the

[22] ICC, Prosecutor v Saif Al-Islam Gaddafi [Decision on the non-compliance by Libya with requests for cooperation by the Court and referring the matter to the United Nations Security Council] (10 December 2014) ICC-01/11-01/11-577 para 23; see also: ICC, The Prosecutor v. Uhuru Muigai Kenyatta [Prosecution Appeal against the "Decision on Prosecutions application for a Finding of Non-compliance under Article 87(7) of the Statute"] (20 March 2015) ICC-01/09-02/11-1006, para 51, where it was held that a decision to refer non-cooperation to the Assembly of States Parties or the Security Council should only be done upon consideration that it would be the most effective manner in which cooperation can be obtained.

[23] *Libya Non-cooperation* Decision, ibid. para 33; Kenyatta Prosecutor's Appeal Decision, ibid. para 53, where it was held that a decision to refer a finding of non-cooperation was not an automatic consequence of the failure to cooperate, but rather a determination that fell within the discretion of the Chamber hearing the decision.

[24] United Nations General Assembly 2005, para 138.

[25] Mills 2015, p. 87, where it is also noted that R2P and the ICC are "ideal complements" in the fight against serious international crimes.

ICC is a legal institution with a mandate to investigate and punish the commission of atrocity crimes.[26]

As this book aims to analyse how R2P can contribute to the development of stronger frameworks for addressing non-cooperation with the ICC, these overlaps and differences should be analysed with a view to establishing an effective and cooperative relationship between the two. In doing so, this study will analyse the relationship between R2P and the ICC through the lens of general international law. This will be done with a view to establishing how certain principles and rules of general international law can assist in strengthening the relationship between the ICC and R2P, as well as developing more effective remedies for preventing and addressing the failure to cooperate.

1.2 Objectives and Structure of this Book

Considering the above, this book aims to answer the following questions:

1. To what extent can the responsibility to protect provide a prism through which to enhance the effectiveness of remedies for non-cooperation with the ICC?
   a. Can R2P be applied to the cooperation regime of the Rome Statute?
   b. Can current tools and institutions at the disposal of the ICC, such as the Assembly of States Parties and the UN Security Council, be enhanced through the application of R2P in relation to responses to instances of non-cooperation?
   c. Does R2P offer any tools not currently available under the Rome Statute to enhance cooperation with the ICC?
2. Outside the framework of the Rome Statute, does general international law provide for additional tools that can assist in the development of more effective responses to non-cooperation with the ICC?
3. To what extent can R2P be applied to allow States to respond to instances of non-cooperation in their individual capacity in the event that more institutionalised frameworks fail to effectively prevent and punish non-cooperation by States?

In light of the problem statement and research questions above, this book aims to identify how the ICC's frameworks for addressing non-cooperation can be strengthened through the lens of the responsibility protect and general international law. Within the framework of this broad objective, this book specifically sets out to achieve the following objectives:

1. Identify how R2P and General International Law can contribute to enhanced remedies for addressing non-cooperation.

---

[26] Birdsall 2015, p. 55.

   a. Analyse the obligation of States to cooperate with the ICC as an erga omnes obligation.
   b. Identify the obligation to respond to instances of non-cooperation as an obligation not to recognise situations as lawful caused by a breach of peremptory norms.
   c. Identify whether specific remedies available under the rules of State Responsibility can be justified as appropriate responses to non-cooperation, namely resort to judicial settlement and the use of countermeasures.
   d. Investigate whether individual States can respond on their own volition to instances of non-cooperation following the failure of institutionalised frameworks.

2. Analyse the role played by the responsibility to protect and general international law in the strengthening of the Assembly of States Parties' procedures for enhancing cooperation and responding to non-cooperation.

   a. Determine how the Assembly of States Parties can assist in building up the capacity of States to cooperate with the ICC through the application of the duties entrenched in R2P.
   b. Through the application of principles developed through the responsibility to protect and general international law, propose the development of potential reforms to the non-cooperation toolkit of the Assembly, with a view to adopting more coercive responses to non-cooperation by States.

3. Investigate how the responsibility to protect and general international law can strengthen the UN Security Council's ability to reach consensus in matters relating to international peace and security, as well as in providing effective follow-up mechanisms for responding to instances of non-cooperation with the ICC.

   a. Identify the Security Council's role in protecting peremptory norms of general international law.
   b. Analyse the decision-making role of the Security Council in the context of the veto right awarded to its permanent members.
   c. Identify how the UN General Assembly can step in a situation where the Security Council has failed in its duty to maintain international peace and security.

1.3 Significance of this Book

This book aims to conduct a deep analysis of the ICC's responses to non-cooperation, with a view to establishing more effective responses, complemented by frameworks and principles recognised in general international law. In conducting this study, the following conclusions as to the academic significance of this book can be made:

1.3.1 Narrow Approaches to Non-cooperation

Existing research on the ICC and its ability to address non-cooperation has shown that the solutions which have been put forward to strengthen the ICC's non-cooperation frameworks have been approached rather narrowly, with most of the focus being on addressing non-cooperation within the scope of the Rome Statute. This can be seen in particular by authors like Sluiter and Barnes who propose amendments to provisions of the Rome Statute.[27] Although there is literature that recognises the use of other international frameworks outside the scope of the Rome Statute in expanding and developing the consequences of a failure to cooperate with the ICC,[28] concrete research on this theme is insufficient and needs to be elaborated further. This research may also assist in identifying frameworks that can be developed to improve promotion of cooperation, and assist in preventing instances of non-cooperation, therefore strengthening the legitimacy of the ICC within the international law system. Therefore, there is a need to expand on this research in order to bridge the legal gap caused by the lack of appropriate mechanisms for addressing non-cooperation with the ICC.

1.3.2 The Relationship between the ICC and R2P

In assessing the relationship between the ICC and R2P, several authors have identified the ICC as a tool for strengthening the R2P doctrine.[29] This is also identified in texts like the ICISS Report, and the UN Secretary-General's *Implementing R2P Report*. However, the purpose of this study is to investigate whether R2P can strengthen the ICC, particularly in the context of remedies for non-cooperation. Research on this topic is limited and has not been addressed in much detail, apart from confirmation that R2P can indeed play a part in strengthening the ICC.[30] International law is constantly developing, with a myriad of sources at its disposal that can assist its development. This can be seen with the introduction of R2P, the development of the Articles on State Responsibility for Internationally Wrongful Acts,[31] and the work of the ILC in better clarifying the content and status of peremptory norms of general international law.[32] This book therefore has value as it aims to bridge the

[27] Barnes 2011, pp. 1617–1618; Sluiter 2018, p. 400.

[28] Sluiter 2010, p. 365; Gillett 2012, p. 63, where both authors suggest strengthening the ICC's cooperation frameworks through the lens of the Genocide Convention.

[29] Birdsall 2015, p. 55; Mills 2015, p. 73.

[30] Megret 2010, pp. 10–11.

[31] A/RES/56/10.

[32] International Law Commission Seventy-Third Session Report of the International Law Commission [Chapter IV(E): Peremptory Norms of General International Law: Text of the Draft Conclusions and Legal Consequences of Peremptory Norms of General International Law (jus cogens)] A/77/10 (18 April—3 June & 4 July—5 August 2022).

aforementioned legal gap caused by a lack of effective mechanisms for addressing non-cooperation with the ICC through the application of these frameworks in the context of the Rome Statute system.

1.3.3 Individual State Responses to Non-cooperation

The content of this book is also crucial for determining whether individual States can respond on their own initiative to cases of non-cooperation if the bodies mandated to assist the Court fail to do so. While the obligations under the UN Charter, the Rome Statute, and the principles entrenched within the responsibility to protect are collective in nature, this book aims to determine whether general international law does provide some room for the execution of individual State remedies as a measure of last resort should all other frameworks and responses fail to be effective.

1.4 Delimitations

Considering the constant development of international law, this book covers legal developments up until November 2024. Therefore, any legal developments after November 2024 are excluded from this book but acknowledged.

The following subjects will be excluded from analysis in this book as they either go beyond the subject matter and goal of this book to establish more effective responses to non-cooperation or are not in line with the principles entrenched within the responsibility to protect and the rules of general international law.

1.4.1 Specific Aspects of Cooperation

This book will exclude any analysis relating to the content of the duty to cooperate with the ICC. In analysing the obligation to cooperate, this study will focus on the obligation to cooperate in the context of the obligation to arrest and surrender ICC suspects under Article 89 of the Statute, considering that most non-cooperation cases that have been heard have dealt with the failure to execute arrest warrants. This study will also not concern itself with the causes of non-cooperation as it is outside the scope of the study. In analysing remedies for addressing non-cooperation, the study will place most of its focus on remedies aimed at addressing the non-cooperation of States Parties to the Rome Statute, as Non-party States do not have a concrete obligation to cooperate with the Court under the Statute.[33]

---

[33] Article 87(5)(a) of the Rome Statute.

1.4.2 Head of State Immunity and Claims of African Bias

While it has been an issue of concern throughout non-cooperation proceedings, issues relating to the immunity of Heads of State shall not be addressed in this book. Under customary international law, heads of State and diplomats possess immunity from the jurisdiction of foreign States.[34] International treaties confer similar immunities upon diplomats and State representatives.[35] These immunities are necessary for the maintenance of a system of peaceful cooperation and co-existence among States.[36] In the context of the work of the ICC, two provisions have caused much confusion and debate during non-cooperation proceedings, particularly among African States Parties as a result of a decision by the African Union which called for member States to not cooperate with the Court's requests to arrest al-Bashir.[37] The first provision is Article 27, which recognises that the Statute applies equally to all persons without any distinction based on official capacity.[38] The second provision is Article 98, which provides that the Court may not proceed with a request for surrender or assistance that would require the requested State to act inconsistently with its obligations under international law to recognise the State or diplomatic immunity of a person or property of a third State, unless the Court can first obtain the cooperation of a third State to waive that immunity.[39]

The issue of non-cooperation has been widely debated in case law, particularly regarding immunity for Heads of State. This matter was resolved by the Appeals Chamber in 2019, which affirmed that under customary international law, Heads of State do not possess immunity before international criminal tribunals.[40] This decision has, for now, clarified the obligations of States in the arrest and surrender of Heads of State to the ICC. However, at the same time, this decision by the Appeals Chamber has led to diverging views among academics as to the correctness of the

[34] Kiyani 2013, p. 474.

[35] Articles 29 and 31 of the Vienna Convention on Diplomatic Relations 1961.

[36] Akande and Shah 2011, p. 818.

[37] Assembly of the African Union 13th Session [Decision on the Meeting of African States Parties to the Rome Statute of the International Criminal Court (ICC)] Doc.Assembly/AU/13(XIII) (3 July 2009) para 10.

[38] RS above n, 1, Article 27(1).

[39] RS above n 1, Article 98(1).

[40] Prosecutor v Omar Hassan Ahmad Al Bashir [Judgment in the Jordan Referral re Al-Bashir Appeal] ICC-02/05-01/09 OA2 (6 May 2019) para 162.

decision.[41] While questions relating to immunity are an important element of non-cooperation procedures, they fall outside the aim and scope of this book to search for effective responses to non-cooperation, and therefore shall not be addressed. A related issue is the African Union's stance that the ICC disproportionately targets African states while neglecting to address situations in other regions.[42] This topic will also be excluded from the study as it is a too broad and contentious topic, therefore detracting from the scope of the study.

1.4.3 Amendment of the Rome Statute

While the law and practice on non-cooperation could benefit from amending the Rome Statute,[43] it is a lengthy process requiring a high threshold of votes for adoption, acceptance and ratification.[44] In addition, therein lies the risk that the ICC may lose States Parties as a result of an amendment. The Statute provides that if an amendment has been accepted by the required majority, any State Party which has not accepted that amendment may withdraw from the Statute with immediate effect.[45] Such a situation would not be in the best interests of the Court, as it cannot risk losing States Parties. Therefore, this book aims to propose for existing frameworks to be strengthened without resorting to an amendment of the Rome Statute.

---

[41] See e.g. Akande D "ICC Appeals Chamber Holds that Heads of State Have no Immunity Under Customary International Law before International Tribunals" (6 May 2019) available at https://www.ejiltalk.org/icc-appeals-chamber-holds-that-heads-of-state-have-no-immunity-under-customary-international-law-before-international-tribunals/ (accessed 15 August 2020), where the Author labels the decision as "stunning and deeply misguided"; Galand AS "A Hidden Reading of the ICC Appeals Chamber's Judgment in the Jordan Referral Re Al-Bashir" (June 6 2019) available at https://www.ejiltalk.org/a-hidden-reading-of-the-icc-appeals-chambers-judgment-in-the-jordan-referral-re-al-bashir/ (accessed 15 August 2020) where the author identifies a number of contradictions and ambiguities in the Court's decision; Sadat L "Why the ICC's Judgment in the al-Bashir Case Wasn't So Surprising" (12 July 2019) *Just Security* available at https://www.justsecurity.org/64896/why-the-iccs-judgment-in-the-al-bashir-case-wasnt-so-surprising/ (accessed 15 August 2020) where the author argues that the decision of the Appeals Chamber was unsurprising, correctly decided, and consistent with the judicial mandate of the Court.

[42] Schuerch 2017, p. 4.

[43] Sluiter 2018, p. 399.

[44] Clark RS 2022, p. 2299; see also Article 121(2) of the Rome Statute *supra,* note. 1, which provides that a majority vote of States present and voting is required to take up a proposed amendment; Article 121(3) which provides that where consensus is not reached, a two-thirds majority vote in favour of the vote should be recorded; and Article 121(4) which provides that an amendment will enter into force one year after seven-eighths of States Parties have deposited instruments of ratification or acceptance with the UN Secretary-General.

[45] Article 121(6) of the Rome Statute *supra,* note. 1; see also Article 127(1) of the Statute which notes that normal withdrawal takes effect one year after the date of receipt of the notification, and Article 127(2) which provides that withdrawal does not discharge a State from obligations towards the Court that still need to be fulfilled.

1.4.4 Regional Tools for Enhancing the ICC's Cooperation Frameworks

Although the general obligation to cooperate with the ICC is placed upon States Parties to the Rome Statute, provision is also made for the inclusion of regional frameworks in this regime. While the Court is authorised to make requests to States Parties for cooperation transmitted through diplomatic or other channels,[46] the Statute also provides that such requests can be made through any appropriate regional organisation.[47] Therefore, regional organisations can contribute to the Court's cooperation frameworks by assisting in encouraging cooperation and ensuring the arrest and surrender of suspects.[48] In turn, these bodies can be essential tools for assisting in developing more effective frameworks for responding to instances of non-cooperation. Such a role has been confirmed in ICC case law.[49]

Regional organisations have developed a variety of tools for assisting the ICC in the execution of its mandate, particularly with regards to the promotion of cooperation, building up the capacities of Member States to cooperate with the Court, and responding to instances of non-cooperation. This is most notable with regards to the European Union's development of specific frameworks for responding to non-cooperation;[50] and the African Union's development of the Protocol on Amendments to the Protocol on the Statute of the African Court of Justice and Human Rights which extends the jurisdiction of the proposed African Court of Justice and Human Rights to include a number of serious international crimes, including those covered by the Rome Statute.[51]

However, as with most new international treaties, the Malabo Protocol is experiencing a few teething problems, which, if not addressed appropriately, may have a negative effect on its proper functioning and enforcement within the African Court of Justice. Most notable is the rate at which the protocol has been signed and ratified by States. The protocol is intended to enter into force thirty days after fifteen AU

---

[46] RS, above, n.1, Article 87(1)(a).

[47] RS, above, n.1, Article 87(1)(b).

[48] UNGA 2011, which highlights the importance of effective communication between the UN and regional groups, particularly when sharing information and assessing ongoing and potential atrocity situations.

[49] *Kenyatta Prosecutors Appeal Decision* (n 21 above) para 53, where the Appeals Chamber made mention of the use of third States and regional organisations as alternative bodies for responding to non-cooperation.

[50] Behrmann 2016, pp. 304–311, where the author identifies frameworks for preventing non-cooperation and responding to non-cooperation.

[51] African Union *Protocol on Amendments to the Protocol on the Statute of the African Court of Justice and Human Rights* (27 June 2014) (Malabo Protocol) Article 28A, which grants the Proposed Court the power to try persons for the Crimes of Genocide, War Crimes, Crimes Against Humanity and Aggression. See also Article 28(B) which recognises genocide, 28(C) which recognises crimes against humanity, 28(D) which recognises war crimes, and 28(M) which recognises the crime of aggression.

members have deposited instruments of ratification with the court.[52] However, as of the time of writing, only fifteen members out of the fifty-five AU members have signed the protocol, with only one State, namely Angola, depositing its instrument of ratification in 2024.[53] In addition, the Protocol does not contain comprehensive cooperation provisions and does not contain provisions which set out how the Court will address and remedy instances of non-cooperation.[54]

Other concerns lie with the potential lack of political will and the ability of individual States to influence the activities of the Court. Regardless of how robust the Malabo Protocol is, the African Court will operate in a climate where political considerations may influence its proper functioning. There appear to be indications of a lack of political commitment among actors to holding persons accountable for international crimes. This can be illustrated by the Protocol's immunity provision,[55] which demonstrates an unwillingness of those in power to hold themselves at the same standards as others; the history of non-cooperation between African States and the ICC; and the slow rate of ratifications of the protocol.[56]

While the potential role that regional organisations may play in strengthening the ICC's cooperation frameworks may be useful for the purposes of this book, such research will be excluded due to the fact that the African Court of Justice is not in operation as of yet, and any proposals for the inclusion of the Court to the ICC discussion will be purely hypothetical as a result of a lack of practice and effective provisions for addressing non-cooperation. However, once the Court is in operation, subject to the required ratifications, and practice is observed, such research could be identified as a potential subject for projects.

[52] Ibid. Article 11.

[53] Ngari A and Machado Z "Angola Becomes first Country to Join African Criminal Court" (14 June 2024) *Human Rights Watch* available at: https://www.hrw.org/news/2024/06/14/angola-becomes-first-country-join-african-criminal-court (accessed 15 October 2024).

[54] Tladi 2019, p. 737, where the author notes that while non-cooperation has not always been handled appropriately by tribunals, provision of remedies for addressing cooperation creates the possibility that action can be taken against such a failure to act.

[55] Article 46A*bis* of the Malabo Protocol (n 41 above) provides that no charges shall be commenced or continued before the Court against any serving head of State or Government or other senor State officials during their time in office.

[56] KPTJ *Seeking Justice or Seeking Suspects? An Analysis of the Malabo Protocol on the African Court* available at http://kptj.africog.org/wp-content/uploads/2016/11/Malabo-Report.pdf (accessed 15 January 2022), p. 19, with regards to the slow rate of ratifications, this appears to indicate that most African States are reluctant to accept a new court, either due to doubts about their capacity to contribute to the Court or as a result of fear of accepting the jurisdiction of the Court.

1.4.5 The Use of Force as a Remedy for Addressing Non-cooperation

While searching for alternative remedies in response to the failure to cooperate, some literature has argued for the use of more coercive measures to respond to instances of non-cooperation. Considering that the use of force is prohibited under international law,[57] such an intervention may not be appropriate in response to non-cooperation or the failure to implement R2P. According to Tams, there lies an argument that the right to use force in defence of core community obligations should be a corresponding right of protection triggered by a breach of an obligation *erga omnes*.[58] However, the concept of *erga omnes* appears to be incapable of justifying additional exceptions to the use of force outside of self-defence and Security Council authorisation. Instead, the legality of the use of force in defence of community interests is typically discussed through the lens of humanitarian intervention and R2P.[59] This book will not look to propose for more coercive measures, such as the use of force, as this is a topic that requires extensive analysis and will therefore distract from the objectives of this study. Instead, this book will aim to propose frameworks that do not have the undesired result of contributing to or otherwise escalating existing atrocity situations.

1.5 Chapter Outline

This book will be divided into six main chapters:

Chapter 2 will analyse the current cooperation frameworks under the Rome Statute. This will include an analysis of the institutions developed to respond to instances of non-cooperation, as well as an analysis of case law on non-cooperation. This chapter will highlight that existing responses to non-cooperation are ineffective.

Chapter 3 will analyse the role of the Assembly of States Parties and the UN Security Council in responding to non-cooperation. This chapter will identify that the current frameworks for addressing non-cooperation are ineffective and need to be strengthened. While identifying the need to strengthen the ICC's cooperation frameworks, this chapter will also propose specific frameworks that can be adopted within the scope of the Rome Statute and the UN Charter that may assist in strengthening responses to non-cooperation.

---

[57] Article 2(4) of the Charter of the United Nations 1945.

[58] Tams 2011, pp. 391–392.

[59] However, see Simma 1999, p. 6, where the author, writing during the aftermath of the Kosovo crisis, warned that the assertion of a right of humanitarian intervention to protect international interests would have to overcome a variety of legal obstacles.

Chapter 4 will introduce the responsibility to protect and its potential for developing a more effective remedies regime under international law. This chapter will also identify the elements within R2P that can be applied to the Rome Statute and its frameworks for responding to non-cooperation. Furthermore, this chapter will analyse the application of R2P within the scope of the UN Charter, highlighting the role of the UN Security Council and the General Assembly in implementing this doctrine.

Chapter 5 will then analyse the role that general international law may have in enhancing the responses to non-cooperation. This analysis will be conducted in the context of the International Law Commission's work on State Responsibility for Internationally Wrongful Acts, as well as the recently developed draft conclusions on peremptory norms of general international law. This chapter will identify that the obligations under the Rome Statute and R2P are peremptory in nature and owed to the international community as a whole, to which all States have a legal interest. This chapter will illustrate these obligations through an analysis of the remedies available under the rules of State responsibility and peremptory norms.

Chapter 6 will then analyse the implications of R2P and general international law for the Assembly of States Parties' role in addressing non-cooperation. Here the elements from R2P that have been identified as applicable within the Rome Statute's cooperation frameworks shall be evaluated in relation to the role of the Assembly in promoting cooperation and preventing instances of non-cooperation. This chapter will also identify the potential for R2P to assist in strengthening the Assembly's cooperation mandate, through the analysis of specific remedies under international law.

Chapter 7 will investigate the implications of R2P and general international law for the UN Security Council, in relation to its role in addressing the non-cooperation of States with the ICC, particularly in situations that the Council has referred to the Court for investigation. This chapter will investigate the potential for UN Reform within the framework of R2P with a view to reviving Security Council support of the ICC, as well as improving the Council's willingness to promote State cooperation with the ICC and its ability to use its UN Charter powers to address and prevent non-cooperation. This chapter will also analyse the role played by the UN General Assembly in the event that the Security Council fails in its primary responsibility to maintain international peace and security.

References

Akande D, Shah S (2010) Immunities of State Officials, International Crimes and Foreign Domestic Courts. European Journal of International Law 21(4): 815–852.

Assembly of the African Union (2009) Decision on the Meeting of African States Parties to the Rome Statute of the International Criminal Court (ICC) Doc.Assembly/AU/13(XIII).

Barnes GP (2011) The International Criminal Courts Ineffective Enforcements Mechanisms: The Indictment of President Omar Al Bashir Fordham International Law Journal 34(6): 1584–1619.

Behrmann C (2016) Strengthening the International Criminal Court Cooperation Regime from the European Union's Perspective. In: Bekou O, Birkett DJ (eds) Cooperation and the International Criminal Court: Perspectives from Theory and Practice. Brill, Leiden, pp. 297–317.
Birdsall A (2015) The Responsibility to Prosecute and the ICC: A Problematic Relationship? Criminal Law Forum 26; 51–72.
Cassese A (1998) On the Current Trends towards Criminal Prosecution and Punishment of Breaches of International Humanitarian Law. European Journal of International Law 9(1): 2–17.
Clark RS (2022) Amendments. In: Ambos K (ed) Rome Statute of the International Criminal Court: Article-by-Article Commentary. Beck/Nomos/Hart, Munich, pp. 2871–2891.
Gillett M (2012) The Call of Justice Obligations under the Genocide Convention to Cooperate with the International Criminal Court. Criminal Law Forum 23, 63–96.
Hillebrecht C, Straus S (2017) Who Pursues the Perpetrators? State Cooperation with the ICC. Human Rights Quarterly 39(1): 162–188.
Jones A (2016) Non-cooperation and the Efficiency of the International Criminal Court. In: Bekou O, Birkett DJ (eds) Cooperation and the International Criminal Court: Perspectives from Theory and Practice. Brill, Leiden, pp. 185–209.
Kiyani AG (2013) Al-Bashir and the ICC: The Problem of Head of State Immunity. Chinese Journal of International Law 12(3): 467–508.
Kress C, Prost K (2022) International Cooperation and Judicial Assistance. In: Ambos K (ed) Rome Statute of the International Criminal Court: Article-by-Article Commentary. Beck/Nomos/Hart, Munich, pp. 2452–2701.
Megret F (2010) ICC, R2P and the International Community's Evolving Interventionist Toolkit" SSRN. https://papers.ssrn.com/sol3/papers.cfm?abstract_id=1933111 (accessed 24 March 2019).
Mills K (2015) R2P and the ICC: At Odds or in Sync? Criminal Law Forum 26, 73–99.
Schuerch R (2017) The International Criminal Court at the Mercy of Powerful States: An Assessment of the Neo-colonialist Claim Made by African Stakeholders. TMC Asser Press, The Hague.
Simma B (1999) NATO, the UN and the Use of Force: Legal Aspects. European Journal of International Law (10)(1): 1–22.
Sluiter G (2010) Using the Genocide Convention to Strengthen Cooperation in the Al Bashir Case. Journal of International Criminal Justice 8(2): 365–382.
Sluiter G (2018) Enforcing Cooperation: Did the Drafters Approach It the Wrong Way? Journal of International Criminal Justice 16(2); 383–402.
Sluiter G, Talontsi S (2016) Credible and Authoritative Enforcement of State Cooperation with the International Criminal Court. In: Bekou O, Birkett DJ (eds) Cooperation and the International Criminal Court: Perspectives from Theory and Practice. Brill, Leiden, pp. 80–113.
Tams CJ (2011) Individual States as Guardians of Community Interests. In: Fastenrath U, Geiger R, Khan D, Paulus A, von Schorlemer S, Vedder C (eds) From Bilateralism to Community Interest; Essays in Honour of Bruno Simma. Oxford University Press, Oxford, pp. 379–405.
Tladi D (2014) When Elephants Collide it is the Grass that Suffers: Cooperation and the Security Council in the Context of the AU/ICC Dynamic. African Journal of Legal Studies (7)(3): 381–398.
Tladi D (2019) Article 46L: Promoting an Effective Cooperation Regime. In: Jalloh CC, Clarke KM, Nmehielle VO (eds) The African Court of Justice and Human and Peoples' Rights in Context: Development and Challenges. Cambridge University Press, New York, pp. 729–740.
Turlan P (2016) The International Criminal Court Cooperation Regime—A Practical Perspective from the Office of the Prosecutor. In: Bekou O, Birkett DJ (eds) Cooperation and the International Criminal Court: Perspectives from Theory and Practice. Brill, Leiden, pp. 58–79.
United Nations General Assembly (UNGA) (2005) World Summit Outcome Document. Resolution A/RES/60/1.
United Nations General Assembly (UNGA) (2011) Report of the Secretary General [The Role of Regional and Subregional Arrangements in Implementing the Responsibility to Protect] (28 June 2011) A/65/877.

Chapter 2
Frameworks for Cooperation under the Rome Statute

Contents

2.1 Introduction 18
2.2 Cooperation 18
    2.2.1 The Obligation to Cooperate 19
    2.2.2 Forms of Cooperation 20
    2.2.3 Non-cooperation 21
2.3 Case Law on Non-cooperation 23
    2.3.1 The Situation in Sudan: The Failure to Arrest Al-Bashir 24
    2.3.2 Upcoming Non-cooperation Responses: The Situation in Ukraine 34
    2.3.3 Case Law on the Discretionary Powers of the Court 38
2.4 Analysing the Content of Current Non-cooperation Case Law 41
    2.4.1 The Court's Exercise of Discretion 42
    2.4.2 The Standard of a Failure to Cooperate 42
2.5 Conclusion 44
References 44

Abstract This chapter examines the frameworks for cooperation under the Rome Statute, with a specific focus on the obligations of States Parties in cooperating with the Court and the challenges associated with non-cooperation. In addition, this chapter seeks to clarify the existing frameworks aimed at regulating State cooperation, identify obstacles to cooperation, and address the development of the law on non-cooperation as highlighted in case law. Divided into two parts, this chapter first outlines the provisions governing cooperation with the Court, followed by an analysis of case law on non-cooperation, and the development of the Court's mechanisms for responding to and remedying such non-cooperation.

Keywords International Criminal Court · Rome Statute · Non-cooperation · Al-Bashir · Remedies · South Africa

M. L. Jacobs, *The Consequences of Non-cooperation with the International Criminal Court*, International Criminal Justice Series 37,
https://doi.org/10.1007/978-94-6265-675-8_2

2.1 Introduction

The establishment of a permanent international criminal tribunal like the ICC demonstrates the will of the international community to address and prevent the commission of serious international crimes through a system of interaction among States, international and regional organizations, and global civil society.[1] In order for such a system to function smoothly, effective procedures need to be in place that are aimed at regulating State cooperation, identifying obstacles to cooperation, and addressing the failure to cooperate. A notable challenge facing the Court is that of non-cooperation by States Parties, particularly in relation to the arrest and surrender of ICC suspects. In observing the practice of the Court in handling instances of non-cooperation, it is noted that existing frameworks at the disposal of the Court and associated bodies tasked with addressing non-cooperation appear to be ineffective. As a result of this ineffectiveness, States appear to avoid any serious consequences for their failure to comply with a request to cooperate transmitted by the Court.[2]

This chapter seeks to clarify the frameworks under the Rome Statute for addressing the failure of States Parties to cooperate with the ICC. In doing so, this chapter is divided into five sections, Sect. 2.1 being the introduction. Section 2.2 will identify the main provisions in place that regulate the obligation to cooperate with the ICC, including the general obligation to cooperate, the forms of cooperation available to the Court, and the procedures that are triggered following a failure to cooperate. This will be followed by an assessment of case law on non-cooperation and the effect of this case law on the development of the ICC's non-cooperation frameworks in Sect. 2.3. This will include a discussion on the implications of these decisions for future instances of non-cooperation. This chapter will then, in Sect. 2.4, conclude by identifying that the Court's responses to non-cooperation are ineffective and require urgent attention.

2.2 Cooperation

Part IX of the Rome Statute contains extensive provisions regulating various aspects of cooperation between States and the Court.[3] As a starting point, cooperation obligations owed to the Court raise concerns relating to State sovereignty and the rights of individuals. These concerns made the drafting negotiations for Part IX difficult, as consensus could not be reached as to the binding nature of cooperation obligations by States towards the Court.[4] A particular area of concern was the uncertainty as to whether cooperation should be defined as a concrete legal obligation that the Court

[1] Wouters and Basu 2009, p. 128.

[2] Bekou 2019, p. 937.

[3] The Rome Statute of the International Criminal Court. (17 July 1998, 2187, UNTS 3, Entry into Force, 1 July 2002) [hereinafter RS], Articles 86–102.

[4] Kress and Prost 2022, p. 2441.

could rely upon, or whether cooperation should be subject to the will or circumstances of a particular State.[5] However, a compromise was reached which specified precise obligations to cooperate and required that States cooperate fully with the Court.[6] This section will briefly discuss the basic provisions on cooperation relevant for the purposes of this book, namely the general obligation to cooperate, the forms of cooperation available to the Court, and the procedure following a failure to cooperate.

2.2.1 The Obligation to Cooperate

Part IX of the Statute opens with the proclamation that "States Parties shall, in accordance with the provisions of this Statute, cooperate fully with the Court in its investigation and prosecution of crimes within the jurisdiction of the Court.[7] This obligation, as well as the obligations that follow, are binding upon States that have signed and ratified the Rome Statute.[8] Seeing that cooperation from States not party to the Statute may be of great importance in certain circumstances, the Statute also makes provision for the creation of a cooperation regime in which a Non-party State may be invited to cooperate with the Court based on an ad hoc arrangement or agreement.[9] By entering into one of these arrangements, a Non-party State has taken up an international responsibility to ensure that the request to cooperate is responded to in an appropriate manner.[10]

In addition to agreements and arrangements between the Court and Non-party States, an obligation to cooperate may also be created as a result of a resolution passed by the UN Security Council.[11] The Rome Statute allows for the Court to exercise jurisdiction over a situation in a State that has been referred to it by the UN Security Council acting under Chapter VII of the UN Charter.[12] Such a mandate includes referrals of situations in the territories of Non-Party States.[13] Therefore, by virtue of the UN Charter, decisions made by the Security Council are binding upon all UN Member States.[14] Therefore a Non-Party State's obligation to cooperate with

---

[5] Machochoko 1999, p. 306.

[6] Schabas 2017, p. 247.

[7] RS, above n 3, Article 86.

[8] Kress and Prost 2022, p. 2452.

[9] RS, above n. 3, Article 87(5)(a); Vienna Convention on the Law of Treaties (23 May 1969 UN Doc A/CONF.39/11/Add.2, Entry into force, 27 January 1980) Article 34, which provides that a treaty does not create either obligations or rights for a third State without its consent.

[10] Kress and Prost 2022, p. 2453.

[11] Wenqi 2006, p. 89.

[12] RS, above n. 3, Article 13(b).

[13] Schabas and Pecorella 2022, p. 841.

[14] The Charter of the United Nations (26 June 1945, 1 UNTS XVI, Entry into Force 24 October 1945) Article 25.

the ICC created through a decision from the UN Security Council takes priority over other obligations and is therefore compulsory and binding upon those States.[15] The obligation to cooperate is restricted to the State as a legal person and does not extend to officials of the State or other private persons in their individual capacity.[16]

2.2.2 *Forms of Cooperation*

The Rome Statute provides for various forms of cooperation obligations required from States towards the Court. Such cooperation includes the obligation to arrest and surrender, and the obligation to further investigation and prosecution procedures.[17]Article 89 of the Statute regulates the obligation to arrest and surrender perpetrators of serious international crimes. The Article opens by proclaiming that States Parties shall comply with requests for arrest and surrender in accordance with the provisions contained in Part IX and under the requested State's national law.[18] Article 89 also addresses issues relating to conflicts in the execution of the cooperation requests, as well as practical questions relating to the transit and surrender of a Suspect.[19] The obligation to arrest and surrender has been the subject of many cases on non-cooperation, with States failing to comply with the request to cooperate when being made aware of the presence or potential presence of an ICC suspect in their territory.[20] Article 93 of the Statute addresses general assistance between the Court and States other than the arrest and surrender of persons.[21] This section opens by describing a detailed list of obligations relating to investigations and prosecutions that States Parties are required to comply with by request of the Court. These obligations read as follows:

(a) *The Identification and whereabouts of persons or the location of items;*
(b) *The taking and production of evidence;*
(c) *Questioning of any person being investigated or prosecuted;*
(d) *Service of documents, including judicial documents;*
(e) *Facilitating the voluntary appearance of persons as witnesses or experts before the Court;*
(f) *The temporary transfer of persons;*
(g) *The exhumation of places and sites, including grave sites;*
(h) *Execution of searches and seizures;*
(i) *The provision of records and documents;*

15 Wenqi 2006, p. 91.
16 Kress and Prost 2022, p. 2454.
17 RS, above n 3 Articles 89 and 93.
18 Ibid. Article 89(1).
19 Ibid. Articles 89(2) and (3).
20 Kress and Prost 2022, p. 2500.
21 Ibid. p. 2532.

(j) *Protecting victims and witnesses and the preservation of evidence;*
(k) *The identification, tracing and freezing or seizure of proceeds, property and assets and instrumentalities of crimes for the purpose of eventual forfeiture;*
(l) *Any other type of assistance which is not prohibited by the law of the requested State with a view to facilitating the investigation and prosecution of ICC crimes.*[22]

The obligations contained in this provision are broad in character and may include obligations that are not of a legal character, such as providing space and infrastructure for conducting inquiries on the territory of the requested State.[23] Article 93 also addresses various practical aspects relating to investigations and prosecutions, including procedures relating to assurances against arrests, addressing the legality of a request, temporary surrender, issues relating to confidentiality and issues relating to competing cooperation requests.[24] Article 93 also makes provision for the situation where the Court may provide assistance to a State Party.[25]

2.2.3 Non-cooperation

Where a State fails to respond to a cooperation request, such a failure has a negative effect upon the proper functioning of the Court and must be addressed accordingly.[26] Several frameworks are set out to address non-cooperation, which apply depending on whether the non-cooperating entity is a State Party, a non-State Party, or a State responding to a cooperation request by the UN Security Council.[27] This section will specifically look at consultation procedures for addressing obstacles to cooperation under Article 97, and the procedures following a situation where non-cooperation has occurred under Articles 87(5)(b) & (7).

2.2.3.1 Consultation Procedures

The Rome Statute provides that where a State Party receives a cooperation request, in which it identifies issues that may negatively affect the execution of the request, the requested State is required to consult with the Court in order to resolve the matter.[28]Article 97 is of practical importance as it creates a mechanism for consultations, which should be used to resolve issues relating to cooperation requests. In

---

[22] RS, above n. 3, Articles 89(1)(a)–(l).

[23] Kress and Prost 2022, p. 2532.

[24] RS, above n 3, Articles 93(2)–(9).

[25] Ibid. Article 93(10).

[26] Kress and Prost 2022, p. 2475.

[27] Bekou 2019, p. 913.

[28] RS, above n. 3 Article 97.

particular it identifies that although there is a clear obligation to cooperate with the Court, there can be various issues that may affect the proper execution of the cooperation request.[29] The provision identifies three specific issues that may affect the execution of a cooperation request:

(a) *Insufficient information to execute the request;*
(b) *In the case of a request for surrender, the fact that despite best efforts the person sought cannot be located or that the investigation conducted has determined that the person in the requested State is clearly not the person named in the warrant;*
(c) *The fact that the execution of the request in its current form would require the requested State to breach a pre-existing treaty obligation undertaken with respect to another State;*[30]

As shall be shown later in this chapter, Article 97 consultation procedures have influenced the outcomes of recent non-cooperation case law.

2.2.3.2 Responding to Non-cooperation

The procedure that follows a failure to cooperate with a request of the Court differs depending on whether the responsible State is a party to the Statute. Regarding States Parties, the Statute proclaims:

> *Where a State Party fails to comply with a request to cooperate by the Court contrary to the provisions of this Statute, thereby preventing the Court from exercising its functions and powers under this Statute, the Court may make a finding to that effect and refer the matter to the Assembly of States Parties or, where the Security Council referred the matter to the Court, to the Security Council.*[31]

In the instance where a non-State Party has entered into a cooperation agreement with the Court and has failed to comply with the obligations requested of it as per the agreement, the Statute provides that the Court may inform the Assembly of States Parties or the Security Council of such a failure.[32] In addressing instances of non-cooperation by non-Party States, consideration is made as to whether the Court is competent to handle such a specific case, which particular organ of the Court is authorised to handle such a situation, as well as which procedures should be followed.[33] This provision on non-cooperation should be read to include cooperation obligations provided for under the Rome Statute, as well as obligations arising from Security Council resolutions.[34]

---

[29] Kress and Prost 2022, p. 2575.

[30] RS above n. 3, Articles 97(a)–(c).

[31] Ibid. Article 87(7).

[32] Ibid. Article 87(5)(b).

[33] Wenqi 2006, p. 107.

[34] Kress and Prost 2022, p. 2471; the authors also note in this regard that the use of weaker language in article 87(5)(b) requiring the Court to "inform" the Assembly of States Parties compared to that

The Regulations of the ICC indicate that the Chamber which made the request to cooperate, is designated as the competent body to make the finding of non-cooperation.[35] Before a finding of non-cooperation is made, the requested State has the opportunity to explain why cooperation did not take place as requested.[36] Following a finding of non-cooperation, the decision is transmitted to the Court President who will then refer the matter to the Assembly of States Parties or the UN Security Council for further consideration.[37] According to Sluiter & Talontsi, a judicial finding of non-cooperation has an important two-sided function for securing the cooperation of States. Firstly, such a finding establishes that an international legal obligation has been violated.[38] Secondly, it serves as the basis for the adoption of further measures aimed at securing cooperation and addressing the lack of cooperation.[39] In addition, the development of case law on non-cooperation is a handy tool to show States what the Court expects from them in responding appropriately to cooperation requests.[40] The various chambers of the Court have heard several Article 87(7) decisions, indicating that instances of non-cooperation have received extensive judicial responses.[41] These decisions will be discussed below with a view to establish the effect such decisions have had on the development of non-cooperation procedures, as well as their potential effect on future non-cooperation cases.

2.3 Case Law on Non-cooperation

This section seeks to analyse the practice of the Court in addressing instances of non-cooperation through a discussion on selected cases that have been heard before Court Chambers. Case law to be discussed will include the multiple cases on the failure to arrest Al-Bashir and the recent failure of Mongolia in arresting Vladimir Putin. This section also seeks to highlight specific issues relating to the failure to cooperate that

of article 87(7) requiring the Court to "make a finding" and "refer the matter" to the Assembly of States Parties highlights the belief during drafting negotiations that stronger language would be an infringement on the rights of third States that chose to cooperate with the Court without a concrete obligation under the Rome Statute.

35 Regulation 109(2) of the Regulations of the International Criminal Court 26 May 2004 ICC-BD/01-01-04.

36 Ibid. Regulation 109(3).

37 Ibid. Regulation 109(4).

38 Kress and Prost 2022, pp. 2475, 2476, where the authors note that this failure to cooperate with the Court constitutes a breach of an international obligation as per the 2001 Articles on State Responsibility, therefore constituting an internationally wrongful act, entailing the responsibility of that non-cooperating State; the applicability of the Articles on State Responsibility to the Rome Statute's cooperation regime shall be elaborated on in Chap. 5.

39 Sluiter and Talontsi 2016, p. 103.

40 Bertrand and Schauder 2016, p. 156.

41 Sluiter 2018, p. 389.

have been identified in Court decisions. This includes the lack of consistent decision-making in court decisions, and uncertainty regarding the discretionary powers of the Court in determining whether referral of non-cooperation is compulsory.

2.3.1 *The Situation in Sudan: The Failure to Arrest Al-Bashir*

The situation in Sudan, which was the first situation to be referred to the ICC by a Security Council Resolution under Article 13(b) of the Statute,[42] investigated allegations of genocide, war crimes and crimes against humanity committed in Darfur since 1 July 2002.[43] The investigations conducted by the Court led to the issuing of several arrest warrants against perpetrators of these crimes, including Sudanese government officials and opposition militia and resistance leaders.[44] Among these perpetrators is the former president of Sudan, Omar Al-Bashir, wanted on five counts of crimes against humanity, two counts of war crimes, and three counts of genocide.[45] Many non-cooperation cases have arisen from the travel of Al-Bashir to the territories of ICC States Parties, with the Court Chambers deciding on the failure of Kenya, Chad, Malawi, the Democratic Republic of Congo, Nigeria, Uganda, Djibouti, South Africa and Jordan in executing his arrest warrant. These cases have assisted in developing the law on non-cooperation and have attempted to answer several contentious questions relating to the obligation to cooperate, including the immunities of heads of State.[46]

Although the immunities of heads of State is relevant and important in the context of present non-cooperation decisions, it will not be addressed in much detail in this book aside from some basic principles considered in case law. Instead, the focus shall be on how these decisions have contributed to the development of the Court's frameworks for responding to non-cooperation. Several gaps in the law on non-cooperation have been identified from these cases, which may have some implications for the further development of non-cooperation frameworks as well as for addressing future non-cooperation scenarios. These developments shall be highlighted in the following cases below.

[42] UNSC 2005, para 1.

[43] ICC, Situation in Darfur, Sudan, ICC-02/05 available at: https://www.icc-cpi.int/darfur (accessed 9 September 2024).

[44] Ibid.

[45] ICC, Prosecutor v Omar Hassan Ahmad Al Bashir, [Warrant of Arrest for Omar Hassan Ahmad Al Bashir] (4 March 2009) ICC-02/05-01/09-1; ICC, Prosecutor v Omar Hassan Ahmad Al Bashir [Second Warrant of Arrest for Omar Hassan Ahmad Al Bashir] (12 July 2010) ICC-02/05-01/09-95.

[46] Kress and Prost 2022, p. 2478.

2.3.1.1 Kenya

In August 2010, the Pre-Trial Chamber addressed the purported presence of Al-Bashir in Kenya, who was invited to attend the celebration of the promulgation of Kenya's new constitution.[47] The Chamber emphasised that Kenya had a clear obligation to cooperate with the Court in relation to the enforcement of the arrest warrants against Al-Bashir.[48] In its decision, the Court found it appropriate to inform the Assembly of States Parties and the UN Security Council about the expected attendance of Al-Bashir in order for them to take any action they deemed appropriate, should such attendance be confirmed.[49] In October 2010, as a result of this decision, as well as international outcry against the hosting of Al-Bashir, the Intergovernmental Authority on Development special summit on Sudan, which was to be held in Kenya, was moved to Ethiopia in order to prevent any diplomatic issues over the attendance of Al-Bashir.[50]

It was confirmed by the Kenyan government that Al-Bashir was indeed in Kenya, with the government citing strategic interest and that arresting Al-Bashir would have "adversely affected peace in Sudan".[51] In response to the failure of Kenya to arrest Al-Bashir, the International Commission of Jurists-Kenya Chapter petitioned the High Court of Kenya to find Kenya in violation of its obligations under the Rome Statute.[52] In November 2011, the Kenyan High Court ruled that Kenya had an obligation to arrest Al-Bashir, and issued a provisional warrant of arrest for him should he ever visit Kenya again, arguing that it was implementing the decision of the ICC to which Kenya, as a State Party to the Rome Statute, had obligations to execute.[53]

In 2018, this decision was heard on Appeal, with the Court of Appeal holding that there was no jurisdiction upon which a provisional arrest warrant against Al-Bashir could be issued, as the required urgency no longer existed at the time the order was issued.[54] However, the Court did hold that Kenya had an obligation to execute the arrest warrants of the ICC and that the failure to do so was a breach of

---

[47] ICC, Prosecutor v Omar Hassan Ahmad Al-Bashir [Decision informing the United Nations Security Council and the Assembly of States Parties to the Rome Statute about Omar Al-Bashir's Presence in the territory of the Republic of Kenya] ICC-02/05-01/09-107 (27 August 2010) ICC-02/05-01/09-107, para 1.

[48] Ibid. para 3.

[49] Ibid. paras 4–5.

[50] Sudan Tribune *IGAD Summit Moved from Kenya as ICC demands arrest of Sudan's Bashir* (26 October 2010) available at: https://sudantribune.com/article36453/ (accessed 5 June 2024).

[51] The Guardian *Kenya Defends Failure to Arrest Sudan's President Omar Al-Bashir* (29 August 2010) available at: https://www.theguardian.com/world/2010/aug/29/kenya-omar-al-bashir-arrest-failure (accessed 5 June 2023).

[52] Nairobi High Court, Kenya Section of the International Commission of Jurists v Attorney General & Another [Miscellaneous Criminal Application 685 of 2010] (28 November 2011) p. 3.

[53] Ibid. p. 20.

[54] Court of Appeal at Nairobi, Attorney General and 2 others v Kenya Section of International Commission of Jurists [Civil Appeal 105 of 2012 & Criminal Appeal 274 of 2011] (16 February 2018) p. 24.

international law, as well as a breach of Kenya's own constitution and legislation.[55] These decisions reaffirmed the obligation of Kenya to arrest Al-Bashir.

2.3.1.2 Malawi

In December 2011, the Pre-Trial Chamber I addressed the non-cooperation of Malawi.[56] In October 2011, Al-Bashir entered Malawi for the purposes of attending a Summit of the Common Market for Eastern and Southern Africa, where he was not arrested as per the requests of the Court.[57] Taking into account the arguments of Malawi regarding Head of State immunity,[58] the Chamber found that Malawi had failed to comply with the request to cooperate in the arrest and surrender of Al-Bashir and decided to refer the matter to the Assembly of States Parties and the UN Security Council.[59]

In 2012 the Bureau of the Assembly of States Parties' first report on non-cooperation addressed the outcomes of interactions held with representatives of Malawi, following the decision on non-cooperation.[60] The report noted that dialogue held with Malawi indicated that it had reaffirmed its intention to follow through with its cooperation obligations.[61] The report also revealed that Malawi had declined to host Al-Bashir at an African Union summit that was planned to be held in the State in June of that year. This summit ended up not being hosted in Malawi and was moved to Ethiopia, a non-State Party to the Statute.[62] From these factors, the Report concluded that Malawi had enhanced the implementation of the Court's decision due to the swift reactions to Assembly communications made to the Government of Malawi, as well as the dialogue conducted that was aimed at ensuring that non-cooperation was not repeated.[63]

2.3.1.3 Nigeria

In 2013, the Pre-Trial Chamber decided on Nigeria's failure to arrest Al-Bashir when he was in the territory to participate in a special AU Summit that was being held in

---

[55] Ibid.

[56] ICC, Prosecutor v Omar Hassan Ahmad Al Bashir [Corrigendum to the Decision Pursuant to Article 87(7) of the Rome Statute on the Failure by the Republic of Malawi to Comply with the Cooperation Requests Issued by the Court with Respect to the Arrest and Surrender of Omar Hassan Ahmad Al Bashir] (13 December 2011) ICC-02/05-01/09-139.

[57] Ibid. para 5(i).

[58] Ibid. paras 10–17.

[59] Ibid. para 47.

[60] ASP 2012.

[61] Ibid. para 5.

[62] ASP 2012, para 10.

[63] Ibid. para 16.

the capital, Abuja.[64] The Chamber reminded Nigeria that it was under an obligation as a State Party to the Rome Statute to execute Court decisions concerning the arrest and surrender of Al-Bashir.[65] Nigeria responded by repeating their commitment to cooperate with the Court, as well as stating that Al-Bashir was not invited to the summit as AU member States do not require invitations by the host government to attend such summits.[66] Nigeria also noted that Al-Bashir left before the official end of the summit while steps were being considered in line with their international obligations towards his arrest.[67] The Pre-Trial Chamber noted this and concluded that in light of its discretionary power by virtue of Article 87(7), it was not necessary to refer Nigeria's non-cooperation to the Assembly of States Parties and/or the UN Security Council, and merely reminded Nigeria of its obligation to arrest and surrender Al-Bashir to the Court as well as requesting that Al-Bashir is immediately arrested and surrendered should a similar situation arise in the future.[68]

2.3.1.4 Democratic Republic of the Congo

In 2014, the Pre-Trial Chamber addressed the failure of the DRC in arresting and surrendering Al-Bashir who was in the country to attend a COMESA summit.[69] The DRC argued that it was not able to cooperate with the Court as a result of time and legal constraints.[70] In relation to the time constraints argument, the DRC gave three reasons for this failure: that the composition of the delegations that were invited to attend the summit was communicated very late to DRC authorities; that Al-Bashir was invited by a regional organisation and not by the DRC; and that Al-Bashir had shortened his visit which made it materially impossible to take such a decision which had massive legal, diplomatic and security implications.[71]

The Pre-Trial Chamber rejected these arguments, reminding the DRC that the obligation to arrest Al-Bashir had existed since the warrants for his arrest were issued in 2009 and 2010.[72] The Chamber also held that the DRC should have consulted or notified the Court as per Article 97 of the Statute upon identification of a problem with the execution of the arrest warrant.[73] The Pre-Trial Chamber decided that the

---

[64] ICC, Prosecutor v Omar Hassan Ahmad Al-Bashir [Decision on the Cooperation of the Federal Republic of Nigeria Regarding Omar Al-Bashir's Arrest and Surrender to the Court] (5 September 2013) ICC-02/05-01/09-159.

[65] Ibid. para 9.

[66] Ibid. para 11.

[67] Ibid. para 12.

[68] Ibid. para 13.

[69] ICC, Prosecutor v Omar Hassan Ahmad Al Bashir [Decision on the Cooperation of the Democratic Republic of the Congo Regarding Omar Al Bashir's Arrest and Surrender to the Court] (9 April 2014) ICC-02/05-01/09 195, para 5.

[70] Ibid. para 11.

[71] Ibid. para 12.

[72] Ibid. para 14.

[73] Ibid. para 15.

DRC had failed to cooperate with the Court in the arrest and surrender of Al-Bashir and that the matter would be referred to the Assembly of States Parties and the UN Security Council.[74] According to the 2014 *Report of the Bureau on Non-cooperation,* Consultations between the Assembly of States Parties and the DRC indicated that it had reaffirmed its commitment and support to the Court.[75]

2.3.1.5 Uganda

In July 2016, the Pre-Trial Chamber decided on Uganda's failure to arrest Al-Bashir when he was in the country in May 2016 to attend an inauguration ceremony.[76] Uganda was invited to provide its observations in order for the Pre-Trial Chamber to determine the Course of action in relation to its non-compliance with the obligation to arrest and surrender Al-Bashir to the Court, including whether resort to measures under Article 87(7) would be warranted in the circumstances.[77] Uganda submitted that inviting Al-Bashir to the inauguration ceremony was for the purpose of maintaining good relations with all countries in the region, which was essential to the maintenance of international peace and security. Uganda also referred to the AU Assembly decision not to cooperate with the ICC's request for the arrest and surrender of Al-Bashir to the Court.[78] Regarding the AU Assembly decision not to cooperate, the Chamber held that this issue had already been addressed in a previous decision and as such was not an impediment to arresting Al-Bashir.[79]

Regarding the claim that inviting Al-Bashir was part of an effort to the realization of permanent peace and stability in the region, the Court held that States Parties to the Rome Statute must pursue any legitimate or desirable political objectives within the boundaries of their legal obligations towards the Court. The Court further held in this regard that it was not the nature of legal obligations that they can be put aside for political reasons.[80] In its final decision, the Court held for these reasons that it was appropriate to make a finding of non-compliance by Uganda and have the matter referred to the Assembly of States Parties and the UN Security Council.[81]

---

[74] Ibid. para 34.

[75] ASP 2014, para 39.

[76] ICC, Prosecutor v Omar Hassan Ahmad Al Bashir [Decision on the non-compliance by the Republic of Uganda with the request to arrest and surrender Omar Al-Bashir to the Court and referring the matter to the United Nations Security Council and the Assembly of State Parties to the Rome Statute] (11 July 2016)ICC-02/05-01/09, paras 4 & 5.

[77] Ibid. para 6.

[78] Ibid. para 7.

[79] Ibid. paras 11–13.

[80] Ibid. para 14.

[81] Ibid. para 15.

2.3.1.6 South Africa

In July 2017, the Pre-Trial Chamber decided on South Africa's failure to arrest Al-Bashir in June 2015 when he was in the country to attend an AU Summit.[82] The Court noted that it was already made aware of Al-Bashir's planned travel to South Africa in May 2015, a month prior to the commencement of the Summit.[83] At the end of May, the Court notified South African authorities that they were requested to arrest Al-Bashir should he enter South African territory, and in the event of any problem that may affect the execution of this request, that they consult with the Court in order to resolve the matter.[84] Prior to Al-Bashir's arrival, Article 97 consultations were entered into between South Africa and the Court in order to resolve any legal questions relating to the arrest of Al-Bashir.[85]

Al-Bashir arrived in South Africa the following day, which prompted a meeting between South Africa's Chief State Law Adviser and representatives of the Court Registry and the Office of the Prosecutor.[86] The Pre-Trial Chamber received an urgent request from the ICC Prosecutor to issue an order which clarified the obligation of South Africa to immediately arrest and surrender Al-Bashir and that there were no obstacles which had the effect of nullifying or delaying this obligation. This request was rejected as it was already made clear that the obligation to arrest and surrender Al-Bashir was still in effect.[87] Al-Bashir left South African territory on the morning of the 15th of June without any resistance from law enforcement authorities.[88] In September 2015, the Pre-Trial Chamber held that these events warranted the opening of Article 87(7) proceedings against South Africa.[89] Prior to non-cooperation proceedings before the Pre-Trial Chamber could be heard, South Africa requested that the Court would give it more time to finalise domestic legal proceedings on the matter. This request was granted, and domestic proceedings took place between December 2015 and May 2016.[90]

In May 2015, prior to the arrival of Al-Bashir in South Africa for the AU Summit, the Southern African Litigation Centre wrote to various branches of the South African Government, reminding them of their obligations in terms of the Rome Statute and

---

[82] ICC, Prosecutor v Omar Hassan Ahmad Al Bashir [Decision Under Article 87(7) of the Rome Statute on the non-compliance by South Africa with the request by the Court for the arrest and surrender of Omar Al-Bashir] (6 July 2017) ICC-02/05-01/09-302.

[83] Ibid. para 5.

[84] Decision Under Article 87(7) of the Rome Statute on the non-compliance by South Africa with the request by the Court for the arrest and surrender of Omar Al-Bashir, above n. 82, para 6.

[85] Ibid. para 7; See also at paras 9–10 where the Pre-trial Chamber noted that previous non-cooperation cases had already answered the legal questions put forward by South Africa, and that entering into such consultation procedures did not have an effect on a State's outstanding obligations towards the Court.

[86] Ibid. paras 11–12.

[87] Ibid. paras 13–14.

[88] Ibid. para 15.

[89] Ibid. para 17.

[90] Ibid. paras 18–19.

South Africa's domestic ICC legislation.[91] A lack of appropriate response by the government prompted the SALC to inform the government that legal action would be taken should Al-Bashir be found in South African Territory.[92] Following the failure to arrest Al-Bashir, the SALC approached the High Court on an urgent basis, seeking the implementation of the arrest warrants.[93] In this decision, the High Court ruled against the South African Government, reaffirming their duty to adhere to South Africa's obligations under domestic and international law.[94] Following this decision, the South African Government sought to appeal the decision, which was heard by the Supreme Court of Appeal in February 2016.[95] The Supreme Court of Appeal ruled against the South African Government, holding that the failure to Arrest Al-Bashir was inconsistent with South Africa's obligations in terms of the Rome Statute and its domestic implementation act, and was therefore unlawful.[96] Following the closing of domestic proceedings, proceedings before the ICC could then resume.[97]

In the ICC Pre-Trial Chamber, South Africa submitted that a number of errors had occurred during the consultations on Article 97 that had taken place prior to the failure to arrest Al-Bashir. The consultation procedures had been wrongly dealt with, the request had been subjected to a quasi-judicial rather than a diplomatic and political process, and that no rules applicable to consultations under Article 97 were available.[98] Previous decisions on non-cooperation were challenged for being inconsistent and not holding any proper legal ground.[99] South Africa also submitted that if the Pre-Trial Chamber were to find that it had been non-compliant, referral to the Assembly of States Parties and/or the UN Security Council would be unwarranted as its only purpose would be to cast South Africa in a negative light, which would not incentivise cooperation in future situations.[100]

Regarding the consultations on Article 97, held between South Africa and the Court prior to the failure to arrest Al-Bashir, the Pre-Trial Chamber held that such interactions did not have an effect on the duty to arrest and surrender a suspect

---

[91] Mudukuti 2016, p. 17.

[92] Ibid. p. 18.

[93] South Africa, North Gauteng High Court, Southern Africa Litigation Centre v Minister of Justice and Constitutional Development and Others (24 June 2015) 27740/2015) [2015] ZAGPPHC 402; 2016 (1) SACR 161 (GP); 2015 (5) SA 1 (GP); [2015] 3 All SA 505 (GP); 2015 (9) BCLR 1108 (GP).

[94] Ibid. para 39.

[95] Supreme Court of Appeal of South Africa, The Minister of Justice and Constitutional Development v The Southern African Litigation Centre (15 March 2016) (867/15) [2016] ZASCA 17.

[96] Ibid. para 113.

[97] Decision Under Article 87(7) of the Rome Statute on the non-compliance by South Africa with the request by the Court for the arrest and surrender of Omar Al-Bashir, above n. 82, paras 20–21.

[98] Ibid. para 27.

[99] Ibid. para 31.

[100] Ibid. para 39.

to the Court.[101] Taking these into consideration, the Pre-Trial Chamber found that South Africa had failed to cooperate with the Court in the arrest and surrender of Al-Bashir.[102] In determining whether a referral of South Africa to the Assembly of States Parties and/or the UN Security Council was warranted, the Chamber came to a number of conclusions. Firstly, in a previous decision of the Appeals Chamber, it was confirmed that an automatic referral to the Assembly or the Security Council was not required as a matter of law and that a Chamber has the discretion to consider all factors relevant in the circumstances of the case.[103] The Chamber took several factors into consideration. Firstly, the way South Africa approached its obligation to cooperate with the Court, including the request for article 97 consultations was particularly significant, as it was the first State Party to invoke article 97 following receipt of a request for arrest and surrender to resolve a perceived legal conflict with this request.[104]

The next factor taken into consideration was whether or not referring South Africa's non-cooperation would be an effective way to promote cooperation.[105] The Chamber noted that South Africa's domestic courts had already found that the South African Government had breached its obligations under domestic laws by failing to arrest and surrender Al-Bashir, with the Supreme Court of Appeal concluding that the conduct of the South African Government was inconsistent with the States obligations under the Rome Statute and South Africa's domestic implementation act and was therefore unlawful.[106]

The Chamber also noted that the South African Government had accepted its obligation to cooperate with the Court under its domestic legal framework.[107] From this, the Chamber concluded that a referral of South Africa's non-cooperation would be of no consequence as a mechanism to obtain cooperation.[108] The Pre-Trial Chamber also observed that in previous decisions, States Parties had been referred to the Assembly of States Parties and the UN Security Council. These referrals had not resulted in any follow up measures against these States. This observation further strengthened the Chamber's belief that a referral of South Africa was not warranted as a way to obtain cooperation.[109] From this the Pre-Trial Chamber decided against referring South Africa to the Assembly of States Parties and/or the UN Security Council.[110]

---

[101] Decision Under Article 87(7) of the Rome Statute on the non-compliance by South Africa with the request by the Court for the arrest and surrender of Omar Al-Bashir, above n. 82, para 122.

[102] Ibid. para 123.

[103] Ibid. paras 124–125.

[104] Ibid. paras 127–130.

[105] Ibid. para 135.

[106] Ibid. para 136; see also The Minister of Justice and Constitutional Development v The Southern African Litigation Centre above n. 95.

[107] Ibid.

[108] Decision Under Article 87(7) of the Rome Statute on the non-compliance by South Africa with the request by the Court for the arrest and surrender of Omar Al-Bashir, above n. 82, para 137.

[109] Decision Under Article 87(7) of the Rome Statute on the non-compliance by South Africa with the request by the Court for the arrest and surrender of Omar Al-Bashir, above n. 82, para 138.

[110] Ibid. para 140.

2.3.1.7 Jordan

In December 2017, the Pre-Trial Chamber decided on the failure of Jordan in arresting and surrendering Al-Bashir when he was in the territory to attend an Arab League summit in March 2017.[111] The Chamber noted that in February 2017, the Court Registry received information that Al-Bashir was expected to travel to Jordan to participate in this summit. Jordan was invited to provide information regarding this visit and was requested to cooperate in his arrest and surrender should he enter their territory.[112] Jordan confirmed in a *note verbale* that Al-Bashir was to attend the summit and announced that they would enter into Article 97 consultations with the Court. Jordan also communicated that it would recognise Al-Bashir's immunity under international law.[113] Al-Bashir reportedly travelled to Jordan to attend the summit and left without any interference from Jordanian law enforcement.[114]

Aside from arguments relating to head of State immunity, Jordan also submitted that it had requested Article 97 consultations with the Court to address potential problems in the execution of their obligation to cooperate. This request was not granted.[115] The Pre-Trial Chamber once again had to address the issue of Head of State immunity and rejected Jordan's arguments on the issue.[116] With regard to Article 97 consultations, the Chamber found that consultations did not take place.[117] The Chamber concluded that any consultations, either pending or ongoing, between the Court and a State Party did not suspend or otherwise affect the validity of a request to cooperate.[118] The Chamber concluded that Jordan had failed to comply with the Court's request to arrest and surrender Al-Bashir.[119] The decision was made to also refer the matter to the Assembly of States Parties and the UN Security Council.[120]

Shortly after the decision of the Pre-Trial Chamber, the Kingdom of Jordan gave notice that it intended to appeal the Chamber's decision.[121] Jordan submitted that the decision made by the Pre-Trial Chamber had several errors of law relating to Head of State immunity and that the Chamber had abused its discretionary powers in deciding

---

[111] ICC, Prosecutor v Omar Hassan Ahmad Al Bashir [Decision under article 87(7) of the Rome Statute on the non-compliance by Jordan with the request by the Court for the arrest and surrender or Omar Al-Bashir] (11 December 2017) ICC-02/05-01/09-309.

[112] Ibid. para 5.

[113] Ibid. para 7.

[114] Ibid. para 8.

[115] Ibid. para 18.

[116] Ibid. paras 44–45.

[117] Ibid. para 47.

[118] Decision under article 87(7) of the Rome Statute on the non-compliance by Jordan with the request by the Court for the arrest and surrender or Omar Al-Bashir, above n. 111, paras 48–49.

[119] Ibid. para 50.

[120] Ibid. para 55.

[121] ICC, Prosecutor v Omar Hassan Ahmad Al Bashir [The Hashemite Kingdom of Jordan's appeal against the "Decision under article 87(7) of the Rome Statute on the non-compliance by Jordan with the request by the Court for the arrest and surrender of Omar Al-Bashir"] (12 March 2018) ICC-02/05-01/09-326.

to refer Jordan to the Assembly of States Parties and the UN Security Council.[122] In response to these submissions, the Appeals Chamber has since upheld the Pre-Trial Chamber's decision, confirming that Heads of State do not have immunity under customary international law before international criminal tribunals.[123]

With regards to the decision to refer Jordan to the Assembly of States Parties and the UN Security Council, the Appeals Chamber held that the Pre-Trial Chamber had erroneously exercised its discretion by treating Jordan differently to South Africa even though their cases shared similar facts.[124] As a result of this finding, the Appeals Chamber decided to reverse the Pre-Trial Chambers decision to refer Jordan to the Assembly of States Parties and the UN Security Council.[125]

2.3.1.8 Repeated Instances of Non-cooperation

The Pre-Trial Chamber has also heard non-cooperation decisions from States who have failed to cooperate in the arrest and surrender of Al-Bashir on multiple occasions: Chad and Djibouti.

Chad's first case on non-cooperation was heard at the end of 2011, relating to its failure to arrest Al-Bashir in August of that year to attend an inauguration ceremony.[126] Chad shared a similar fate to Malawi, with the Pre-Trial Chamber finding that it had failed to comply with the cooperation requests communicated to it and that the matter would be referred to the UN Security Council and the Assembly of States Parties.[127] Another non-cooperation decision against Chad was heard in 2013.[128] The Chamber recognised that Chad had been engaging in a consistent pattern of deliberately disregarding not only the decisions of the Court and its orders related to the obligation to arrest Al-Bashir, but also Security Council Resolution 1593 which referred the situation in Sudan to the Court. This decision was also referred to the Assembly of States Parties and the UN Security Council.[129] The Assembly of States Parties addressed the continued non-cooperation of Chad at the eleventh, twelfth

[122] Ibid. paras 4(a)–(d).

[123] Prosecutor v Omar Hassan Ahmad Al Bashir [Judgment in the Jordan Referral re Al-Bashir Appeal] (6 May 2019) ICC-02/05-01/09 OA2, para 162.

[124] Ibid. paras 211–212.

[125] Ibid. para 216.

[126] Prosecutor v Omar Hassan Ahmad Al Bashir [Decision pursuant to article 87(7) of the Rome Statute on the Refusal of the Republic of Chad to comply with the cooperation requests issued by the Court with respect to the arrest and surrender of Omar Hassan Ahmad Al Bashir] (13 December 2011) ICC-02/05-01/09-140, para 3.

[127] Ibid. para 14.

[128] Prosecutor v Omar Hassan Ahmad Al Bashir [Decision on the Non-compliance of the Republic of Chad with the cooperation requests issued by the Court regarding the Arrest and Surrender of Omar Hassan Ahmad Al Bashir] (26 March 2013) ICC-02/05-01/09-151.

[129] Ibid. para 23.

and thirteenth sessions. The thirteenth session noted that Chad finally expressed its commitment to support the work of the Court with regards to non-cooperation.[130]

In the case of Djibouti, its first decision on non-cooperation was also heard in 2011 and addressed the failure to arrest Al-Bashir while he was in Djibouti to attend an inauguration ceremony.[131] In this decision, the Pre-Trial Chamber reminded Djibouti of its obligation to cooperate with the Court by virtue of its obligation as a State Party to the Rome Statute, and decided not to refer the non-cooperation to the Assembly of States Parties and the UN Security Council, but instead informed these bodies that Al-Bashir was not arrested.[132]

In 2016, a second case was heard where Djibouti failed to arrest Al-Bashir while he was in the territory to attend another inauguration ceremony.[133] Djibouti submitted four reasons for its failure to cooperate with the Court: that it lacked national procedures for the arrest and surrender of suspects to the Court, Al-Bashir enjoyed immunity by virtue of Article 98(1) of the Statute, that it aligned itself with the position of the African Union regarding the arrest and surrender of sitting heads of State, and that it was part of peace negotiations between Sudan and South Sudan.[134] The Pre-Trial Chamber rejected all of these arguments.[135] The fact that Djibouti had already failed to arrest Al-Bashir on a previous occasion was also taken into consideration.[136] The Chamber found that Djibouti had failed to comply with the Court's requests to cooperate and that the matter would be referred to the Assembly of States Parties and the UN Security Council.[137]

2.3.2 *Upcoming Non-cooperation Responses: The Situation in Ukraine*

While there have been no non-cooperation decisions since Jordan's failure to cooperate in 2017, the recent issuing of an arrest warrant for Vladimir Putin with regard to the situation in Ukraine has highlighted the need to revisit the ICC's regime for responding to instances of non-cooperation.

---

[130] ASP 2014, para 39.

[131] Prosecutor v Omar Hassan Ahmad Al Bashir [Decision informing the United Nations Security Council and the Assembly of the States Parties to the Rome Statute about Omar Al-Bashir's recent visit to Djibouti] (12 May 2011) ICC-02/05-01/09, para 1.

[132] Ibid. paras 3, 5.

[133] Prosecutor v Omar Hassan Ahmad Al Bashir [Decision on the Non-compliance by the Republic of Djibouti with the Request to Arrest and Surrender Omar Al-Bashir to the Court and Referring the matter to the United Nations Security Council and the Assembly of States Parties to the Rome Statute] (11 July 2016) ICC-02/05-01/09-266, para 4.

[134] Ibid. para 6.

[135] Ibid. paras 8–14.

[136] Ibid. para 15.

[137] Ibid. paras 16–18.

Prior to becoming a State Party to the Rome Statute in 2024,[138] Ukraine accepted the ICC's jurisdiction over alleged crimes occurring on its territory under Article 12(3) of the Statute on two separate occasions. In April 2014, Ukraine lodged its first declaration which accepted the ICC jurisdiction over alleged crimes committed in Ukrainian territory from 21 November 2013 to 22 February 2014.[139] A second declaration was lodged in September 2015, which extended the period on an open-ended basis to cover alleged crimes committed throughout Ukraine from February 2014 onwards.[140]

Between March and April 2022, the ICC Office of the Prosecutor received referrals of the situation in Ukraine from 43 States Parties as per Article 14 of the Statute, with the ICC Prosecutor announcing on the Second of March 2022 the opening of an investigation into the situation in Ukraine on the basis of the referrals received from States.[141] The scope of the situation encompasses any past and present allegations of serious international crimes committed on any part of Ukrainian territory by any person from 21 November 2013 onwards.[142]

2.3.2.1 The Arrest Warrant for Vladimir Putin and the 2023 BRICS Summit

In March 2023, the ICC issued a warrant of arrest for Vladimir Vladimirovich Putin, the President of the Russian Federation, for the war crimes of unlawful deportation of population, and the unlawful transfer of population from occupied areas of Ukraine to Russia. These crimes were allegedly committed in Ukrainian occupied territory from February 2022, following the Russian invasion of Ukraine. While the existence of these arrest warrants is known to the public, the Pre-Trial Chamber has considered

---

[138] The New Voice of Ukraine "Ukraine Adapts Criminal Codes to ICC's Rome Statute Norms" (22 October 2024) available at: https://english.nv.ua/nation/ukraine-enacts-law-to-prosecute-war-crimes-meeting-icc-rome-statute-obligations-50460419.html (accessed 22 October 2024).

[139] Letter Dated 9 April 2014 to the Registrar of the International Criminal Court from the Embassy of Ukraine to the Kingdom of the Netherlands, available at: https://www.icc-cpi.int/sites/default/files/itemsDocuments/997/declarationRecognitionJuristiction09-04-2014.pdf (accessed 22 October 2024).

[140] Letter Dated 8 September 2015 to the Registrar of the International Criminal Court from the Minister for Foreign Affairs of Ukraine, available at: https://www.icc-cpi.int/sites/default/files/icc docs/other/Ukraine_Art_12-3_declaration_08092015.pdf#search=ukraine (accessed 1 June 2024).

[141] ICC Statement of ICC Prosecutor, Karim A.A. Khan QC, on the Situation in Ukraine: Receipt of Referrals *from 39 States Parties and the Opening of an Investigation* (2 March 2022) available at: https://www.icc-cpi.int/news/statement-icc-prosecutor-karim-aa-khan-qc-situation-ukraine-rec eipt-referrals-39-states (accessed 1 June 2024).

[142] Ibid.

it necessary to keep the warrants secret to protect victims and witnesses, and to safeguard the investigation.[143]

This arrest warrant was almost put to the test in 2023 at a BRICS summit that was hosted in South Africa. As already noted above, South Africa already has a history of non-cooperation with the requests of the ICC to arrest a sitting head of State. It was reported that Putin was invited to attend this summit as the head of State of a BRICS State.[144] However, considering that there was an ICC arrest warrant issued out for Putin, it was agreed that he would not attend the summit, and instead attend remotely in a video conference format.[145] If Putin were to attend the summit, South Africa would have had an obligation to arrest Putin. While this may have had the effect of placing South Africa in bad favour with its BRICS partners, the execution of the arrest warrant would have shown the international community South Africa's dedication to the fight against impunity for serious international crimes. It would also have had the effect of legitimizing the ICC's image as an effective international criminal tribunal.[146]

2.3.2.2 Mongolia's Failure to Arrest Putin

Mongolia has been a State Party to the Rome Statute since 11 April 2002, when it deposited its instrument of ratification.[147] In turn, Mongolia therefore has an obligation under the Rome Statute to cooperate with requests from the Court.[148] Mongolia is further represented within the ICC by Judge Erdrenebalsuren Damdin, who was elected in March 2024 and assigned to the appeals division of the Court.[149] Additionally, in June 2024, Mongolia declared its "unwavering support" for the ICC "as

[143] ICC Press Release "Situation in Ukraine: ICC judges issue arrest warrants against Vladimir Vladimirovich Putin and Maria Alekseyevna Lvova Belova" (17 March 2023) available at: https://www.icc-cpi.int/news/situation-ukraine-icc-judges-issue-arrest-warrants-against-vladimir-vladimirovich-putin-and (accessed 6 June 2024).

[144] Khoza A 'Russia's Vladimir Putin invited to attend Brics summit in SA, Pandor Confirms' (23 March 2023) *Times Live* available at: https://www.timeslive.co.za/politics/2023-03-23-russias-vladimir-putin-invited-to-attend-brics-summit-in-sa-pandor-confirms/ (accessed 1 June 2024).

[145] "Putin to Miss BRICS summit by mutual agreement, South Africa says" (19 July 2023) *Al-Jazeera* available at: https://www.aljazeera.com/news/2023/7/19/south-africa-putin-to-miss-brics-summit-by-mutual-agreement (accessed 1 June 2024).

[146] Sithole L 'Should South Africa Arrest Putin at the 2023 BRICS Summit?' African Business (14 April 2023) available at: https://african.business/2023/04/politics/should-south-africa-arrest-putin-at-the-2023-brics-summit (accessed 1 June 2024).

[147] ICC *States Parties to the Rome Statute—Mongolia,* available at: https://asp.icc-cpi.int/states-parties/asian-states/mongolia (accessed 5 September 2024).

[148] RS, above n. 3. Article 86.

[149] ICC *Judges—Judge Erdenebalsuren Damdin* available at: https://www.icc-cpi.int/judges/judge-erdenebalsuren-damdin (accessed 5 September 2024).

an independent and impartial judicial institution" in a joint statement endorsed by 93 ICC States Parties following several threats to ICC States Parties and employees.[150]

In September 2024, the ICC arrest warrant against Putin was put to the test when he arrived in Mongolia to attend a ceremony that commemorated a 1939 victory of Soviet and Mongolian troops over Japan.[151] Prior to this visit, there were calls by various organisations for Mongolia to either refuse Putin entry into their territory or otherwise arrest him.[152] Unfortunately, Putin was not arrested, with Mongolia citing the visit as a furtherance of national interests due to its reliance on Russia for energy resources.[153]

In October 2024, Pre-Trial Chamber II of the ICC decided on Mongolia's failure to arrest Putin.[154] As in the *South Africa* and *Jordan* decisions, the Court noted that Mongolia had requested consultations prior to his arrival to address challenges related to the cooperation request, namely the purported immunities held by Putin as a sitting head of State. In particular, the *note verbale* transmitted to the Court highlighted that Mongolia recognised Putin's immunities and had not identified any rule in customary international law that excludes or renders the immunity of heads of State inapplicable when their arrest is sought by an international criminal tribunal.[155] In granting immunity to the Putin, the Pre-Trial Chamber held that Mongolia was acting inconsistently with its international obligations under the Rome Statute, thereby preventing the Court from exercising its functions and powers under the Statute.[156] The Pre-Trial Chamber concluded that Mongolia's failure to arrest Putin while in the territory, and not promptly informing the Court of its intentions with regard to the Article 97 consultations, was a failure on the part of Mongolia to comply with the Court's request for cooperation as per Article 87(7) of the Statute.[157]

---

[150] Government of Canada "Joint Statement in support of the International Criminal Court" (17 June 2024) available at: https://www.canada.ca/en/global-affairs/news/2024/06/joint-statement-in-support-of-the-international-criminal-court.html (accessed 5 September 2024).

[151] Associated Press (2024) Putin Arrives in Mongolia, a Member of the ICC that Issued an Arrest Warrant for Him. available at: https://apnews.com/article/russia-mongolia-putin-icc-warrant-b9c04dff1849164010de92b5564f7e60 (accessed 5 September 2024).

[152] Human Rights Watch (2024) Mongolia: Arrest Putin. available at: https://www.hrw.org/news/2024/09/02/mongolia-arrest-putin (accessed 5 September 2024); Amnesty International (2024) Mongolia: Putin must be arrested and surrendered to the International Criminal Court available at: https://www.amnesty.org/en/latest/news/2024/09/mongolia-putin-must-be-arrested-and-surrendered-to-the-international-criminal-court/ (accessed 5 September 2024).

[153] Lkhaajav B "In Welcoming Putin, Mongolia Prioritizes National Interest over Russia's War with Ukraine" (9 September 2024) *The Diplomat* available at: https://thediplomat.com/2024/09/in-welcoming-putin-mongolia-prioritizes-national-interest-over-russias-war-with-ukraine/ (accessed 10 September 2024).

[154] ICC, Situation in Ukraine [Finding under article 87(7) of the Rome Statute on the Non-compliance by Mongolia with the request by the Court to cooperate in the arrest and surrender of Vladimir Vladimirovich Putin and Referral to the Assembly of States Parties] (24 October 2024) ICC-01/22-90.

[155] Ibid. para 6.

[156] Ibid. para 37.

[157] Ibid. para 38.

In determining whether referral to the Assembly of States Parties was warranted, the Court held that Mongolia's obligation to arrest Putin was sufficiently clear. Despite this clear obligation, Mongolia failed to fulfil this obligation, did not provide any valid justifications for its breach of obligations, and did not indicate its intention to cooperate with the Court in future situations. In view of the seriousness of Mongolia's failure to cooperate, the Chamber found it appropriate to refer Mongolia's non-cooperation to the Assembly of States Parties.[158] At the time of writing, the Assembly of States Parties is yet to respond to Mongolia's referral.

2.3.3 *Case Law on the Discretionary Powers of the Court*

According to Ntahiraja, referrals of instances of non-cooperation to the Assembly of States Parties or the UN Security Council are not mandatory, and are therefore not necessary consequences of a finding of non-compliance.[159] In determining whether or not to refer a decision of non-cooperation to the Assembly of States Parties and/ or the UN Security Council, the various chambers of the Court have addressed the discretionary power granted to them and have raised questions as to whether alternative measures could be used to address non-cooperation more effectively. Some of these decisions will be referred to below.

2.3.3.1 Libya: Availability of Measures to Address Non-cooperation

In the case of *The Prosecutor v Saif Al Islam Gaddafi*, the Pre-Trial chamber addressed Libya's failure to cooperate with the Court in the arrest and surrender of the suspect, as well as failing to return legal documents seized by Libyan authorities from former legal representatives of the suspect.[160] The Chamber held that the use of measures under Article 87(7) was not a mandatory course of action, but one of many tools available to the Court to use as a measure of last resort or part of a wide-ranging strategy aimed at promoting cooperation.[161] The Chamber also confirmed that Article 87(7) was not designed to punish or criticise a non-compliant State, but instead make additional tools available to the Court to assist it in eliminating obstacles to cooperation.[162] In this decision the Chamber found it appropriate to make a finding of non-cooperation and refer the matter to the UN Security Council for it to consider

---

[158] Finding under Article 87(7) of the Rome Statute on the Non-compliance by Mongolia with the request by the Court to cooperate in the arrest and surrender of Vladimir Vladimirovich Putin and Referral to the Assembly of States Parties, above n 154, para 40.

[159] Ntahiraja 2017, p. 28.

[160] Prosecutor v Saif Al-Islam Gaddafi [Decision on the non-compliance by Libya with requests for cooperation by the Court and referring the matter to the United Nations Security Council] (10 December 2014) ICC-01/11-01/11-577, para 4.

[161] Ibid. para 23.

[162] Ibid. para 33.

any possible measures that would achieve cooperation from Libya with regard to its outstanding obligations towards the Court.[163]

2.3.3.2 Kenya: The Discretionary Powers of the Court

In the case of *The Prosecutor v Uhuru Muigai Kenyatta,* Kenya's failure to cooperate in the arrest of former President Kenyatta was addressed by both the Trial Chamber and the Appeals Chamber.

In 2014, the Pre-Trial Chamber was tasked with determining whether it was appropriate to proceed with a decision on non-cooperation and refer the matter to the Assembly of State Parties.[164] The Chamber held that even where a determination has been made that a State has failed to comply with a cooperation request, a Chamber still has to determine the appropriateness of making a finding of non-cooperation, taking into account the circumstances of the case.[165] The Chamber held that a certain amount of restraint is appropriate when hearing a decision on non-cooperation. In particular, it was held that not every instance of non-compliance with a request to cooperate will constitute a failure to comply under Article 87(7). It was the view of the Trial Chamber that cooperation was a continuing process that that both the Court and the requested State should make genuine efforts to resolve any issues that may have an effect on the proper execution of a request to cooperate.[166]

It was further held was that where non-cooperation arose from a genuine and confirmed lack of capacity or ability, such inaction will be condoned as a valid justification.[167] The Chamber also noted that the main reason for making a finding of non-cooperation was to further the proceedings in the main case.[168] It was also the view of the Chamber that referring a matter to the Assembly of States Parties could be made, irrespective of whether or not action by the Assembly would promote compliance with a request to cooperate. Such a referral should be made as a sanction or disciplinary measure and assist in enhancing the work of the Court by promoting future cooperation.[169] Noting that the Kenyan Government continued to not cooperate with the requests of the Court, the Chamber found it appropriate to make a decision on non-cooperation as further delays would not be in the interests of justice.[170] However,

[163] Decision on the non-compliance by Libya with requests for cooperation by the Court and referring the matter to the United Nations Security Council, above n. 160, para 34.

[164] The Prosecutor v. Uhuru Muigai Kenyatta [Decision on Prosecution's application for a finding of non-compliance under Article 87(7) of the Statute] (3 December 2014) ICC-01/09-02/11-982.

[165] Ibid. para 39.

[166] Ibid. para 40.

[167] Ibid. para 41.

[168] Ibid. para 82.

[169] Ibid. para 84.

[170] Decision on Prosecution's application for a finding of non-compliance under Article 87(7) of the Statute, above n. 164, para 89.

the Chamber found it unnecessary to refer the matter to the Assembly and rejected the Article 87(7) application.[171]

This decision was appealed by the ICC prosecutor on the grounds that the Trial Chamber had erred in law by not referring Kenya to the Assembly of States Parties upon its finding of non-cooperation; and alternatively, if the Trial Chamber had the discretion to refer Kenya to the Assembly, it erred in its exercise of discretion by taking irrelevant factors into consideration when making its decision.[172] In the Appeals Chamber, issues surrounding the scope of a Chambers discretion under Article 87(7) were raised.[173] The Appeals Chamber confirmed that exercising discretion under Article 87(7) was subject to two conditions: that the target State failed to comply with a request to cooperate; and that this failure was of a nature serious enough to prevent the Court from exercising its functions and powers under the Statute.[174] The Chamber also held that the decision to refer a matter to external actors should only be done upon concluding that it is the most effective way to obtain cooperation.[175]

It was further held that a decision not to refer a matter to the Assembly of States Parties or the UN Security Council did not imply acceptance of the non-cooperation, but instead is based upon the conclusion that referral may not be effective in addressing the failure to cooperate in a specific case.[176] The Chamber also confirmed that a decision to refer an instance of non-cooperation was not an automatic consequence of the failure to cooperate, but rather a determination that fell within the discretion of the Chamber hearing the Article 87(7) decision.[177] These principles were applied in the decision on South Africa's non-cooperation,[178] where the Pre-Trial Chamber decided against referring the matter further;[179] as well as in the Jordan Appeal decision,[180] where the Appeals Chamber reversed the Pre-Trial Chambers decision to refer Jordan to the Assembly of States Parties and/or the UN Security Council.[181]

---

[171] Ibid. para 90.

[172] The Prosecutor v. Uhuru Muigai Kenyatta [Prosecution Appeal against the "Decision on Prosecutions application for a Finding of Non-compliance under Article 87(7) of the Statute"] (20 March 2015) ICC-01/09-02/11-1006, para 4.

[173] Prosecutor v Uhuru Muigai Kenyatta [Judgment on the Prosecutor's appeal against Trial Chamber V(B)'s "Decision on Prosecution's application for a finding of non-compliance under Article 87(7) of the Statute"] (19 August 2015) ICC-01/09-02/11-1032, para 21.

[174] Ibid. para 39.

[175] Ibid. para 51.

[176] Ibid. para 52.

[177] Ibid. para 53.

[178] Decision Under Article 87(7) of the Rome Statute on the non-compliance by South Africa with the request by the Court for the arrest and surrender of Omar Al-Bashir, above, n. 82, para 61.

[179] Ibid. paras 124–126 and 139–140.

[180] Judgment in the Jordan Referral re Al-Bashir Appeal, above, n. 123, para 183.

[181] Ibid. paras 212–215.

2.4 Analysing the Content of Current Non-cooperation Case Law

The above decisions on non-cooperation have both positive and negative implications for the practice of the Court. On the one hand, these decisions are positive for the practice of the Court as they indicate that instances of non-cooperation are being responded to and receiving increased judicial responses.[182] On the other hand, the mere occurrence of non-cooperation cases has negative implications for the Court as it highlights the extent to which States are choosing not to comply with cooperation requests.[183] In addition, these decisions on non-cooperation have not led to any effective measures against States aimed at promoting cooperation and preventing non-cooperation.[184] The Pre-Trial Chamber has recognised that the current frameworks for addressing non-cooperation have been ineffective and have not appropriately addressed non-cooperation issues.[185]

According to Hunter, current case law is not robust enough to deter instances of non-cooperation, with these decisions lacking "consistency, quality and authority of legal reasoning.[186]" This can be illustrated by the manner in which cases with similar facts have been treated differently by Chambers; noting the DRC and Nigeria cases in addressing time constraints, the Djibouti and Chad cases in handling repeated instances of non-cooperation and the South Africa and Jordan Cases with regards to the application of Article 97 consultation procedures.[187] These cases also indicate the need to fix the legal and procedural provisions within the ICC's cooperation frameworks to ensure proper and effective support of the work of the Court.[188] While recognising that each case of non-cooperation before the Court needs to be examined on its own merits and facts, adopting a consistent approach to legal findings and responses to non-cooperation may assist in sending a coherent message to non-cooperating States, as well as deter future instances of non-cooperation by the same or other States.[189]

---

182 Sluiter 2018, p. 389.

183 Magliveras and Naldi 2013, p. 141, where the authors argue that the non-cooperation of States, particularly in the context of the Al-Bashir case, has reached the level of a "rebellion" against the ICC; Smith-van Lin 2016, pp. 115, 124, where the author highlights the growing list of States Parties not cooperating with the Court and that non-cooperation "has become the bane of the ICC's existence"; Behrmann 2016, p. 304, where the author notes that non-cooperation has turned into an established practice where arrest warrants are repeatedly ignored and requested States expressly refuse to abide by their obligations.

184 Sluiter 2018, p. 389.

185 Decision Under Article 87(7) of the Rome Statute on the non-compliance by South Africa with the request by the Court for the arrest and surrender of Omar Al-Bashir, above, n. 82, para 138.

186 Hunter 2016, p. 374.

187 Sluiter and Talontsi 2016, p. 92.

188 Ngari A "The Real Problem Behind South Africa's Refusal to Arrest al-Bashir" (10 July 2017) *ISS Today* available at https://issafrica.org/iss-today/the-real-problem-behind-south-africas-refusal-to-arrest-al-bashir (accessed 1 April 2020).

189 Bekou 2019, p. 931.

2.4.1 The Court's Exercise of Discretion

In looking at decisions that address the Court's exercise of discretion to refer a matter to the Assembly of States Parties and/or the UN Security Council, there is some uncertainty as to the exact standard required for such referrals, with there being noticeable differences in opinion as to the proper exercise of discretion.[190] Sluiter & Talontsi recognise that the various ICC chambers have been inconsistent in developing the precise standard of a failure to cooperate that may begin a judicial finding of non-cooperation.[191] In observing case law, there is uncertainty whether a judicial finding of non-cooperation is reserved for States acting in bad faith, or whether its application applies to all instances of non-cooperation.

2.4.2 The Standard of a Failure to Cooperate

Case law has identified three standards of failure to cooperate: an apparent failure, an objective failure and a complete failure.[192] In the decision on the DRC's non-cooperation in the arrest and surrender of Al-Bashir, the Pre-Trial Chamber held that an "apparent failure" to cooperate is sufficient for a judicial finding and its referral.[193] In Libya's non-cooperation decision, the Pre-Trial Chamber held that there must be an "objective failure" on the part of the State to comply with a request to cooperate.[194] This suggests that the motives behind the failure to cooperate are irrelevant.[195] In the decision on Kenya's failure to cooperate, the Trial Chamber held that a finding of non-cooperation should be based on a "complete failure" to cooperate.[196] In addition, for non-cooperation to meet the requirements of Article 87(7), there should be an unjustified inaction, delay or clear failure to have appropriate measures for executing the request to cooperate.[197] The Trial Chamber further held that the party going forward with a determination under Article 87(7) should be able to show that the requested State breached the standard of good faith required from States Parties.[198] In the Appeals Chamber, it was held that in determining whether a referral would be appropriate, the Chamber responsible for the decision needs to take into account

[190] Sluiter and Talontsi 2016, p. 90.

[191] Ibid. p. 92.

[192] Ibid. pp. 92–93.

[193] Decision on the Cooperation of the Democratic Republic of the Congo Regarding Omar Al Bashir's Arrest and Surrender to the Court, above n. 69, para 33.

[194] Decision on the non-compliance by Libya with requests for cooperation by the Court and referring the matter to the United Nations Security Council, above n. 160, paras 24 and 33.

[195] Sluiter and Talontsi 2016, p. 93.

[196] Decision on Prosecution's application for a finding of non-compliance under Article 87(7) of the Statute, above n. 164, para 21.

[197] Ibid. para 42.

[198] Ibid. paras 42 and 67.

certain considerations that are distinct from the factual assessment of whether the State has failed to cooperate with the Court.[199]

These cases indicate that there is much uncertainty and confusion as to the proper Standard of a failure to cooperate. This uncertainty fuels concerns that discretion under article 87(7) is used in a manner that is inconsistent and possibly illogical.[200] In this regard, Sluiter holds that this discretionary power granted by the Appeals Chamber is problematic and sends the wrong message to non-cooperating States.[201] In addition, Kress and Prost hold that while there is no strict duty to reach a finding of non-cooperation and refer such non-cooperation to the appropriate organs, it is in the best interests of the efficiency of the Court's cooperation regime that such discretion is exercised consistently.[202]

As it stands, current case law on non-cooperation gives the impression that States have nothing to fear for failing to cooperate with the Court. As a result, such non-cooperation appears to have become "business as usual" for States.[203] This can be illustrated by State reactions to the Court's recent issuing of an arrest warrant for Israeli prime minister, Benjamin Netanyahu, for war crimes and crimes against humanity.[204] While some States Parties have indicated their support for the Court's decision to issue the arrest warrant, other States indicate their intention not to fulfil their obligation to arrest and surrender should such a situation arise.[205] A notably glaring example of defiance of the Court's decision by a State Party is the statement by the Hungarian government that they would invite Netanyahu to visit Hungary and guarantee that they would not follow the contents of the arrest warrant.[206]

---

[199] Judgment on the Prosecutor's appeal against Trial Chamber V(B)'s "Decision on Prosecution's application for a finding of non-compliance under Article 87(7) of the Statute", above, n. 173, para 53.

[200] Sluiter and Talontsi 2016, *supra*, note 39, p. 94.

[201] Sluiter G "Key Reforms for the Next Decade of the ICC—Towards a Stronger Judicial Role in the Investigations and a More Robust System of Enforcing State Cooperation" (2018) *ICC Forum* available at https://iccforum.com/anniversary#Sluiter (accessed 15 August 2020).

[202] Kress and Prost 2022, p. 2490.

[203] Sluiter 2020, p. 312.

[204] ICC, 21 November 2024, Situation in the State of Palestine: ICC Pre-Trial Chamber I rejects the State of Israel's challenges to jurisdiction and issues warrants of arrest for Benjamin Netanyahu and Yoav Gallant available at: https://www.icc-cpi.int/news/situation-state-palestine-icc-pre-trial-chamber-i-rejects-state-israels-challenges (accessed 22 November 2024).

[205] See e.g. Ingber R "Mapping State Reactions to the ICC Arrest Warrants for Netanyahu and Gallant (23 November 2024) *Just Security* available at: https://www.justsecurity.org/105064/mapping-state-reactions-icc/ (accessed 24 November 2024) where it is highlighted that there are largely varied political responses to the Court's decision to issue the arrest warrant.

[206] Than K and Heine F "Orban Invites Netanyahu to Hungary as ICC Warrant Divides Europeans" (22 November 2024) *Reuters* available at: https://www.reuters.com/world/europe/pm-orban-says-he-will-invite-israeli-pm-netanyahu-hungary-after-icc-move-2024-11-22/ (accessed 23 November 2024); see also the tweet by Viktor Orban on X, "The #ICC arrest warrant against Prime Minister @netanyahu is brazen, cynical and completely unacceptable. I invited Prime Minister Netanyahu for an official visit to Hungary, where we will guarantee his freedom and safety", 22 November 2024, available at: https://x.com/PM_ViktorOrban/status/1859905807577726996 (accessed 23 November 2024).

2.5 Conclusion

This chapter looked to identify the frameworks under the Rome Statute for enforcing State obligations to cooperate with the ICC, as well as the procedure following a failure to comply with such obligations. This chapter has in particular highlighted several challenges faced by the Court chambers in responding to instances of non-cooperation, including a lack of consistent decision-making, and uncertainty regarding various aspects of a State's obligation to comply with requests to cooperate. A particularly notable aspect of current non-cooperation case law is the fact that referrals of non-cooperation have not led to any meaningful action being taken by either the Assembly of States Parties or the UN Security Council.[207]

As already noted above in the decision on South Africa's non-cooperation, the Pre-Trial Chamber observed that previous referrals of non-cooperation had not been effective in securing cooperation and was one of the factors that influenced its decision not to refer South Africa to the Assembly of States Parties and/or the Security Council.[208] Such inaction within the growing practice of the Court in responding to non-cooperation is a significant blow to the effectiveness of the ICC's cooperation regime and to the overall running of the Court itself.[209] The conclusion that can be drawn by such decisions is that the Court appears to have given up on its referral and enforcement mechanisms in anticipation of them failing to secure cooperation in the future.[210]

The chapter to follow seeks to analyse the procedure following a referral of a decision of non-cooperation to the ICC Assembly of States Parties and/or the UN Security Council. Here the remedies that have been developed by these bodies shall be analysed with a view to determining whether they are effective measures for following up on a judicial finding of non-cooperation. This chapter also seeks to highlight how these bodies can be better equipped to fulfilling their mandate to the Court through the application of frameworks already established within the Rome Statute and the United Nations System.

References

Ambach P (2022) Article 112, Assembly of States Parties. In: Ambos K (ed) Rome Statute of the International Criminal Court: Article-by-Article Commentary. Beck/Nomos/Hart, Munich, pp. 2767–2811.

Assembly of States Parties (2012) Eleventh Session Report of the Bureau on non-cooperation ICC-ASP/11/29.

---

[207] Ambach 2022, p. 2783.

[208] Decision Under Article 87(7) of the Rome Statute on the non-compliance by South Africa with the request by the Court for the arrest and surrender of Omar Al-Bashir, above n. 82, paras 138–140.

[209] Kress and Prost 2022, p. 2490.

[210] Sluiter 2018, p. 392.

Assembly of States Parties (2014) Thirteenth Session Report of the Bureau on non-cooperation ICC-ASP/13/40.

Behrmann C (2016) Strengthening the International Criminal Court Cooperation Regime from the European Union's Perspective. In: Bekou O, Birkett DJ (eds) Cooperation and the International Criminal Court: Perspectives from Theory and Practice. Brill, Leiden, pp. 297–317.

Bekou O (2019) Dealing with Non-cooperation at the ICC: Towards a More Holistic Approach. International Criminal Law Review 19(6): 911–937.

Bertrand A, Schauder N (2016) Practical Cooperation Challenges Faced by the Registry of the International Criminal Court. In: Bekou O, Birkett DJ (eds) Cooperation and the International Criminal Court: Perspectives from Theory and Practice. Brill, Leiden, pp. 152, 184.

Hunter E (2016) Using 'Managerial Compliance' to Strengthen ICC Cooperation. In: Bekou O, Birkett DJ (eds) Cooperation and the International Criminal Court: Perspectives from Theory and Practice. Brill, Leiden, pp. 366–395.

Kress C, Prost K (2022) International Cooperation and Judicial Assistance. In: Ambos K (ed) Rome Statute of the International Criminal Court: Article-by-Article Commentary. Beck/Nomos/Hart, Munich, pp. 2452–2701.

Machochoko P (1999) International Cooperation and Judicial Assistance. In Lee RS (ed) The International Criminal Court, The Making of the Rome Statute, Issues, Negotiations, Results. Kluwer Law International, The Hague, pp. 305–317.

Magliveras K, Naldi G (2013) The ICC Addresses Non-cooperation by States Parties: The Malawi Decision. African Journal of Legal Studies 6(1): 137–151.

Mudukuti A (2016), Judicial Integrity and Independence: The South African Omar Al Bashir Matter. In: Southern Africa Litigation Centre Goal 16 of the Sustainable Development Goals. South African Litigation Centre, Johannesburg, pp. 16–21.

Ntahiraja B (2017) Enforcing Cooperation Differently: Time to Criminalise Active Non-cooperation in the Rome Statute. In: Van der Merwe HJ, Kemp G (eds) International Justice in Africa, 2016. Strathmore University Press, Nairobi, pp. 21–49.

Schabas WA (2017) An Introduction to the International Criminal Court, 5th edn. Cambridge University Press, Cambridge.

Schabas WA, Pecorella G (2022) Article 13, Exercise of Jurisdiction. In: Ambos K (ed) Rome Statute of the International Criminal Court: Article-by-Article Commentary. Beck/Nomos/Hart, Munich, pp. 834–853.

Sluiter G (2018) Enforcing Cooperation: Did the Drafters Approach It the Wrong Way? Journal of International Criminal Justice 16(2): 383–402.

Sluiter G (2020) Reforms to Enhance State Cooperation and Address Witness Interference. In: Steinberg RH (ed) The International Criminal Court: Contemporary Challenges and Reform Proposals. Koninklijke Brill NV, Leiden, pp. 303–313.

Sluiter G, Talontsi S (2016) Credible and Authoritative Enforcement of State Cooperation with the International Criminal Court. In: Bekou O, Birkett DJ (eds) Cooperation and the International Criminal Court: Perspectives from Theory and Practice. Brill, Leiden, pp. 80–113.

Smith-van Lin L (2016) Non-compliance and the Law and Politics of State Cooperation: Lessons from the Al-Bashir and Kenyatta Cases. In: Bekou O, Birkett DJ (eds) Cooperation and the International Criminal Court: Perspectives from Theory and Practice. Brill, Leiden, pp. 114–151.

UN Security Council (2005) Resolution 1593 [Sudan] S/RES/1593.

Wenqi Z (2006) On Co-operation by States not Party to the International Criminal Court. International Review of the Red Cross 88(861): 87–110.

Wouters J, Basu S (2009) The Creation of a Global Criminal Justice System: The European Union and the International Criminal Court. In: Ryngaert C (ed) The Effectiveness of International Criminal Justice. Hart Publishing, Oxford, pp. 117–142.

Chapter 3
The Role of the Assembly of States Parties and the UN Security Council in Responding to Instances of Non-cooperation

Contents

3.1 Introduction ... 48
3.2 The Assembly of States Parties ... 48
3.2.1 The Assembly Procedures Relating to Non-cooperation ... 49
3.2.2 The Bureau Toolkit ... 51
3.2.3 Analysing the Assembly's Responses to Non-cooperation ... 54
3.2.4 Highlighting the Need to Strengthen Assembly Responses to Non-cooperation ... 56
3.2.5 Analysing the Effectiveness of the Assembly's Responses to Non-cooperation ... 59
3.3 The UN Security Council ... 60
3.3.1 The Security Council's Mandate Towards the ICC ... 61
3.3.2 Analysing the Security Council's Responses to Non-cooperation ... 66
3.3.3 Enhancing Security Council Responses to Non-cooperation ... 71
3.4 Conclusion ... 74
References ... 76

Abstract This chapter examines the mechanisms and remedies available to the Assembly of States Parties (ASP) and the UN Security Council in addressing instances of non-cooperation referred to it by a decision of the Court. It highlights the shortcomings in the enforcement of State cooperation obligations under the Rome Statute, with focus on the lack of effective follow-up measures or enforcement actions following such referrals, as evidenced by previous decisions of the Court. Such inaction undermines the effectiveness of the ICC's cooperation regime and its broader mandate for ensuring accountability for international crimes. This chapter begins its investigation by analysing the role of the ASP in responding to non-cooperation, exploring the procedural and substantive limitations that affect its ability to enforce compliance with obligations under the Rome Statute. It then evaluates the tools at the disposal of the UNSC for responding to non-cooperation, including its capacity to take binding measures under Chapter VII of the UN Charter, considering the political and structural constraints that often block its ability to act decisively. Building on these analyses, this chapter proposes strategies for strengthening these bodies' ability to respond to non-cooperation in an effective manner.

M. L. Jacobs, *The Consequences of Non-cooperation with the International Criminal Court*, International Criminal Justice Series 37,
https://doi.org/10.1007/978-94-6265-675-8_3

Keywords Non-cooperation · Referral · Rome Statute · Assembly of States Parties · UN Security Council · UN Charter

3.1 Introduction

Following a decision of non-cooperation by a chamber of the ICC, such a decision is referred to the Assembly of States Parties, and/or the UN Security Council for the consideration of further remedies against the non-cooperating State.[1] However, as noted by the Court itself in its decision on the non-cooperation of South Africa,[2] while States had been referred to the Assembly or the UN Security Council for further consideration, such referrals had not resulted in any follow-up measures or enforcement of a State's cooperation obligations. Such an observation placed the Court under the impression that a referral of South Africa's non-cooperation would not be an effective way of obtaining cooperation in the future.[3] The inaction on the part of these bodies represents a significant blow to the effectiveness of the Rome Statute's cooperation regime and to the overall efficiency of the Court.[4]

This chapter therefore looks to identify the remedies available to the Assembly of States Parties and the UN Security Council for responding to instances of non-cooperation and assess the effectiveness of these remedies. This chapter also seeks to identify ways in which these bodies can be strengthened to effectively respond to non-cooperation situations that have been referred to them. This chapter shall open through a discussion on the work of the Assembly of States Parties in responding to non-cooperation.

3.2 The Assembly of States Parties

The Assembly of States Parties is made up of representatives of ICC States Parties and is the management oversight and legislative body of the Court.[5] Among the vast powers granted to the Assembly is that of considering any question relating to non-cooperation.[6] This general provision on non-cooperation is complimented by a range of resolutions passed by the Assembly, indicating the measures that can

[1] The Rome Statute of the International Criminal Court. (17 July 1998, 2187, UNTS 3, Entry into Force, 1 July 2002) [hereinafter Rome Statute/RS] Article 87(7).

[2] ICC, Prosecutor v Omar Hassan Ahmad Al Bashir [Decision Under Article 87(7) of the Rome Statute on the non-compliance by South Africa with the request by the Court for the arrest and surrender of Omar Al-Bashir] (6 July 2017) ICC-02/05-01/09-302.

[3] Ibid. para 138.

[4] Kress and Prost 2022, p. 2490.

[5] RS, above n. 1, Article 112(1); see also ICC, Assembly of States Parties available at https://www.icc-cpi.int/asp (accessed 4 April 2020).

[6] Ibid. Article 112(2)(f).

be adopted to respond to instances of non-cooperation.[7] Seeing as no guidance was given by the drafters of the Statute as to the procedure that the Assembly could take to address non-cooperation, and the fact that the Statute and other legal texts are notably silent concerning the course of action to be taken by the assembly to address non-cooperation, the development of further regulations and practices aimed at addressing non-cooperation was left to the Assembly.[8] As a result of this uncertainty and silence, it has taken some time to develop a more structured approach to addressing non-cooperation.[9]

3.2.1 The Assembly Procedures Relating to Non-cooperation

At its tenth session in 2011, the Assembly of States Parties adopted the *Assembly Procedures Relating to Non-cooperation*.[10] These were updated further at the Assembly's seventeenth session,[11] and outline the general procedure to be taken by the Assembly following a finding of non-cooperation.[12] Under these procedures, non-cooperation is defined as the failure by a State to comply with a specific Court request for cooperation as defined in Articles 87(5)(b) and (7) of the Statute.[13] Any response to non-cooperation by the Assembly is to be non-judicial in nature and based upon what the Assembly is authorised to do under Article 112 of the Statute. These procedures reflect the Assembly's efforts to support the effectiveness of the Statute through the deployment of political and diplomatic efforts in promoting cooperation and responding to non-cooperation.[14]

The Assembly Procedures provide for different scenarios of non-cooperation which require specific formal or informal measures on the diplomatic and political level to respond to such situations.[15] These procedures aim to enhance the implementation of the Court's decisions. All actors involved in these procedures must ensure that their participation does not in any way undermine the findings of the Court.[16]

In the first scenario, the Court has referred a matter of non-cooperation under Article 87 and urgent action may be necessary to bring about cooperation.[17] The first scenario requires a response that is formal in nature and includes some public

[7] Assembly of States Parties *Non-cooperation available at* https://asp.icc-cpi.int/en_menus/asp/non-cooperation/pages/default.aspx (accessed 4 April 2020).

[8] Smith-van Lin 2016, p. 140; Ambach 2022, p. 4, 2874.

[9] Sluiter 2018, p. 393.

[10] ASP 2011.

[11] ASP 2018a [Annex II Assembly Procedures relating to non-cooperation].

[12] Ambach 2022, p. 2782.

[13] ASP 2018a, para 4.

[14] Ibid. para 6

[15] Ambach 2022, p. 2782.

[16] ASP 2018a, para 12.

[17] Ibid. para 7.

elements as it has been triggered through a decision by the Court to refer the matter to the Assembly. This scenario also recognises the possibility of pursuing an informal and urgent response in the event where it is still possible to achieve cooperation.[18] Following a decision of non-cooperation made by the Court, the following actions are recommended to address the situation:

(a) *An emergency Bureau meeting, where a report on any action taken by the Assembly President would be received, followed by a decision on what further action should be taken;*
(b) *The sending of an open letter to the requested State from the Assembly President that reminds the State of the obligation to cooperate and requesting its views on the matter as part of a formal response procedure within a specified time. This letter should be transmitted to all States Parties to encourage them to raise the matter with the requested State;*
(c) *A representative of the requested State should be invited to the next Bureau meeting to discuss the implications of the Court's decision on non-cooperation and present its views on how it would cooperate in future situations;*
(d) *Holding a public meeting at the next session of the Assembly to allow for open dialogue with the requested State, including participation from States Parties, observers, and representatives of civil society;*
(e) *Noting the decision of the Court in a resolution adopted by the Assembly at its next or ongoing session;*
(f) *At the next session of the Assembly a report of the Bureau should be discussed in a plenary session of the Assembly with a view to enhance future cooperation with the Court. This could include the appointment of a facilitator to consult on a draft resolution that contains concrete recommendations on the matter;*
(g) *In cases of a finding of non-cooperation referred by the Court to the UN Security Council the Assembly President could write to the Security Council president to follow up on its own referrals to encourage cooperation with the Court and outline what the Assembly has done in response to the Court's referral.*[19]

Any action taken in accordance with these steps should then be submitted to the next or ongoing Assembly session, as well as any concrete recommendations on the matter.[20]

In the second scenario, the Court has yet to refer a matter of non-cooperation, but there are reasons to believe that a specific and serious incident of non-cooperation is about to occur or is currently ongoing and urgent action may help bring about cooperation.[21] This scenario requires an urgent, but informal response at diplomatic and political levels.[22] Flexible mechanisms are therefore needed to take urgent action

[18] Ibid. paras 10, 13.
[19] ASP 2018a, paras 14(a)–(g).
[20] Ibid. para 15.
[21] Ibid. para 7.
[22] Ibid. para 11.

and ensure that cooperation can still take place.[23] These procedures require the setting up of regional focal points tasked with assisting the Assembly President in responding to instances of non-cooperation, triggered either by the President or by a decision of the Assembly Bureau.[24] Where the offices of the Assembly President are triggered, this matter should be raised after consultations with the Court with the requested State and other relevant stakeholders with a view to promoting full cooperation. These interactions would serve the purpose of raising awareness of the issue and promoting full cooperation while still possible.[25]

These procedures aim to enhance the implementation of the Court's decisions. All actors involved in these procedures must ensure that their participation does not in any way undermine the findings of the Court.[26]

3.2.2 *The Bureau Toolkit*

The Bureau of the Assembly of States Parties assists the Assembly in the discharge of its responsibilities.[27] In relation to non-cooperation, the *Assembly Procedures* requires that the Bureau submits reports on the outcomes of the Assembly's responses to non-cooperation, including any recommendations on the matter.[28] These reports describe interactions between the Bureau and States that have been the subject of non-cooperation decisions, followed by a description of preventative steps that have been taken to ensure cooperation in future situations.[29] Later reports on non-cooperation appear not to address consultations held with non-cooperating States.[30] In addition, as the Court did not refer South Africa and Jordan to the Assembly, such non-cooperation dialogues did not take place.

At the Assembly's Fourteenth Session, the Bureau recommended in its report on non-cooperation that the non-cooperation focal points should collaborate with any interested States, the Court and other relevant bodies to finalise a toolkit aimed at improving the implementation of the informal procedures relating to non-cooperation.[31] At the Fifteenth Session of the Assembly, this toolkit was finalised

---

[23] Ibid. para 16.

[24] Ibid. paras 17–19.

[25] Ibid. 20.

[26] Ibid. para 12.

[27] RS, above n. 1, Article 112(3).

[28] ASP 2018a, para 15.

[29] ASP 2012, para 17, which highlighted that the dialogue with Chad was not successful in securing future cooperation; ASP 2013, para 24, which cited Chad's continued failure to cooperate with the Court; ASP 2014, para 39, where Chad, the Central African Republic and the Democratic Republic of the Congo explained the circumstances that prevented them from executing their arrest warrants and expressed their willingness to cooperate in future circumstances.

[30] ASP 2016, paras 9–15, which took note of the non-cooperation of Djibouti, Uganda and Kenya that was referred to the assembly. No consultations were held with these States to secure cooperation.

[31] ASP 2015, para 8.

and published in the *Bureau Report on Non-cooperation*.[32] The toolkit was amended at the seventeenth session of the Assembly and appeared in that sessions *Report of the Bureau on Non-cooperation*.[33] The resources included in this toolkit are aimed at encouraging States to meet their cooperation obligations with the ICC in relation to the arrest and surrender of persons subject to a warrant of arrest.[34]

The Toolkit makes provision for standardised responses to potential instances of non-cooperation, as well as removing any political influence from actions taken to encourage States to meet their cooperation obligations.[35] The depoliticization of actions taken to encourage States to fulfil their cooperation obligations aims to shift the focus towards objective criteria and established norms, rather than political interests. Such an approach helps maintain the integrity of the cooperation process and reduces the influence of political dynamics that can hinder effective cooperation. The toolkit includes measures that establish clear criteria for addressing and responding to instances of non-cooperation.

3.2.2.1 Information on the Travel of ICC Suspects

The first set of responses aim to encourage the obtaining and sharing of information relating to the travel of persons wanted by the Court.[36] States Parties are encouraged to monitor the travel of persons wanted by the Court by communicating with diplomatic networks.[37] States Parties are also encouraged to monitor these movements through the use of internet and social media platforms. In particular, the use of Google Alerts is encouraged to assist States Parties in keeping up to date with the travel of persons subject to an ICC arrest warrant:

(a) *Go to* https://www.google.com/alerts;
(b) *Enter key search terms, such as the name of the individual wanted by the court e.g., Al-Bashir, "Travel" "International Criminal Court;"*
(c) *Enter email address and click CREATE ALERT;*
(d) *Google then sends a confirmation email that has to be verified.*[38]

Links to relevant articles, news items and other information will then be regularly transmitted to the email address that set up the alert.[39] Representatives of States Parties can also be appraised of the travel of persons wanted by the ICC through the

---

[32] ASP 2016 [Addendum: Toolkit for the Implementation of the Informal dimension of the Assembly procedures relating to non-cooperation].

[33] ASP 2018b [Annex: Toolkit for the Implementation of the Informal Dimension of the Assembly Procedures relating to non-cooperation].

[34] Ibid. para 1.

[35] Ibid. para 10

[36] Ibid. para 11.

[37] Ibid. para 12.

[38] ASP 2018b [Annex: Toolkit for the Implementation of the Informal Dimension of the Assembly Procedures relating to non-cooperation], para 13.

[39] Ibid. para 14.

use of social media platforms by specifically using hashtags in combination with key search terms.[40]

States Parties are also encouraged to share information with the Court and the non-cooperation focal points through two email addresses.[41] The non-cooperation focal points are required to share the information they have received with members of their regional group to enable States Parties to take any action they determine as appropriate.[42] The focal points are also required to share information received with civil society representatives in order to enable these bodies to transmit appropriate information through their regional and local networks.[43]

3.2.2.2 Preventing Non-cooperation

The next set of responses contained in the Toolkit are aimed at assisting in the prevention of instances of non-cooperation. These consist of templates prepared by the non-cooperation focal points to encourage States to meet their cooperation obligations.[44] These templates include draft statements, notes verbale, talking points, media releases and "tweets" that are aimed at addressing the travel of ICC suspects as well as reminding States of their obligations to arrest them.[45] The next set of tools aim to assist in discussing and promoting awareness of issues relating to non-cooperation. States Parties are encouraged to express support for the Court in all meetings in which subjects relating to the rule of law, international law or accountability for serious international crimes are discussed.[46]

States Parties are also encouraged to communicate with State representatives responsible for handling issues relating to international cooperation and justice to ensure that support for the Court and the importance of cooperation is raised in all meetings.[47] States Parties are also encouraged to develop contacts with civil society groups that encourage States to follow through with their cooperation obligations.[48] This section also proposes the setting up of workshops and seminars that may assist in maintaining public attention to issues relating to non-cooperation.[49] Lastly, the

---

[40] Ibid. para 15.

[41] Ibid. paras 16–21.

[42] Ibid. paras 22–25.

[43] Ibid. paras 26 & 27.

[44] Ibid. para 28.

[45] Ibid. paras 29–42.

[46] Ibid. paras 43–44.

[47] ASP 2018b [Annex: Toolkit for the Implementation of the Informal Dimension of the Assembly Procedures relating to non-cooperation], para 45.

[48] Ibid. para 46.

[49] Ibid. para 47.

toolkit contains proposals to adjust the language of future Security Council referral resolutions in order to strengthen the obligation of all States, including those not party to the Rome Statute, to cooperate with the ICC.[50]

3.2.3 Analysing the Assembly's Responses to Non-cooperation

While the Assembly has developed its own frameworks for responding to instances of non-cooperation that have been referred to it, these frameworks have not been able to address non-cooperation in an effective manner. Sluiter and Talontsi argue that the Assembly has acted below expectations in this respect as no concrete and effective measures have been taken to address non-cooperation. Soft, diplomatic initiatives, such as the initiation of dialogue with uncooperative States, have not had any real impact upon non-cooperation procedures and there has been no improvement in State cooperation as a result of involvement by the Assembly.[51] In addition, they hold that the enforcement of cooperation within the assembly appears to be highly politicised, with powerful blocs of States opposing the implementation of concrete and effective enforcement measures.[52] The Assembly itself is also aware of the difficulties associated with improving cooperation. Delegates at the 14th session of the Assembly in 2015 reiterated the importance of being attentive to non-cooperation issues, as instances of non-cooperation should not be normalised and ignored.[53] However, this has not been the case, and no State has been subjected to serious consequences because of their failure to cooperate.[54]

3.2.3.1 The Efficacy of the Assembly Procedures Relating to Non-cooperation

As already noted above, the formal and informal response procedures are aimed at enhancing the implementation of the Court's decisions and are not intended to be a continuation of judicial processes. The actors involved in these procedures must ensure that their participation does not open up discussions or otherwise undermine the findings of the Court.[55] However, this does not seem to be the case with various States Parties raising issues regarding decisions on non-cooperation made

[50] Ibid. paras 49–54.

[51] Sluiter and Talontsi 2016, p. 108.

[52] Ibid.

[53] ASP 2015, para 45.

[54] Sluiter 2018, p. 398; Hunter 2016, p. 374, where the author recognises that the absence of formal action from the Assembly has had the effect of muting the Court and disincentivising cooperation.

[55] ASP 2018a, para 12.

by the Court.[56] These debates are concerning as they reveal the continuation of the ICC's Article 87(7) procedures within the Assembly.[57] These continued discussions indicate that the Court could do better at ensuring that it passes decisions that are consistent and of a good quality.[58]

In assessing the responses developed by the *Assembly Procedures*, several issues and tensions can be identified. With regard to the formal responses to non-cooperation and the steps required to implement them, Sluiter observes tensions between the consequences of these steps and their actual purpose.[59] As an example, one of the steps requires for the holding of dialogue with the non-cooperating State to allow it to present its views on how it intends to cooperate in future situations.[60] Such a step raises questions as to the reasoning behind organising an open dialogue with the non-cooperating State after such dialogues have already been conducted in Court chambers. Allowing the continuation of such dialogues following the decision of the Court may open up the potential for a non-cooperating State to challenge or otherwise undermine the judicial finding of non-cooperation.[61]

Also of concern are the steps that refer to follow up measures and recommendations on further action by the Assembly.[62] These references to follow up action are held to unlikely have any coercive effect on present or future non-cooperating States and raise questions as to the scope and content of these measures.[63] Regarding informal discussions on non-cooperation, Bekou observes that dialogue, letters to States and media releases aimed at ensuring cooperation are useful in that they provide a timely response to instances of non-cooperation.[64] However, the nature of the Assembly as a political body means that the type and intensity of the response depends wholly on particular political and regional affiliations and cannot provide a consistent or reliable course of action to address non-cooperation effectively.[65]

---

[56] ASP 2014, para 24, where Chad raised the issue of non-cooperation with regard to the AU's legal position on the arrest and surrender of heads of State; see also Politi M "Statement By The Chair of COJUR-ICC, Prof. Mauro Politi, on Behalf of the European Union, at the General Debate of The Thirteenth Session of the Assembly of States Parties to The Rome Statute of the International Criminal Court" (10 December 2014) https://italyun.esteri.it/rappresentanza_onu/en/comunicazione/archivio-news/2014-12-10-politi-icc.html (accessed 1 September 2020) where EU States Parties discussed the irrelevance of an official capacity of an ICC Suspect.

[57] Sluiter and Talontsi 2016, p. 107.

[58] Sluiter 2018, p. 394.

[59] Ibid. p. 395.

[60] ASP 2018a, para 14(c).

[61] Sluiter 2018, p. 395.

[62] ASP 2018a, paras 14(a) and (e).

[63] Sluiter 2018, p. 396.

[64] Bekou 2019, pp. 929–930.

[65] Ibid. p. 930.

3.2.3.2 The Efficacy of the Assembly Bureau's Work on Non-cooperation

In Assessing how the Bureau of the Assembly of States Parties handles instances of non-cooperation communicated to it, it can be observed that there is a lack of effective follow-up on communications between the Bureau and States Parties that have failed to cooperate with the Court. Two scenarios can be identified where the Bureau has shown an inability to follow up with States. States Parties that have acknowledged their actions and undertake to cooperate in the future no longer form part of the attention of the Assembly; while those States who have not responded to cooperation request merely remain on the Assembly's agenda for future consideration.[66]

In analysing the effectiveness of the *Bureau Toolkit*, Bekou notes that its efficacy is yet to be tested practically but applauds the *Toolkit* as a much-needed addition to the Assembly's non-cooperation frameworks, seeing that all action taken to address non-cooperation has been based on the informal procedures.[67] However much emphasis is put on reminding States of their obligation to cooperate, which is unnecessary as the Statute already performs this function. In addition, the *Toolkit* does not contain measures of a more punitive or remedial nature to assist in responding to and addressing non-cooperation.[68]

3.2.4 Highlighting the Need to Strengthen Assembly Responses to Non-cooperation

According to Sluiter and Talontsi, ICC's judicial findings of non-cooperation, as per Article 87(7) of the Rome Statute, are the basis for the adoption of further measures aimed at enforcing these decisions. Therefore, a judicial finding of non-cooperation without appropriate follow-up action has the effect of potentially weakening the authority of cooperation obligations, as well as the authority and legitimacy of the ICC within the international legal sphere.[69]

While the Assembly has contributed to the development of procedures and remedies aimed at addressing non-cooperation, such measures have been less than effective.[70] Radical transformation and improvement of the Assembly's non-cooperation frameworks should therefore be an absolute priority.[71] The fact that the Assembly does not have a stricter set of sanctions mechanisms at its disposal, only strengthens the non-cooperating State's ability to oppose or reject these obligations.[72] In order to

[66] Sluiter 2018, p. 397.

[67] Bekou 2019, p. 930.

[68] Sluiter 2018, p. 398.

[69] Ambach 2022, p. 2784.

[70] Babaian 2018, p. 97.

[71] Sluiter and Talontsi 2016, p. 108.

[72] Babaian 2018, p. 98.

ensure the effective implementation of the Assembly's non-cooperation toolkit, these mechanisms must be adopted promptly and routinely in response to any existing or imminent instance of non-cooperation that has or will be the object of a referral by the Court. Effective channels of communication must therefore be kept open between the Assembly, the Court, and the Office of the Prosecutor.[73]

This section will look at the Assembly's General Powers granted to it by the Rome Statute and its application through the lens of other international law frameworks. This will be analysed through the application of the Assembly's general powers to perform any other function, as well as the potential for the Assembly to resort to the ICJ to settle disputes between States regarding instances of non-cooperation through the lens of other international law cooperation obligations. This will be followed by an analysis of potential methods for strengthening the Assembly's responses to non-cooperation both within the structure of the Rome Statute and through the application of other international law frameworks.

3.2.4.1 The Assembly's General Powers

While the Assembly is granted specific powers under the Rome Statute, which includes the power to address instances of non-cooperation,[74] the Assembly is also granted with a general power to perform "any other function" in line with the Statute or the Rules of Procedure and Evidence.[75] The consideration of remedies for non-cooperation could therefore also be done through the application of this general power.[76] This provision has been specified and complemented by Assembly resolutions indicating the political, diplomatic or administrative measures that can be adopted in response to non-cooperation. In particular, the application of this provision could be read into the Assembly's procedures relating to non-cooperation, particularly in the context of its informal non-cooperation procedures. Such procedures would come into effect where there is reason to believe that that a specific and serious incident of non- cooperation in respect of a request for arrest and surrender of a person is about to occur or is currently ongoing and urgent action by the Assembly may help bring about cooperation.[77]

With regard to the formal procedures, whereby non-cooperation has already occurred, the Assembly would be tasked with public communications with the non-cooperating State in order to enhance future cooperation with the Court and deter potential instances of non-cooperation before they occur.[78] Such procedures are

[73] Akande and De Souza Dias 2019, p. 12.
[74] RS, above n. 1 Articles 112(2)(f).
[75] Ibid. Article 112(2)(g).
[76] Ambach 2022, p. 2787, where the author also notes that the practical application of this provision in the context of non-cooperation will however be subject to the test of overall compatibility with the Statute.
[77] ASP 2018a, para 7(b).
[78] Ibid. paras 7(a); 10 and 14(a)–(g).

advantageous as they allow the Assembly to act more quickly than the ICC itself and even allow it to pre-empt a situation of non-cooperation involving the arrest and surrender of an ICC suspect. However, these procedures also restrict the circumstances under which the Assembly can act informally without a judicial decision on non-cooperation.[79]

3.2.4.2 Clarifying the Obligation to Cooperate

In most of the non-cooperation cases before the ICC, the failure to cooperate has occurred due to the lack of clarity surrounding the obligations of States under the Rome Statute. This has been particularly notable regarding the immunities question which was addressed and clarified by the Appeals Chamber in the Jordan non-cooperation decision.[80] In this regard, Akande and De Souza Dias propose that the Assembly could assist in clarifying uncertainties by adopting resolutions in the form of understandings or interpretative declarations.[81]

Although the Assembly has the competency to adopt amendments to the Statute,[82] it can also propose its own interpretations of the Statute. Although these interpretative resolutions aren't binding on the Court, they can qualify as a subsequent agreement or subsequent practice as per the Vienna Convention on the Law of Treaties if adopted with the agreement of all parties.[83] If these resolutions qualify, they can be considered by the Court when interpreting the relevant provisions of the Statute. Such interpretative resolutions may therefore be helpful in developing the Assembly's procedures on consultations.[84]

3.2.4.3 Settlement of Disputes

Issues relating to non-cooperation could also be addressed through the Statute's provisions on the settlement of disputes under Article 119. The Statute provides specifically that any dispute concerning the judicial functions of the Court shall be settled by the decision of the Court.[85] According to Clark and Meisenberg, the term "dispute" in this section is broad in nature,[86] and can be defined through case law as a disagreement on a point of law or fact, a conflict of legal views or of interests between

---

[79] Jones 2016, p. 203.

[80] ICC, Prosecutor v Omar Hassan Ahmad Al Bashir [Judgment in the Jordan Referral re Al-Bashir Appeal] (6 May 2019) ICC-02/05-01/09 OA2, para 162.

[81] Akande and De Souza Dias 2019, p. 13.

[82] RS, above n. 1, Article 121.

[83] Vienna Convention on the Law of Treaties (23 May 1969 UN Doc A/CONF.39/11/Add.2, Entry into force, 27 January 1980), Article 31(b).

[84] RS, above n. 1 Article 119(1).

[85] Ibid.

[86] Clark and Meisenberg 2022, p. 2847.

parties.[87] Clark also notes that the definition of judicial functions is rather broad in nature, and suggests a non-exhaustive list of judicial functions that may possibly be subject to dispute. Among these functions includes questions concerning cooperation with and judicial assistance to the Court.[88] Article 119 also provides:

> *Any other dispute between two or more States Parties relating to the interpretation or application of this Statute which is not settled through negotiations within three months of their commencement shall be referred to the Assembly of States Parties. The Assembly may itself seek to settle the dispute or may make recommendations on further means of settlement of the dispute, including referral to the International Court of Justice in conformity with the Statute of that Court.*[89]

Among the disagreements, which according to Clark and Meisenberg fit the category of "any other dispute ... relating to the interpretation or application of the Statute'" includes disputes relating to the failure by a State to comply with a request to cooperate.[90] This provision does not state expressly the party responsible for referring a matter to the Assembly, but it is presumed that each party to the dispute owes the obligation to refer the matter.[91] In an attempt to settle the dispute, the Assembly has explicit powers to set up subsidiary bodies for that specific purpose.[92] In exercising its power to make recommendations on further means of settlement, the Assembly should consider relying on a range of options under the UN Charter for pacific settlement of disputes, which includes judicial settlement.[93]

3.2.5 Analysing the Effectiveness of the Assembly's Responses to Non-cooperation

While the Assembly is in theory given a great extent of power to promote cooperation through the application of various diplomatic or political measures, it has not used this power effectively and appears to prefer strictly implementing the various procedures it has developed to get the attention and respect as one of the executive organs of the ICC, as well as to strengthen the Court itself.[94] Considering that the Assembly of States Parties is a political organ of the Court, rather than a judicial one, the

[87] ICJ Case Concerning East Timor [Portugal v Australia] (30 June 1995) ICJ Rep. 1995 90, para 22.

[88] Clark and Meisenberg 2022, pp. 2848–2849.

[89] RS, above n. 1, Article 119(2).

[90] Clark and Meisenberg 2022, pp. 2850–2851.

[91] Ibid. p. 2851.

[92] Article 122(4) of the Rome Statute note. 3.

[93] Clark and Meisenberg 2022, pp. 2852–2853; the Charter of the United Nations (26 June 1945, 1 UNTS XVI, Entry into Force 24 October 1945), [UN Charter] Article33, "... negotiation, enquiry, mediation, conciliation, arbitration, judicial settlement, resort to regional agencies or arrangements or other peaceful means of their own choice."

[94] Babaian 2018, p. 106.

successful enforcement and adoption of measures for addressing non-cooperation is largely reliant on the political will of its Member States.[95]

Legal theory professes that law, and politics should be independent from one another, so as to not allow specific interests to influence the development of the law.[96] In this regard, Shaw notes that there can never be a complete separation between law and politics. He states that "no matter what theory of law of political philosophy is professed, the inextricable bonds linking law and politics must be recognised".[97] Therefore, law and political considerations have to interact with each other in order to obtain a certain outcome, which in this instance is ensuring that States cooperate with the requests of the Court, and are deterred from disobeying cooperation obligations as a result of increased political willingness effectively combat the commission of serious international crimes.[98]

The Assembly must therefore use its ability to put diplomatic and political pressure upon States to encourage and incentivise cooperation and prevent and address non-cooperation.[99] Sluiter holds that the original idea behind Article 87(7) of the Statute was to create a clear distinction between the tasks and responsibilities of the Court and those of its political organs, the Assembly and the UN Security Council.[100] However this has not been the case, especially considering the South Africa decision, where the Pre-Trial Chamber held that referring South Africa to the Assembly and the Security Council would not be an effective way to ensure cooperation.[101] This gives off the impression that the Pre-Trial Chamber is interfering with the enforcement mechanisms of the Assembly and the Security Council by anticipating that such measures will have no effect on the non-cooperating State.[102]

3.3 The UN Security Council

As the organ of the United Nations with the primary responsibility for the maintenance of international peace and security,[103] the UN Security Council has a special role to play in the effective functioning of the ICC. Unlike the *ad hoc* tribunals of

95 Babaian 2018, p. 176.

96 Crear 2009, p. 23.

97 Shaw 2021, p. 8.

98 Babaian 2018, p. 202.

99 Smith-van Lin 2016, p. 141.

100 Sluiter 2018, p. 391.

101 Decision Under Article 87(7) of the Rome Statute on the non-compliance by South Africa with the request by the Court for the arrest and surrender of Omar Al-Bashir, para 138.

102 Sluiter 2018, p. 392.

103 UN Charter above n. 93, Article 24.

the 1990s and the specialised hybrid courts set up through UN resolutions,[104] the ICC does not form part of the UN System.[105] The UN Security Council and the ICC have however developed a relationship which is regulated by the Rome Statute and a special relationship agreement signed between the two bodies.[106]

3.3.1 The Security Council's Mandate Towards the ICC

Under the Rome Statute, the Security Council has three specific roles to play in its relationship with the ICC, namely referral of situations to the Court, deferral of such situations, and responding to instances of non-cooperation that have been referred to it by ICC Chambers.

3.3.1.1 ICC Referral

Article 13(b) of the Rome Statute grants the Security Council with the power to refer situations to the ICC Prosecutor.[107] This mechanism has the effect of extending the jurisdiction of the Court to cover atrocity crimes committed in territories of States not Party to the Rome Statute, or crimes committed by nationals of such States.[108] The ICC's jurisdiction to address a situation triggered by a Security Council referral is rooted in the Council's powers under Chapter VII of the UN Charter to adopt measures for the maintenance of international peace and security.[109] Such measures range from the use of enforcement mechanisms, to more coercive measures requiring the use of force.[110] In addition to the Rome Statute and the UN Charter, the Negotiated Agreement between the International Criminal Court and the United Nations requires that the Court keep the Security Council informed of any developments in a situation

---

[104] International Criminal Tribunal for the Former Yugoslavia S/Res/827 (1993); International Criminal Tribunal for Rwanda S/Res/955 (1995); the Special Court for Sierra Leone S/Res/1315 (2000); Special Tribunal for Lebanon S/Res/1757 (2007).

[105] Alamuddin 2014, p. 103.

[106] RS, above note 1, Article 13(b); UNGA 2004.

[107] Coutre 2015, p. 12, where the author notes that this power is discretionary, and referrals have to be done within the parameters of the Rome Statute.

[108] Schabas and Pecorella 2022, p. 842; see also Arbour 2014, p. 195, where the author notes that the power of the Security Council to refer situations to the ICC can be seen as a chance to expand the reach of international criminal justice by offering the opportunity to hold perpetrators of international crimes, who might otherwise be exempt from prosecution and punishment, accountable for their crimes.

[109] Galand 2019, p. 52.

[110] UN Charter, above n. 93, Article 41 "… complete or partial interruption of economic relations, and of rail, sea, postal, telegraphic, radio and other means of communication, and the severance of diplomatic relations;" Article 42, "… action by air, sea or land forces as may be necessary to maintain or restore international peace and security."

arising from a Security Council resolution.[111] These referral resolutions also require that the ICC Prosecutor addresses the Security Council every six months on actions taken pursuant to these resolutions.[112]

However, expanding the jurisdiction of the Court to include States and nationals of States not party to the Rome Statute can be seen to be in conflict with the *pacta tertiis* rule of customary international law, which recognises that a treaty does not create obligations or rights for a third State without the consent of that State.[113] Under classic international law, it is therefore within the sovereign right of a State to choose to designate an international court to exercise jurisdiction over a crime committed on the territory of that State by virtue of signing onto a multilateral treaty like the ICC.[114] The UN Charter protects State sovereignty by proclaiming that the UN cannot interfere in the domestic matters of the State.[115] However, the UN Charter does grant the Security Council with the power to intervene in matters which are within the domestic jurisdiction of any State where such matters are determined to be a threat to the peace, breach of the peace or an act of aggression.[116]

The Security Council has passed two resolutions referring situations to the ICC under article 13(b) of the Rome Statute, namely the situations in Libya and Sudan.[117] These resolutions place an obligation upon the situation States, which are not parties to the Rome Statute, to cooperate fully with the Court.[118] Under the UN Charter, these States have an obligation to accept and carry out decisions made by the Security Council.[119] These States therefore have a binding obligation to cooperate with the ICC.[120] The obligation to cooperate with the Court in these resolutions does not extend to other Non-party States.[121] These referrals can be read as enforcement measures under Article 41 of the UN Charter. This is based on the argument raised by the ICTY Appeals Chamber in the *Tadic* case that the measures set out in Article 41 are merely illustrative examples which do not exclude other measures, and therefore include the establishment of international criminal tribunals.[122] However, the ICC is not part of the UN System and has a separate legal personality with its own rights

111 UNGA 2004, Article 17(1).

112 UNSC 2005, para 8; UNSC 2011, para 7.

113 Galand 2019, p. 49; see also article Vienna Convention on the Law of Treaties (23 May 1969 UN Doc A/CONF.39/11/Add.2, Entry into force, 27 January 1980) Article 34.

114 Lentner 2014, pp. 11–12.

115 UN Charter, above n. 93, Article 2(7).

116 Ibid. Article 39.

117 UNSC 2005, para 1; UNSC 2011, para 4.

118 Ibid. paras 2, 5.

119 UN Charter, above n. 93, Article 25.

120 Akande 2012, p. 306.

121 Ciampi 2016, p. 39.

122 ICTY Prosecutor v Dusko Tadic [Decision on the Defence Motion for Interlocutory Appeal on Jurisdiction] (2 October 1995) IT-94-1, para 35.

and obligations.[123] As a result, it does not become a subsidiary organ of the Security Council following a referral of a situation.[124]

In addition, while the ICC has a close relationship with the United Nations, it is neither a member nor one of the specialised agencies within the UN System.[125] Building on what was stated in the *Tadic* case, the Security Council's referral resolutions stated that it was acting under Chapter VII of the UN Charter.[126] Therefore Article 41 of the UN Charter is broad enough in nature to confer additional jurisdictional power to an already existing criminal tribunal like the ICC. This has been accepted by UN Member States, considering the number of ratifications of the Rome Statute and the unanimous referral of the situation in Libya.[127] Therefore, the Security Council's referrals to the ICC as enforcement measures under chapter VII of the UN Charter implies that the ICC's exercise of jurisdiction over the territory and nationals of Non-party States or States not consenting to the Court's jurisdiction does not conflict with the principles of State sovereignty.[128]

3.3.1.2 Deferral

The Rome Statute also empowers the Security Council to adopt a resolution, under Chapter VII of the UN Charter, aimed at preventing or stopping an ICC investigation or prosecution for a period of 12 months.[129] This mechanism allows the Security Council to request that the Court does not investigate or prosecute where a majority vote concludes that judicial action may have the effect of doing more harm than good to the Security Council's efforts in the maintenance of international peace and security.[130] Such a view raises issues relating to selectivity and political control over the discretion exercised by the ICC.[131] The ability of the Security Council to defer ICC proceedings is controversial, as it codifies the right of a political body to interfere

---

[123] UNGA 2004, Article 2(1).

[124] Galand 2019, p. 53; see also Jia 2020, p. 365, where the author notes that cooperation between the ICC and the Security Council is "no more than voluntary in substance."

[125] Ibid. p. 210.

[126] UNSC 2005, pre para 6; UNSC 2011, pre para 16, this paragraph also noted that the Security Council was taking measures under article 41 of the UN Charter.

[127] Galand 2019, p. 53.

[128] Ibid. p. 54.

[129] RS, above n. 1, Article16.

[130] Bergsmo and Zhu 2022, p. 933; see also Aloisi 2013, p. 150, where the author notes that this power was based on the need to reconcile peace and justice in situations in which the presence of peace talks of security concerns makes justice a secondary goal to the international community.

[131] Ibid. pp. 937–938; the authors also note that the Permanent Members of the Security Council that are States Parties to the Rome Statute have a responsibility to balance political considerations with the maintenance of international peace and security.

in the workings of a judicial institution, which therefore undercuts the legitimacy of the ICC as an independent judicial body.[132]

Under such a mechanism, State obligations to cooperate in the investigation and prosecution of ICC crimes would therefore fall away until the expiration of the deferral term.[133] According to Mistry and Verduzco, there lies the risk that resort to deferral may result in negative consequences for the Security Council and the ICC. For example, if the Security Council is successfully convinced by a State under investigation to make a deferral on the basis that an investigation presents a threat to international peace and security, it may be faced with permanent threats by a regime in that States to renew the deferral.[134] In addition, there lies concerns as to what would happen to ongoing proceedings should a deferral be made, with regards to the collection of evidence and the status of investigations.[135]

There have been several attempts to invoke deferral proceedings, which have been proven to be controversial.[136] For example, Resolution 1422, which was passed shortly after the Rome Statute's entry into force, granted peacekeeping troops from non-State Parties to the Rome Statute immunity from prosecution under the basis of Article 16 deferral proceedings.[137] In the context of the situation in Sudan, adopted through Security Council *Resolution 1593,* the African Union called for deferral proceedings following the issuing of the arrest warrant against former Sudanese President Al-Bashir.[138] However, apart from peacekeeping resolutions, the Security Council has not approved any deferral requests in relation to ongoing ICC situations.[139] Noting the abovementioned concerns surrounding deferral proceedings, the likelihood of such proceedings being resorted to may be slim.[140]

---

[132] Mistry and Verduzco 2012, p. 14; the authors also note that since the exercise of such powers is recognised as controversial, they are rarely used.

[133] Bergsmo and Zhu 2022, p. 940, where the authors note that prosecution as defined under the Rome Statute would encompass the totality of actions undertaken by the ICC Prosecutor to secure the conviction of a person against whom charges have been confirmed. This would include requesting a State to cooperate with the Court and the subsequent consequences of a failure to cooperate.

[134] Mistry and Verduzco 2012, p. 16; the authors note that this may have the effect of enabling regimes to continually delay the administration of justice, as well as counter the Security Council's primary responsibility for the maintenance of international peace and security.

[135] As above.

[136] Bergsmo and Zhu 2022, p. 938; Mistry and Verduzco 2012, p. 15.

[137] UNSC 2002, para 1; see also UNSC 2003, which was basically a renewal of Resolution 1422.

[138] AU 2009, para 8; see also Mistry and Verduzco 2012, p. 15, where the authors observe that arguments in favour of this deferral rested on the basis that any arrest warrant against Al-Bashir would block the possibility of peace talks in the country. However, such an argument is, according to the authors, not convincing.

[139] Bergsmo and Zhu 2022, p. 939.

[140] Mistry and Verduzco 2012, p. 16.

3.3.1.3 Responding to Non-cooperation

Following a decision of non-cooperation by the Pre-Trial Chambers under Articles 87(5)(b) and 87(7) of the Rome Statute, such a decision is transmitted to the Security Council in which further remedies against the non-cooperating State are considered. Under the ICC/UN Relationship agreement, the Security Council is required to inform the Court of any action taken by it to address such non-cooperation.[141] Following a referral, the Security Council may act against the responsible State in accordance with Chapter VII of the UN Charter.[142] This Chapter authorises the Security Council to make recommendations or decide upon measures that can assist in the maintenance of international peace and security.[143] Under this Chapter, the Security Council can either use measures not requiring the use of force, such as the cessation or interruption of economic activities and the severance of diplomatic relations,[144] or measures requiring the use of force by UN Member States, which includes the use of blockades and demonstrations.[145]

However, while the Relationship Agreement fully recognises the importance of the UN's Assistance to the ICC, it does not contain any enforceable provisions to make that assistance available when needed.[146] In addition, although the Court has notified the Security Council of instances of non-cooperation by States in their failure to execute ICC arrest warrants, the Council has not taken any action pursuant to these notifications.[147]

According to Aloisi, the Security Council has done very little to acknowledge the difficulties through which the ICC has worked and has not threatened the enforcement of mechanisms under the UN Charter following clear instances of non-cooperation.[148] Security Council's failure to take up any follow up measures to assist the Court in its proper functioning does not convincingly demonstrate that the Security Council is committed to assisting the Court in achieving its goal of crime prevention and ensuring international accountability.[149] State failure to cooperate with the ICC has been addressed primarily through the application of adversarial strategies such as shaming the responsible State. Such strategies aim to activate international pressure against the non-cooperating State, as well as raise the political costs of the

[141] UNGA 2004, Article 17(3).

[142] Kress and Prost 2022, p. 2470.

[143] UN Charter, above n. 93, Article 39.

[144] UN Charter, above n. 93, Article 41.

[145] Ibid. Article 42

[146] Jia 2020, p. 365, where the author notes that if States Parties to the Rome Statute cannot be enforced against by the ICC, it is unlikely that the Court will be able to enforce agreements with the UN following a failure to cooperate.

[147] Akande and De Souza Dias 2019, p. 10, "... the UNSC remains idle in the face of violations of cooperation obligations incumbent upon Sudan, Libya and states parties to the Rome Statute."

[148] Aloisi 2013, p. 154.

[149] Mistry and Verduzco 2012, p. 9.

failure to cooperate.[150] However, resort to shaming may not have the desired effect of ensuring increased cooperation, as it may undermine future cooperation, as well as the tribunal's reputation among States.[151]

In addition, referring instances of non-cooperation to the Security Council represents a high-profile strategy to shame a non-cooperating State. The combination of frequent complaints of non-cooperation and inaction by the Security Council gives off the message that a State can withhold cooperation without any effective consequences or remedies.[152] The Security Council's lack of commitment to the work of the ICC therefore has a negative effect on the proper functioning of international justice.[153] In order to better respond to instances of non-cooperation, the Security Council should be encouraged to apply existing measures more effectively, or develop more appropriate measures to follow up on situations it has referred to the Court and address instances of non-cooperation.[154]

3.3.2 Analysing the Security Council's Responses to Non-cooperation

This section will look at the Security Council's record in responding to instances of non-cooperation by States Parties in their obligations towards international criminal tribunals. While focus will still be placed upon cooperation obligations towards the ICC, this section will also briefly analyse the Security Council's handling of non-cooperation cases in the *Ad Hoc* tribunals that preceded the ICC.

3.3.2.1 Cooperation with the Ad-hoc Tribunals

The UN Security Council has a history of not appropriately addressing non-cooperation before international criminal tribunals prior to the establishment of the ICC. The International Criminal Tribunals for Rwanda and the former Yugoslavia were established through the passing of Security Council resolutions 827 and 955

---

[150] Peskin 2008, p. 238.

[151] Ibid. p. 238, where the author also notes that even if a State does end up being shamed into cooperating, the pressure placed upon it by the international criminal tribunal may have the effect of increasing hostility towards the tribunal and maintain the perception that that tribunal is unfairly targeting that State.

[152] Peskin 2008, p. 239.

[153] Aloisi 2013, p. 167.

[154] Akande and De Souza Dias 2019, p. 10; they also note that the Security Council should consider such matters both in cases arising from situations it has referred to the Court, as well as in other cases and situations; see also Mistry and Verduzco 2012, p. 19; Trahan 2013 p. 473, where the authors recognise that the Security Council should take consistent action in responding to instances of non-cooperation.

in response to the atrocities committed in those regions.[155] These tribunals were granted with the power to prosecute persons responsible for serious violations of international law committed in those regions.[156] Similar to the ICC, these tribunals placed an obligation upon States Parties to cooperate with them in the investigation and prosecution of serious international crimes.[157] By virtue of the UN Charter, these obligations prevailed over other obligations under any other international agreements.[158] Therefore, the obligation to comply with the requests of the Tribunals was placed upon any UN Member State receiving an order, regardless of the role played by the State during the conflicts in the regions.[159]

The preambular paragraphs of the Security Council resolutions establishing the *Ad Hoc* tribunals recognised that these situations constituted threats to international peace and security.[160] Therefore, as the Security Council is empowered to take any measures against situations that constitute as a threat to international peace and security, the failure to cooperate with these tribunals, established with the purpose of maintaining peace and security, can be equated as a threat to peace, which the Security Council has the right to respond to accordingly.[161]

In the *Blaskic* case, the ICTY Appeals Chamber held that when a State failed to comply with a binding order issued by the Tribunal, the Tribunal was granted with the power to make a judicial finding of non-cooperation and request that the president of the tribunal transmit such a finding to the Security Council.[162] The Security Council and Member States could then take steps to address the judicial finding of non-cooperation.[163] The Appeals Chamber also noted that the finding of non-cooperation by the Tribunal must not include recommendations or suggestions as to the course of action that could be taken by the Security Council as a consequence of that finding.[164] However responses to non-cooperation were less than effective, with repeated notifications of non-compliance by States leading to no sanctions other

[155] UNSC 1993, para 2; UNSC 1994, para 1.

[156] Article 1 of the Statute of the International Criminal Tribunal for the Former Yugoslavia 1993; Article 1 of the Statute of the International Criminal Tribunal for Rwanda 1994.

[157] UNSC 1993, para 4; UNSC 1994, para 2.

[158] Ciampi 2016, p. 11; see also UN Charter, above n. 93 Article103, which confirms the primacy of UN Decisions over any other international agreement.

[159] Stroh 2001, p. 254; the author also notes that the neutrality or active participation of States in those conflicts had no effect on the obligation to cooperate with the Tribunals.

[160] UNSC 1993, pre para 4; UNSC 1994, pre para 5.

[161] Dushimimana 2013, p. 87.

[162] ICTY Prosecutor v Tihomir Blaskic [Judgment on the Request of the Republic of Croatia for Review of the Decision of Trial Chamber II of 18 July 1997] (29 October 1997) IT-85-14-T, para 33.

[163] Harmon and Gaynor 2004, p. 418.

[164] *Judgment on the Request of the Republic of Croatia for Review of the Decision of Trial Chamber II of 18 July 1997*, para 36; see also Harmon and Gaynor 2004, p. 418, where the authors note that no guidance was given as to a State's liability following a failure to abide by an order of the ICTY.

than reprimands through the issuing of resolutions or presidential statements which called on non-cooperative States to cooperate fully with the Tribunal.[165]

According to Harmon and Gaynor, reliance on the Security Council as a mechanism to address non-cooperation with the ICTY was unpredictable, time-consuming and ineffective.[166] For example, the Security Council failed to impose sanctions or otherwise punish Serbia for its failure to cooperate with the ICTY, despite blatant evidence of non-cooperation.[167] The failure of the Security Council to enforce measures under the UN Charter to address non-cooperation had the effect of undermining the authority of the Tribunals, as well as the knock on effect of showing States that there was no real incentive to cooperate.[168] Therefore, faced with the lack of support to compel cooperation under threat of penalty, the tribunals had to rely on States and other third parties acting in good faith and exerting political and economic pressure on behalf of the tribunals in order for them to function effectively.[169]

3.3.2.2 The Situations in Sudan and Libya

The obligation of States to cooperate with the ICC in the situations in Libya and Sudan, while entrenched in the Rome Statute, was further strengthened through the Security Council's referral resolutions which placed duties upon parties to the conflict to cooperate fully with the Court. However, while UN Member States are under an obligation to cooperate with all obligations contained within Security Council resolutions as per the UN Charter, resolutions 1593 and 1970 did not extend this obligation to other UN Member States and instead urged all UN Member States to cooperate fully with the Court.[170]

The ICC Prosecutor has recognised that the Security Council has not taken any action against any decisions on non-cooperation that have been referred to it. The Prosecutor's reports to the Security Council highlight that the Council has not shown any ongoing commitment to ensure that investigations and prosecutions actually proceed.[171] As a result, former ICC Prosecutor Bensouda has openly expressed frustration towards the Security Council. In December 2013, at her briefing to the Security Council, the Prosecutor asked:

> *"What is the point of the Office of the Prosecutor's briefings if there is no concrete follow-up action taken by the Council?"*[172]

---

[165] Rastan 2008, p. 443; Harmon and Gaynor 2004, p. 419.

[166] Harmon and Gaynor 2004, p. 419.

[167] Peskin 2008, p. 35.

[168] Dushimimana 2013, p. 88.

[169] Meernik 2015, p. 931; Rastan 2008, p. 438.

[170] UNSC 2005, para 2; UNSC 2011, para 5.

[171] ICC OTP 2018 at para 16, "... none of the decisions finding compliance and/or referring the matter to the ASP and UNSC have been responded to by the Council." Aloisi 2013, p. 154.

[172] UNSC 2013, p. 3. The Prosecutor also notes in this Statement that the silence of the Council in this context "only serves to add insult to the plight of Darfur's victims."

The following year, the former Prosecutor expressed her continued frustration with the lack of support being received from the Council. In particular she noted that:

> *"It is becoming increasingly difficult for me to appear before you to update you when all I am doing is repeating the same things I have aid over and over again, most of which are well known to this Council."*[173]

The lack of cooperation from the Security Council, together with the limited resources available to the Court, led to the former Prosecutor halting activities in Sudan in order to shift resources to other urgent cases. In her report she stated that:

> *"Unless there is a change of attitude and approach to Darfur in the near future, there shall continue to be little or nothing to report to you for the foreseeable future."*[174]

While the former Prosecutor later made reassurances that investigations in Sudan had continued,[175] the failure of the Security Council to cooperate with the ICC continues to have a negative impact on the efficiency of its investigations by increasing the length and costs of its proceedings.[176]

In addition, the *Report of the Court on Non-cooperation* at the 17th Session of the Assembly of States Parties observed that 16 communications on non-cooperation had been transmitted to the Security Council, of which none were addressed further.[177] This raises questions as to whether the Security Council considers the failure to cooperate with the Court a threat to international peace and security; if there is distrust of the ICC's frameworks for addressing non-cooperation; or whether the Security Council simply lacks the political will to support the work of the Court.[178] Bureau reports on non-cooperation note that interactions with the Security Council seem to indicate that the permanent members have been unwilling to use their powers, in accordance with Chapter VII, to address non-cooperation.[179]

This present section has identified that the UN Security Council has been less than effective in responding to issues relating to international criminal law. This is particularly notable in its ineffective responses to non-cooperation by a State that have been transmitted to it. Prior to the establishment of the ICC, the *Ad Hoc* international criminal tribunals experienced a lack of support from the Security Council in responding to the non-cooperation of States. Apart from condemning instances of non-cooperation, the Security Council has not used its powers available to it under the UN Charter to effectively sanction uncooperative States.[180] It is therefore crucial for the sake of the institutional credibility of the ICC and the Security Council, as

---

[173] ICC OTP 2018, para 2.

[174] Ibid. para 4.

[175] ICC OTP 2018, para 25, "... I must emphasise that my Office's investigations into the alleged crimes committed in Darfur are continuing, albeit not at the pace or intensity we would have liked."

[176] Jones 2016, p. 190.

[177] ASP 2018a, para 36.

[178] Sluiter and Talontsi 2016, p. 104.

[179] ASP 2014, paras 25–30.

[180] Rastan 2008, p. 438.

well as for the Security Council to be shown as a responsible actor in the face of large-scale atrocity crimes, for there to be consistency and objectivity when passing referral resolutions.[181]

In addition, the failure of the Security Council to respond to instances of non-cooperation transmitted to it by the Court highlights the need for the Security Council to make more an effort to follow up on its referrals to ensure that they actually succeed and that States are discouraged from choosing to not cooperate with the Court.[182] Therefore, while the Security Council can strengthen the Court by referring situations to it and obliging UN Member States to cooperate with investigations and arrests, the likelihood of referral is largely dependent on the strategic interests of powerful States holding permanent seats on the Council.[183] This can be highlighted by the selective manner in which the Security Council has referred certain situations to the Court, while failing to refer other situations, namely the situation in Syria.

3.3.2.3 The Selectivity of the UN Security Council

The UN Charter provides that decisions of the Security Council on non-procedural matters shall be made by an affirmative vote of nine members, including the concurring votes of the permanent members.[184] The veto right gives the permanent members of the Security Council the power to block the passing of any council resolution which they do not support.[185] This veto power is used by the permanent members as a way to defend their national interests, uphold foreign policy or promote a single issue of particular importance to a State.[186]

In particular, the Security Council's decision to selectively refer situations to the ICC gives off an impression to States that those with allies among the permanent members of the Security Council are beyond the reach of international criminal law.[187] This failure can be illustrated by the Security Council's inability to refer the situation in Syria to the ICC because of the veto. In 2014, two permanent members of the Security Council, namely Russia and China, vetoed the draft referral resolution.[188]

---

[181] Trahan 2013, p. 433.

[182] Ibid. p. 466.

[183] Tiemessen 2014, p. 454; the author also notes that linking the Security Council to the Court invites politicisation.

[184] UN Charter, above, n. 93 Article 27(3).

[185] Genser 2018, p. 500.

[186] Illingworth 2020, p. 388, "The veto is not just a means to realise national interests of the P5 but exists to prevent great power conflict by guaranteeing their participation into the UN system."

[187] Holvoet and Meman 2016, p. 29; Coutre 2015, p. 27, where the author notes that the use of the veto has allowed the permanent members of the Security Council to influence which situations have been referred to the ICC.

[188] UNSC 2014a, paras 2–3; UN News *Russia, China block Security Council referral of Syria to International Criminal Court* (22 May 2014) available at https://news.un.org/en/story/2014/05/468962-russia-china-block-security-council-referral-syria-international-criminal-court (accessed 15 November 2020).

According to Russia, the draft resolution revealed an attempt to use the ICC to further inflame political tensions and lay the groundwork for outside military intervention. Russia also noted that previous referral resolutions, particularly in Libya, did not do much to resolve the crisis but instead worsened the conflict.[189] China's reasons to use the veto power, lay with its belief that any action to seek recourse to the ICC to prosecute perpetrators of serious violations of international law should be conducted on the basis of respect for State judicial sovereignty and complementarity.[190]

3.3.3 Enhancing Security Council Responses to Non-cooperation

The lack of follow-up by the Security Council to its own referrals and failure to act on notifications of non-cooperation is detrimental to the credibility of the Council.[191] This failure on the part of the Security Council can be attributed partly by the unwillingness of the Council to address issues related to the ICC, and partly by a lack of a permanent mechanism within the Council for dealing with ICC related issues.[192] Identical to the Assembly of States Parties, the Security Council is a political, rather than judicial body.[193] The successful enforcement and adoption of measures aimed at addressing the failure to cooperate is therefore reliant on the political will of its members.[194] Decisions made by the Council will therefore be influenced by considerations of State sovereignty, as well as the geo-political interests of member States. It is therefore of utmost importance that an effort is made to promote and enhance the political will of the Security Council to address non-cooperation.

---

[189] UNSC 2014b, p. 13, Statement by Russia: "After the cessation of hostilities, the ICC did not exactly rise to the occasion ... It did not contribute to a return of normality of justice to Libya and instead evaded the most pressing issues."

[190] Ibid. p. 13, where China also noted that it has had serious reservations to Security Council referrals of particular country situations to the ICC; see also at p. 14, where China held that referral of the situation in Syria to the ICC was not conducive to the building of trust among all parties in Syria and would only jeopardize the efforts by the international community to push for a political settlement of the crisis. China also held the opinion that alternative measures should be resorted to in order to resolve the situation, such as holding consultations in order to avoid undermining Council unity and obstructing coordination and cooperation on issues of serious international concern.

[191] UNSC 2012a, paras 14–16.

[192] Saba and Akbarzadeh 2020, p. 99.

[193] Babaian 2018, p. 200; UNSC 2012b Statement by Mochochoko P of the Office of the Prosecutor of the ICC at the 6849th Meeting of the UN Security Council, p. 6.

[194] Ibid. p. 176.

3.3.3.1 Strengthening the Obligation to Cooperate with Security Council Resolutions

Noting that the Security Council referral resolutions only place an obligation to cooperate upon the States subject to the referral,[195] there remains a gap in the law regarding the obligations of UN Member States not Party to the Rome Statute towards such resolutions.[196] For example, in the *Gadaffi and Al-Sennusi* case, the Pre-Trial Chamber has attempted to clarify these obligations by confirming that Libya was under an obligation to cooperate with the Court by virtue of the UN Charter and the Security Council resolution. Therefore, the order to cooperate fully with the Court means that the Rome Statute is the legal framework within, which Libya must comply with the request to arrest and surrender.[197] However, the inapplicability of the Rome Statute to Non-Party States continues to be an impediment to the proper execution of the Court and the Security Council's mandate in this regard.

This lack of a concrete obligation is also recognised in the context of the Assembly of States Parties' non-cooperation procedures. This absence of a legal duty on Non-Party States to cooperate has made it difficult for the ICC to effect the arrest and surrender of some of its suspects.[198] In order to strengthen the obligations of all States towards the ICC's cooperation frameworks, the Assembly of States Parties proposed in its Non-cooperation Toolkit that future Security Council referral resolutions contain language that places an obligation upon all UN Member States to cooperate with the requests of the ICC:

> *Decides that [X State] [Y authorities], shall cooperate fully with and provide any necessary assistance to the Court and the Prosecutor pursuant to this resolution and the Rome Statute of the International Criminal Court, the Elements of Crimes and the Rules of Evidence and Procedure of the International Criminal Court and, while recognizing that other States not party to the Rome Statute have no obligation under the Statute, urges all States and concerned regional and other international organizations to cooperate fully with the Court and the Prosecutor.*[199]

This template reflects the language used to describe State cooperation obligations in the Security Council resolutions that established the ICTY and ICTR.[200] According

---

[195] UNSC 2005, para 2; UNSC 2011, para 5, in which ICC States Parties are "obliged" to cooperate with the Court, while Non-Party States are only urged to cooperate with the Court.

[196] Trahan 2013, p. 462; Ayeni and Olong 2017, p. 252, "... no legal obligation on non-state parties to cooperate with the ICC."

[197] ICC, Prosecutor v Saif Al-Islam Gaddaffi and Abdullah Al-Senussi [Decision on Libya's Submissions Regarding the Arrest and Surrender of Saif Al-Islam Gaddafi]. (7 March 2012) ICC-01/11-01/11-72, para 12.

[198] Ayeni and Olong 2017, p. 252.

[199] ASP 2018b [Annex: Toolkit for the Implementation of the Informal Dimension of the Assembly Procedures relating to non-cooperation], para 54.

[200] UNSC 1993, para 4, "Decides that all States shall cooperate fully with the International Tribunal and its organs in accordance with the present resolution and the Statute of the International Tribunal and that consequently all States shall take any measures necessary under their domestic law to implement the provisions of the present resolution and the Statute..." UNSC 1994. Para 2, "Decides

to Bekou, the suggested template may have the effect of assisting in removing the ambiguity associated with the obligations of Non-Party States.[201] In the context of peacekeeping operations, the extension of cooperation to all UN Member States may have the potential to strengthen the mandate of these operations in situation States. This opens the possibility of the Security Council to take more effective action under Chapter VII, to impose sanctions or freeze the assets of non-cooperating States. In addition, the setting up of a task force, established to deal with the execution of arrest warrants may also assist in strengthening the Security Council's ability to follow up on ICC situations it has referred.[202]

3.3.3.2 Following Up on ICC Situations

While the Security Council has referred situations to the ICC, and thus has assisted in contributing to the prevention and prosecution of serious international crimes, it has not effectively followed up on these situations, particularly where instances of non-cooperation have been referred to it.[203] This failure to follow up is detrimental to the credibility of the Security Council in its role in maintaining international peace and security.[204] Such a failure also has a knock-on effect upon the effective functioning of the ICC. In the decision on Chad's failure to cooperate in the arrest and surrender of Sudan's Al-Bashir, the ICC Pre-Trial Chamber observed:

> *...if there is no follow up action on the part of the Security Council, any referral by the Council to the ICC under Chapter VII would never achieve its ultimate goal, namely, to put an end to impunity. Accordingly, any such referral would become futile.*[205]

The lack of enforcement mechanisms in cases referred to the Court by the Security Council not only weakens the Court's ability to improve the application of universal justice, but also deters other States from ratifying the Statute or implementing legislation aimed at responding to and prosecuting atrocity crimes.[206]

---

that all States shall cooperate fully with the International Tribunal and its organs in accordance with the present resolution and the Statute of the International Tribunal and that consequently all States shall take any measures necessary under their domestic law to implement the provisions of the present resolution and the Statute, including the obligation of States to comply with requests for assistance or orders issued by a Trial Chamber…".

[201] Bekou 2019, p. 940.

[202] Hamilton 2016, p. 362.

[203] ICC OTP 2018, para 17.

[204] Sluiter and Talontsi 2016, p. 105; see also: UNSC 2012, *Statement by Colombia at the 6849th meeting of the UN Security Council*, p. 10, "… when the Court issues arrest warrants and they are not carried out, what is at stake is the credibility of the Council's decisions and authority."

[205] Prosecutor v Omar Hassan Ahmad Al Bashir [Decision pursuant to article 87(7) of the Rome Statute on the Refusal of the Republic of Chad to comply with the cooperation requests issued by the Court with respect to the arrest and surrender of Omar Hassan Ahmad Al Bashir] (13 December 2011) ICC-02/05-01/09-140, para 22.

[206] Aloisi 2013, p. 154.

The lack of follow up on ICC situations by the Security Council has highlighted the need for the development of a forum within the Council that would be tasked with monitoring the implementation and enforcement of State obligations towards the ICC. In addition, such a forum would decide on consequences for the failure to cooperate with such obligations through the lens of the UN Charter.[207] The development of such a forum has been proposed at Security Council meetings. For example, at the 6849th meeting of the Security Council in 2012, the delegation of Togo suggested the establishment of a committee or working group on the ICC within the Security Council which would be tasked to ensure that matters relating to the implementation of the Security Council's mandate towards the ICC are monitored more effectively.[208]

Ensuring better follow up on matters relating to the ICC, particularly within the scope of non-cooperation, could also be conducted through the expansion of the mandate of the Informal Working Group on International Tribunals.[209] At the 6849th Meeting of the Security Council, France proposed that the mandate of this working group should be broadened in order to better organise dialogue and follow up of international criminal law matters.[210] This working group was established in 2000, following a proposal by members of the Security Council.[211] It addresses issues relating to the Rwanda, Yugoslavia and Lebanon tribunals, and has over the years expanded its mandate to address other matters relating to international criminal tribunals.[212]

3.4 Conclusion

This chapter has identified that the frameworks currently in place to address and remedy non-cooperation have not been effective, and have yet to successfully function as intended. The ineffectiveness of these frameworks can be attributed to failure of the institutions tasked with addressing non-cooperation to take appropriate, concrete action against uncooperative States. These institutions also have limited remedies at their disposal to address instances of non-cooperation.[213] Their inability to appropriately address non-cooperation can also be attributed to a lack of political

---

[207] Akande and De Souza Dias 2019, p. 9.

[208] UNSC 2012, Statement by Togo at the 6849th Meeting of the UN Security Council, p. 22.

[209] Akande and de Souza Dias 2019. p. 9.

[210] UNSC 2012, Statement by France at the 6849th Meeting of the UN Security Council, p. 23.

[211] UNSC 2000; see the Statements by Bangladesh, Canada, and Tunisia at pp. 13, 14 and 17, where these States supported the development of such a working group.

[212] UN Security Council Working Groups, available at: https://www.un.org/securitycouncil/content/repertoire/working-groups (accessed 1 September 2020); this mandate also includes the International Residual Mechanism for Criminal Tribunals.

[213] Tladi 2014, p. 398.

will, within the Assembly of States Parties and the UN Security Council expressing apathy towards efforts at taking effective measures against non-cooperating States.[214]

According to Hunter, the ICC's judicial decisions on non-cooperation, together with the lack of appropriate formal action from the Assembly of States Parties and the Security Council, have muted the coercive powers of the Court and have not been effective in incentivising compliance with cooperation obligations.[215] It is therefore necessary for the remedies and procedures aimed at addressing non-cooperation to be developed and strengthened. If these remedies are still not sufficient for addressing non-cooperation, this may identify the need to develop additional remedies outside the scope of the Rome Statute, which could enhance the ICC's ability to address non-cooperation. In this regard, it may be necessary to look at the rules of general international law, particularly those rules that address the responsibility of States.

As already noted in Chap. 2 of this Book, several decisions on non-cooperation have recognised that the frameworks for addressing non-cooperation under Article 87(7) are but one of the many tools available for remedying the failure to cooperate.[216] This suggests that there may be remedies other than those within the ICC's classical frameworks that may be implemented to assist in improving responses to non-cooperation. Sluiter and Talontsi recognise the potential use of other international law frameworks for addressing non-cooperation. However, noting the current political climate, they also recognise that States would not likely seek alternative avenues for enforcing cooperation obligations.[217] From this they suggest that enhancing the political will of all parties involved is crucial for introducing a more effective regime for responding to non-cooperation.[218]

The chapter to follow will investigate the frameworks associated with the Responsibility to Protect, an international doctrine which affirms a global commitment by States and the larger international community to protect populations from the most serious of international crimes. This chapter will identify how R2P and the ICC can interact with each other in the context of the ICC's cooperation frameworks. In doing so, this chapter will investigate how R2P can strengthen the ICC's frameworks for addressing instances of non-cooperation, thus creating a more effective cooperation regime for preventing and punishing serious international crimes.

---

[214] Sluiter and Talontsi 2016, p. 109; Tladi 2014, p. 398.

[215] Hunter 2016, p. 374.

[216] Prosecutor v Saif Al-Islam Gaddafi [Decision on the non-compliance by Libya with requests for cooperation by the Court and referring the matter to the United Nations Security Council] (10 December 2014) ICC-01/11-01/11-577, para 23; Prosecutor v Uhuru Muigai Kenyatta [Judgment on the Prosecutor's appeal against Trial Chamber V(B)'s "Decision on Prosecution's application for a finding of non-compliance under Article 87(7) of the Statute"] (19 August 2015) ICC-01/09-02/11-1032. para 51.

[217] Sluiter and Talontsi 2016, p. 103.

[218] Ibid. p. 109.

References

African Union (AU) (2009) Decision of the Meeting of African States Parties to the Rome Statute of the International Criminal Court. Assembly/AU/Dec.245 (XIII) Rev.1.

Assembly of States Parties (ASP) (2011) Tenth Session Strengthening the International Criminal Court and the Assembly of States Parties ICC-ASP/10/Res.5.

Assembly of States Parties (ASP) (2012) Eleventh Session Report of the Bureau on non-cooperation ICC-ASP/11/29.

Assembly of States Parties (ASP) (2013) Twelfth Session Report of the Bureau of Cooperation ICC-ASP/12/36.

Assembly of States Parties (ASP) (2014) Thirteenth Session Report of the Bureau on Non-cooperation ICC-ASP/13/40.

Assembly of States Parties (ASP) (2015) Fourteenth Session Report of the Bureau on non-cooperation ICC-ASP/14/38.

Assembly of States Parties (ASP) (2016) Fifteenth Session Report of the Bureau on non-cooperation ICC-ASP/15/31.

Assembly of States Parties (ASP) (2018a) Seventeenth Session Strengthening the International Criminal Court and the Assembly of States Parties Resolution ICC-ASP/17/Res.5 [Annex II Assembly Procedures Relating to Non-Cooperation].

Assembly of States Parties (ASP) (2018b) Seventeenth Session Report of the Bureau on non-cooperation [Annex: Toolkit for the Implementation of the Informal dimension of the Assembly procedures relating to non-cooperation] ICC-ASP/17/31. Annex III.

Akande D (2012) The Effect of Security Council Resolutions and Domestic Proceedings on State Obligations to Cooperate with the ICC. Journal of International Criminal Justice 10(2), 299–324.

Akande D, de Souza Dias T (2019) Cooperation with the ICC: What the Security Council and ASP Must Do. ISS Africa Report 1–15, available at: https://issafrica.s3.amazonaws.com/site/uploads/ar15.pdf (accessed 12 October 2024).

Alamuddin A (2014) The Role of the Security Council in Starting and Stopping Cases at the International Criminal Court. In: Zidar A, Bekou O (eds) Contemporary Challenges for the International Criminal Court. British Institute of International and Comparative Law, London.

Aloisi R (2013) A Tale of Two Institutions: The United Nations Security Council and the International Criminal Court. International Criminal Law Review 13(1) 147–168.

Ambach P (2022) Article 112, Assembly of States Parties. In: Ambos K (ed) Rome Statute of the International Criminal Court: Article-by-Article Commentary. Beck/Nomos/Hart, Munich, pp. 2767–2811.

Arbour L (2014) The Relationship Between the ICC and the UN Security Council. Global Governance 20(2), 195–201.

Ayeni VO, Olong MA (2017) Opportunities and Challenges to the UN Security Council Referral Under the Rome Statute of the International Criminal Court. African Journal of International and Comparative Law 25(2), 239–260.

Babaian S (2018) The International Criminal Court—An International Criminal World Court. Springer International Publishing AG, Cham.

Bekou O (2019) Dealing with Non-cooperation at the ICC: Towards a More Holistic Approach. International Criminal Law Review 19(6): 911–937.

Bergsmo M, Zhu D (2022) Article 16, Deferral of Investigation or Prosecution. In: Ambos K (ed) Rome Statute of the International Criminal Court: Article-by-Article Commentary. Beck/Nomos/Hart, Munich, pp. 933–945.

Ciampi A (2016) Legal Rules, Policy Choices and Political Realities in the Functioning of the Cooperation Regime of the International Criminal Court In: Bekou O, Birkett DJ (eds) Cooperation and the International Criminal Court: Perspectives from Theory and Practice. Brill, Leiden, pp. 7–57.

Clark RS, Meisenberg SM (2022) Article 119, Settlement of Disputes. In: Ambos K (ed) Rome Statute of the International Criminal Court: Article-by-Article Commentary. Beck/Nomos/Hart, Munich, pp. 2846–2855.
Cerar M (2009) The Relationship Between Law and Politics. Annual Survey of International and Comparative Law 15(1) 19–41.
Coutre A (2015) The Politicals of International Justice: The Security Council's Impact on the Independence, Effectiveness and Legitimacy of the International Criminal Court International Human Rights Internship Working Paper Series 3(2) 1–33.
Dushimimana L (2013) States' Cooperation with the International Criminal Tribunal for Rwanda. Rwanda Journal, Series B: Social Sciences 1(1) 71–91.
Galand AS (2019) UN Security Council Referrals to the International Criminal Court: Legal Nature, Effects and Limits. Brill Nijhoff, Leiden.
Genser J (2018) The United Nations Security Council's Implementation of the Responsibility to Protect: A Review of Past interventions and Recommendations for Improvement. 18(2) Chicago Journal of International Law 18(2) 420–501.
Hamilton K (2016) The Role of Peacekeeping Operations in International Criminal Justice: Obstacles to Assistance following Security Council Referrals to the ICC. Journal of International Peacekeeping 20(3-4) 342–362.
Harmon MB, Gaynor F (2004) Prosecuting Massive Crimes with Primitive Tools: Three Difficulties Encountered by Prosecutors in International Criminal Proceedings. Journal of International Criminal Justice 2(2) 403–426.
Holvoet M, Meman M (2016) The International Criminal Court and the Responsibility to Protect. In: Fiott D, Koops J (eds) The Responsibility to Protect and the Third Pillar: Legitimacy and Operationalization. Palgrave Macmillan, London, pp. 21–38.
Hunter E (2016) Using 'Managerial Compliance' to Strengthen ICC Cooperation. In: Bekou O, Birkett DJ (eds) Cooperation and the International Criminal Court: Perspectives from Theory and Practice. Brill, Leiden, pp. 366–395.
ICC Office of the Prosecutor (2018) Twenty-Eighth Report of the Prosecutor of the International Criminal Court to the United Nations Security Council Pursuant to UNSCR 1593 (2005) available at https://www.icc-cpi.int/itemsDocuments/181214-rep-otp-UNSC-1593_ENG.pdf (accessed 4 April 2020).
Illingworth R (2020) Responsible Veto Restraint: a Transitional Cosmopolitan Reform Measure for the Responsibility to Protect. Global Responsibility to Protect 12(4) 385–414.
Jia BB (2020) Reflections on the ICC's Relationship with the United Nations and Regional Courts. In: Steinberg RH (ed) The International Criminal Court: Contemporary Challenges and Reform Proposals. Koninklijke Brill NV, Leiden, pp. 358–366.
Jones A (2016) Non-cooperation and the Efficiency of the International Criminal Court. In: Bekou O, Birkett DJ (eds) Cooperation and the International Criminal Court: Perspectives from Theory and Practice. Brill, Leiden, pp. 185–209.
Kress C, Prost K (2022) International Cooperation and Judicial Assistance. In: Ambos K (ed) Rome Statute of the International Criminal Court: Article-by-Article Commentary. Beck/Nomos/Hart, Munich, pp. 2452–2701.
Lentner GM (2014) The Role of the UN Security Council vis-à-vis the International Criminal Court—Resolution 1970 (2011) and its Challenges to International Criminal Justice. International and Comparative Law Review, 14(2) 7–23.
Meernik JD (2015) Why do Individuals Surrender to the International Criminal Tribunals? International Criminal Law Review 15(5) 926–948.
Mistry H, Verduzco RH (2012) International Law Meeting Summary, with Parliamentarians for Global Action: The UN Security Council and the International Criminal Court. Chatham House, pp. 1–22.
Peskin V (2008) International Justice in Rwanda and the Balkans: Virtual Trials and the Struggle for State Cooperation. Cambridge University Press, New York.

Rastan R (2008) Testing Co-operation: The International Criminal Court and National Authorities. Leiden Journal of International Law 21(2) 431–456.
Saba A, Akbarzadeh S (2020) The ICC and R2P: Complementary or Contradictory? International Peacekeeping 28(1), 84–109.
Schabas WA, Pecorella G (2022) Article 13, Exercise of Jurisdiction. In: Ambos K (ed) Rome Statute of the International Criminal Court: Article-by-Article Commentary. Beck/Nomos/Hart, Munich, pp. 834–853.
Shaw MN (2021) International Law, 9th edn. Cambridge University Press, Cambridge.
Sluiter G (2018) Enforcing Cooperation: Did the Drafters Approach It the Wrong Way? Journal of International Criminal Justice 16(2): 383–402.
Sluiter G, Talontsi S (2016) Credible and Authoritative Enforcement of State Cooperation with the International Criminal Court. In: Bekou O, Birkett DJ (eds) Cooperation and the International Criminal Court: Perspectives from Theory and Practice. Brill, Leiden, pp. 80–113.
Smith-van Lin L (2016) Non-compliance and the Law and Politics of State Cooperation: Lessons from the Al-Bashir and Kenyatta Cases. In: Bekou O, Birkett DJ (eds) Cooperation and the International Criminal Court: Perspectives from Theory and Practice. Brill, Leiden, pp. 114–151.
Stroh D (2001) State Cooperation with the International Criminal Tribunals for the Former Yugoslavia and for Rwanda. Max Planck Yearbook of United Nations Law 5, 249–283.
Tiemessen A (2014) The International Criminal Court and the Politics of Prosecutions. The International Journal of Human Rights 18(4-5), 444–461.
Tladi D (2014) When Elephants Collide it is the Grass that Suffers: Cooperation and the Security Council in the Context of the AU/ICC Dynamic. African Journal of Legal Studies (7)(3): 381–398.
Trahan J (2013) The Relationship between the International Criminal Court and the UN Security Council: Parameters and Best Practices. Criminal Law Forum 24, 417–473.
UN General Assembly (UNGA) (2004) Relationship Agreement Between the United Nations and the International Criminal Court, A/58/874.
UN Security Council (UNSC) (1993) Resolution 827 [International Criminal Tribunal for the former Yugoslavia (ICTY)] S/RES/827.
UN Security Council (UNSC) (1994) Resolution 955 [Establishment of the International Criminal Tribunal for Rwanda] S/RES/955.
UN Security Council (UNSC) (2000) 4161st Meeting, S/PV.4161.
UN Security Council (UNSC) (2002) Resolution 1422 [on suspension for 12 months of investigation or prosecution cases involving personnel from States not parties to the Rome Statute of the International Criminal Court] S/RES/1422.
UN Security Council (UNSC) (2003) Resolution 1487 [on extension for 12 months of suspension of investigation or prosecution cases involving personnel from States not parties to the Rome Statute of the International Criminal Court] S/RES/1487.
UN Security Council (UNSC) (2005) Resolution 1593 [Sudan] S/RES/1593.
UN Security Council (UNSC) (2011) Resolution 1970 [Peace and Security in Africa] S/RES/1970.
UN Security Council (UNSC) (2012a) Letter dated 1 October 2012 from the Permanent Representative of Guatemala to the United Nations addressed to the Security Council S/2012/731.
UN Security Council (UNSC) (2012b) 6849th Meeting of the UN Security Council S/PV.6849.
UN Security Council (UNSC) (2013) 7080th Meeting [Statement by the Prosecutor of the International Criminal Court] S/PV.7080.
UN Security Council (UNSC) (2014a) Draft Resolution [Syria] S/2014/348.
UN Security Council (UNSC) (2014b) 7180th Meeting of the UN Security Council. S/PV.7180.

Chapter 4
Enhancing Responses to Non-cooperation Through the Responsibility to Protect

Contents

4.1 Introduction 80
4.2 The Origins of R2P 81
  4.2.1 Origins: Humanitarian Intervention 81
  4.2.2 Origins: The International Commission on Intervention and State Sovereignty 83
  4.2.3 Origins: Reports of the Secretary General 85
  4.2.4 The Recognition and Development of R2P 86
4.3 The Pillars of R2P 89
  4.3.1 Pillar One 90
  4.3.2 Pillar Two 90
  4.3.3 Pillar Three 91
  4.3.4 Assessing the Implementation of the Three Pillars of R2P 92
4.4 R2P and the ICC 93
  4.4.1 The ICC in R2P Texts 93
  4.4.2 Overlaps and Differences Between the ICC and R2P 94
  4.4.3 The ICC Analysed through the Lens of the Three Pillars of R2P 98
  4.4.4 The Role of R2P in Strengthening the ICC 102
4.5 R2P and the UN System 104
  4.5.1 The Security Council and R2P 104
  4.5.2 The General Assembly and R2P 107
4.6 Conclusion 118
References 119

Abstract This chapter aims to examine the development of the Responsibility to Protect (R2P) in the international legal landscape and assess the potential of this doctrine to strengthen or otherwise compliment the ICC's frameworks for responding to non-cooperation. By analysing the elements of R2P that align with the Rome Statute's provisions on cooperation, this chapter seeks to determine how these principles might enhance the effectiveness of the Court's current frameworks. Ultimately, the goal of this chapter is to explore how R2P can contribute to a more robust and comprehensive regime for enforcing State cooperation with the ICC, thereby addressing the limitations of existing non-cooperation remedies. This chapter also seeks to highlight the role of R2P in enhancing the United Nations' collective security mechanisms as tools for enhancing cooperation between States and the ICC.

M. L. Jacobs, *The Consequences of Non-cooperation with the International Criminal Court*, International Criminal Justice Series 37,
https://doi.org/10.1007/978-94-6265-675-8_4

Keywords R2P · Responsibility to Protect · United Nations · Atrocity Crimes · Non-cooperation · ICC · Rome Statute

4.1 Introduction

The Responsibility to Protect (also referred to as R2P) is a global political commitment endorsed by all UN Member States to address concerns relating to the prevention of atrocity crimes. Under this doctrine, States have a primary responsibility to protect its populations from genocide, war crimes, crimes against humanity and ethnic cleansing, as well as a collective responsibility to assist other States, in accordance with the UN Charter, in ensuring that this commitment is upheld.[1] The doctrine emerged out of an interest among the international community to address issues relating to the use of force in order to prevent the commission of atrocity crimes.[2] In particular, the failure of the United Nations to respond to the commission of atrocities in various territories in the 1990s increased the need to find solutions for improving frameworks for protection and prevention.[3] Developments in several fields associated with protection for humanitarian purposes placed much focus on international attention on the duty to protect people from serious international crimes.[4]

Aside from assessing the effectiveness of the ICC's responses to non-cooperation, this book aims to investigate whether other sources of international law could assist in strengthening or otherwise complement the Court's remedies for addressing non-cooperation. This chapter will analyse whether R2P could be used as a prism through which such remedies could be introduced. Therefore, the ultimate purpose of this chapter is to investigate the development of R2P within the international legal sphere, and its potential to contribute to the development of a more effective remedies regime for the ICC. In addition, this chapter will identify the elements from R2P that can be applied to strengthen the Rome Statute and its cooperation frameworks.

---

[1] Global Centre for the Responsibility to Protect *What is R2P?* available at https://www.globalr2p.org/what-is-r2p/ (accessed 20 April 2020); United Nations Office on Genocide Prevention and the Responsibility to Protect *About* available at https://www.un.org/en/genocideprevention/about-responsibility-to-protect.shtml (accessed 17 July 2020) "Ultimately, the Responsibility to Protect principle reinforces sovereignty by helping states to meet their existing responsibilities. It offers fresh programmatic opportunities for the United Nations system to assist states in preventing the listed crimes and violations and in protecting affected populations through capacity building, early warning, and other preventive and protective measures, rather than simply waiting to respond if they fail."

[2] Hehir 2019, p. 30.

[3] Ibid. pp. 30–32.

[4] Bellamy and Dunne 2016, p. 6.

4.2 The Origins of R2P

This section seeks to identify the origins of R2P. This section will specifically look at the precursor to R2P, humanitarian intervention, and the subsequent adoption of the doctrine within the framework of international protection from serious breaches of international law.

4.2.1 Origins: Humanitarian Intervention

The responsibility to protect is rooted in principles developed from humanitarian intervention, which can be defined as:

> *The protection by a State or group of States of fundamental human rights, in particular the right to life of nationals of, and residing in, the territory of other States, involving the use of force or threat of force, such protection taking place neither upon the authorisation by the relevant organs of the United Nations, nor upon invitation by the legitimate government of the target State.*[5]

According to the UN Charter, the threat or use of force against the territorial integrity or political independence of a State is expressly prohibited.[6] In addition, the UN Charter recognises the principle of non-intervention, stating that:

> *Nothing contained in the present Charter shall authorize the United Nations to intervene in matters which are essentially within the domestic jurisdiction of any state or shall require the Members to submit such matters to settlement under the present Charter; but this principle shall not prejudice the application of enforcement measures under Chapter VII.*[7]

Exceptions to this prohibition are where the UN Council has authorised the use of force in the maintenance or restoration of international peace and security,[8] and where a State acts in self-defence in response to an armed attack by another State.[9] The UN Charter also requires that Member States actively enforce human rights standards.[10] States therefore have the duty to refrain from relying on the use of force, as well as the duty to enforce human rights standards.[11]

---

[5] Kritsiotis 1998, p. 1005.

[6] The Charter of the United Nations (26 June 1945, 1 UNTS XVI, Entry into Force 24 October 1945), Article 2(4).

[7] Ibid. Article 2(7).

[8] Ibid. Article 42.

[9] Ibid. Article 51.

[10] UN Charter, above n. 6, Article 55.

[11] Merriam 2001, p. 114; the author also notes that as a result of these conflicting duties, "… some States have opted to use force as a means of last resort to prevent humanitarian tragedy, while at the same time seeking to establish a self-defence argument in order to avoid a UN sanction."

4.2.1.1 The Legality of Humanitarian Intervention

The right to humanitarian intervention opened several debates as to the legality of its use, especially within the current international legal climate. Under the UN Charter, humanitarian intervention is not expressly referred to as an exception to the prohibition of the use of force. The case for the illegality of humanitarian intervention rests on the black letter of the UN Charter, in that all justifications for resorting to military force which are not authorised by the UN Charter, are illegal and infringe upon the sovereignty of the target State, irrespective of the humanitarian goals or nature of the act.[12] Nothing in the UN Charter opens up the possibility that the use of force for humanitarian purposes should be interpreted differently from other uses of force.[13] In addition, customary international law does not recognise humanitarian intervention as a legitimate ground for the use of force and has been considered as an excuse for powerful States to intervene in the affairs of less powerful States.[14]

However, those in favour of humanitarian intervention argue that it is permitted under the Charter, and therefore qualifies as an exception to the prohibition of the use of force alongside with self defence and Security Council authorisation exceptions.[15] The case for the legality of humanitarian intervention can be made through the application of various distinct arguments. According to Benjamin, the prohibition of the use of force, entrenched in Article 2(4) of the UN Charter, has lost its legal force due to its repeated violation by States. This argument suggests that permitting humanitarian intervention would not undermine the prohibition of the use of force, as force is only prohibited when it operates against the integrity and political independence of other States, and when it is inconsistent with the spirit and purport of the United Nations.[16]

In addition, there are arguments that rebut the claim that humanitarian intervention is an infringement of State sovereignty and non-intervention.[17] In this regard, it is argued that sovereignty and humanitarian intervention are complementary to each other. Under this view, humanitarian intervention is lawful because the legal protections for sovereign States fall away if the State engages in serious abuses of its

---

[12] De Beer and Tladi 2019, pp. 213–214.

[13] Hurd 2011, p. 298.

[14] De Beer and Tladi 2019, p. 222; see also Breau 2018, p. 536, where the author confirms that there is general agreement that unilateral humanitarian intervention is not a recognised exception to the prohibition of the use of force.

[15] See for discussion: De Beer and Tladi 2019, pp. 211–212, the authors note that such a proposal suggests that humanitarian intervention is not directed against the territory or political independence of the target State but is instead conducted to give effect to UN-recognised principles such as the protection of human rights; Hurd 2011, p. 301; "Two forces in international politics have repeatedly pressed humanitarian intervention onto the international legal agenda despite Article 2(4): the extension of the ideology of cosmopolitanism and human rights, which provides a moral imperative to respond to outrages against people regardless of their citizenship; and the strategic manipulation by states who see in humanitarianism a useful instrument to justify their military interventions."

[16] Benjamin 1992, pp. 149–150.

[17] Kritstosis 1998, p. 1005.

population.[18] Those in favour of humanitarian intervention also argue that the UN has recognised that sovereignty is secondary in importance to the protection of the right to life.[19] It is further argued that humanitarian intervention is not in conflict with the customary principle of non-intervention but instead complements it, as the purpose of both principles is the protection and promotion of State sovereignty.[20]

Although humanitarian intervention has been used on rare occasions, its practice has been objected to by several States. In the 1990s the use of humanitarian intervention led to debates on the legitimacy and appropriateness of the use of force for humanitarian purposes.[21] In particular the controversy surrounding the failure of the UN Security Council in responding to intra-state atrocity crimes, such as in the case of Rwanda and the Former Yugoslavia, as well as NATO intervention in Kosovo indicated that existing frameworks aimed at addressing, preventing and punishing the commission of atrocity crimes were influenced and hampered by political considerations.[22]

4.2.2 Origins: The International Commission on Intervention and State Sovereignty

As a result of these continued failures by the UN system and the international community in responding to and addressing atrocity crimes, the UN Secretary-General challenged UN Member States to develop clearer and more effective frameworks to assist in the protection of human rights and the prevention of serious international crimes.[23] The Canadian Government responded to this challenge through the establishment of the International Commission on Intervention and State Sovereignty (hereinafter referred to as the "ICISS"). This Commission consisted of a panel of experts that aimed to find consensus on a proper strategy to prevent and end the commission of atrocity crimes.[24]

---

[18] Hurd 2011, p. 302; Merriam 2001, p. 115, "... human rights are so valuable that even the sanctity of sovereignty should not serve as a bar to their protection;", and pp. 117–118, "It is thus in the general interest of all states to cooperate to prevent and punish war crimes..."

[19] Merriam 2001, p. 122; see also Benjamin 1992, p. 150, where the author argues that the legality of humanitarian intervention should be determined by the action or inaction of international organisations tasked with maintaining international peace and security. The ability to rely on the use of force should be phased out when those organisations are able to prevent atrocities more effectively.

[20] Gulati and Khosa 2013 p. 411.

[21] Weiss 2016, p. 57.

[22] Hehir 2019, p. 33; see also Franchini and Tzanakopoulos 2018, pp. 594–622, for a discussion on the legitimacy of the intervention in Kosovo which was conducted without the authorisation of the UN Security Council.

[23] Annan K (2000) "We the Peoples: The Role of the United Nations in the 21st Century" available at: https://www.un.org/en/events/pastevents/pdfs/We_The_Peoples.pdf (accessed 14 April 2019) p. 48.

[24] Thakur 2016, p. 107.

In 2001, the ICISS published a report which introduced the concept of R2P and discussed the approach that States should follow in its further development.[25] The report recognised that the international environment of the 21st century had changed drastically since the formation of the United Nations in 1945, with the emergence of new realities and changes, as well as new expectations for action and standards of conduct in national and international affairs.[26] The report recognised the increase in the number of international actors, with a range of new voices, perspectives, interests, experiences, and aspirations. The emergence of these new actors forced a debate on the manner in which humanitarian intervention should be conducted, with special regard being given to the rise in global security issues, the increase in non-international armed conflicts, the rise of affordable and destructive weapons, and the increased vulnerability of civilian populations.[27] The ICISS Report noted that the measures aimed at addressing and remedying atrocity crimes needed to be reassessed in order to meet the foreseeable needs of the 21st century.[28]

This report did not propose a change in the laws that governed the means by which the UN and the general international community should respond to intra-State atrocity crimes, but instead argued that the aim was to build the capacity of these bodies to appropriately respond to these crimes.[29] Regarding this, the report noted that new approaches to intervention on the grounds of human protection needed to meet four basic objectives:

> *to establish clearer rules, procedures, and criteria for determining whether when and how to intervene;*
>
> *to establish the legitimacy of military intervention when necessary and after all other approaches have failed;*
>
> *to ensure that military intervention, when it occurs, is carried out only for the purposes proposed, is effective and is undertaken with proper concern to minimize the human costs and institutional damage that will result;*
>
> *to help eliminate, where possible, the causes of conflict while enhancing the prospects for durable and sustainable peace.*[30]

---

[25] ICISS 2001.

[26] Ibid. para 1.10.

[27] ICISS 2001, paras 1.11–1.18.

[28] Ibid. para 2.2.

[29] Hehir 2019, pp. 34–35.

[30] ICISS 2001 para 2.3.

4.2.3 Origins: Reports of the Secretary General

In 2004, the UN Secretary General added to the discussion on R2P with the *Report of the High-Level Panel on Threats, Challenges and Change.*[31] This report saw to depict R2P as a means to strengthen the collective security system under the UN Charter. In its opening pages, the report mentioned the link between sovereignty and the responsibility of States.[32] In a section of the report titled "Chapter VII of the Charter of the United Nations, internal threats and the responsibility to protect", the report developed the concept within the framework of the use of force.[33] This section endorsed the emerging norm of a collective international responsibility to protect, exercisable by the Security Council authorising military intervention as a last resort to address serious international crimes where States have proved to be unable or unwilling to prevent such crimes.[34]

The Secretary-General released an additional report in 2005, which addressed proposals for UN Reform, while also discussing a then fledgling R2P, and the primary responsibility of States.[35] While drawing much from the report of the High-Level Panel, this report discussed a more moderate approach to R2P, placing stronger emphasis on the need to implement R2P through more peaceful means.[36] This was done to ease concerns held by some States against the military dimension of R2P and the risk that it could be abused.[37] This report opened up the floor for more elaborate discussions on what R2P may entail for each State. In particular, States were urged to ratify and implement all treaties relating to the protection of civilians,[38] build

---

[31] UNGA 2004.

[32] Ibid. para 29, "Whatever perceptions may have prevailed when the Westphalian system first gave rise to the notion of State sovereignty, today it clearly carries with it the obligation of a State to protect the welfare of its own peoples and meet its obligations to the wider international community."

[33] UNGA 2004, para 201, "There is a growing recognition that the issue is not the 'right to intervene' of any State, but the 'responsibility to protect' of *every* State when it comes to people suffering from avoidable catastrophe ... And there is a growing acceptance that while sovereign Governments have the primary responsibility to protect their own citizens from such catastrophes when they are unable or unwilling to do so that responsibility should be taken up by the wider international community.

[34] Ibid. para 203.

[35] UNGA 2005a.

[36] Ibid. para 135 "If national authorities are unable or unwilling to protect their citizens then the responsibility shifts to the international community to use diplomatic, humanitarian and other methods to help protect the human rights and well-being of civilian populations."

[37] Amneus 2013, p. 9.

[38] UNGA 2005a, para 136.

up effective national judicial institutions,[39] cooperate fully with the ICC and other criminal tribunals,[40] and strengthen the work of the International Court of Justice.[41]

4.2.4 The Recognition and Development of R2P

At its inception, R2P was considered controversial as it was feared that the doctrine would be used by more powerful States to intervene in the affairs of smaller States.[42] The doctrine was also not well received among more powerful States due to the lack of political will on their side to respond and act according to R2P guidelines.[43]

4.2.4.1 The World Summit Outcome Document

In 2005, R2P was officially recognised at the UN World Summit. The Summit's *Outcome Document* confirmed that:

> *Each individual State has the responsibility to protect its populations from genocide, war crimes, ethnic cleansing, and crimes against humanity. This responsibility entails the prevention of such crimes, including their incitement, through appropriate and necessary means. ... The international community should, as appropriate, encourage and help States to exercise this responsibility and support the United Nations in establishing an early warning capability.*[44]

The *Outcome Document* also reaffirmed the responsibility of the international community to use appropriate means in accordance with the UN Charter and other rules of international law to assist in the protection of populations from serious international crimes.[45] These paragraphs were reaffirmed by the UN Security Council in resolutions 1674 and 1706, passed in 2006.[46] In 2009, the UN Secretary-General published his first report on R2P, which outlined the strategy for its proper implementation.[47] This report analyses paragraphs 138 and 139 of the *World Summit Outcome*

---

[39] Ibid. para 137, "Effective national legal and judicial institutions are essential to the success of all our efforts to help societies emerge from a violent past."

[40] Ibid. para 138.

[41] Ibid. para 139, "I also urge all parties to bear in mind, and make greater use of, the Court's advisory powers. Measures should also be taken, with the cooperation of litigating States, to improve the Court's working methods and reduce the length of its proceedings."

[42] Thakur and Weiss 2009, p. 22, where the authors describe R2P as a more sophisticated, more broadly acceptable reformulation of humanitarian intervention; see also Tladi 2019, p. 2 at n4, where the author notes that the responsibility to protect is viewed as a replacement of humanitarian intervention, which is not the case.

[43] Hehir 2019, p. 36.

[44] UNGA 2005b, para 138.

[45] Ibid. para 139.

[46] UNSC 2006a, para 4; UNSC 2006b, pre para 2.

[47] UNGA 2009a.

Document and identifies three pillars of R2P.[48] The Secretary-General has since released annual reports on R2P, all addressing various issues relating to the R2P regime. At the time of writing, the most recent report addresses the commitment of the international community in preventing and protecting populations from atrocity crimes.[49]

4.2.4.2 Debates and Discussions on R2P

Following the publication of the R2P Report, the first General Assembly debate on R2P was held in July 2009, in which 92 governments and two observers signed up and spoke over a period of two and a half days over the implementation of R2P.[50] Matters discussed included: that it was the task of the General Assembly to discuss ideas and challenges for the implementation of R2P, rather than attempt to renegotiate it;[51] that the definition of R2P should be confined to the four crimes illustrated in the *World Summit Outcome Document;*[52] full support for the pillar system, aside from some questions regarding the implementation of the third pillar;[53] and recognising that R2P is rooted in existing international law.[54]

The debates also gave Member States the opportunity to get clarity over certain aspects of R2P. This included fears that the application of R2P would legitimise the use of unilateral coercive measures;[55] that there was a lack of political will among Member States to react appropriately to mass atrocities;[56] calls for the reform of the

48 Ibid. para 11.

49 UNGA 2024.

50 UNGA 2009b, 97th–101st Plenary Meetings.

51 Ibid. Statement by Ghana at the 98th Plenary Meeting, "this debate should not be about renegotiating the concept ... instead the primary focus of our ongoing dialogue must be on how to garner the needed collective political will to act and take on concrete measures at the national, regional and international levels towards the prevention of those four crimes."

52 Ibid. statement by The Philippines at the 97th Plenary Meeting "Any attempt to enlarge its coverage even before R2P is effectively implemented will only delay, if not derail, such implementation; or worse yet, diminish its value or devalue its original intent and scope."

53 Ibid. Statement by Mali at the 98th Plenary Meeting, "my delegation believes that discussion on the third pillar must continue in the General Assembly"; Statement by Mexico at the 99th Plenary Meeting, "The third pillar ... requires more specifics."

54 Ibid. Statement by Israel at the 98th Plenary Meeting, "The Responsibility to Protect lies primarily in enhancing existing tools and mechanisms, rather than creating them anew"; Statement by Slovenia at the 99th Plenary Meeting, "R2P is based on existing international law, and nothing about the concept implies any alterations to the provisions of the Charter of the United Nations."

55 Ibid. Statement by India at the 99th Plenary Meeting, "The responsibility to protect should in no way provide a pretext for humanitarian intervention or unilateral action"; Statement by Kyrgyzstan at the 101st Plenary Meeting, "A neighbouring country used it (R2P) as a false pretext to actually carry out the ethnic cleansing of entire provinces of our country through a unilateral large-scale military invasion."

56 UNGA 2009b, Statement by the USA at the 97th Plenary Meeting, "The greatest obstacle to swift action in the face of sudden atrocity is the lack of political will"; Statement by Iran at the 100th

Security Council;[57] and for an enhanced role for the General Assembly in implementing R2P.[58] These debates also highlighted a number of general issues, concerns and misconceptions. These included, the similarity between R2P and humanitarian intervention;[59] issues with Security Council reform;[60] the view that R2P was a violation of sovereignty;[61] and false and misrepresentative arguments on the legal status of R2P.[62] A few months after this debate, the General Assembly adopted its first resolution on R2P, in which it showed support for the *Implementing R2P Report* and the debates.[63]

Plenary Meeting ibid, "there is no illusion that tragic cases of genocide, crimes against humanity and outrageous acts of aggression have been left unanswered not because of a lack of empowering legal norms, but simply due to a lack of political will dictated by power politics."

[57] Ibid. Statement by South Africa at the 98th Plenary Meeting, "... our delegation agrees with the Secretary-General that the General Assembly needs to develop guidelines for response, including the curtailment of the veto when considering issues related to these four crimes"; Statement by India at the 99th Plenary Meeting, "A necessary ingredient is real reform of decision-making bodies in the United Nations, especially the Security Council and its permanent membership stricture, to reflect contemporary realities and make them forces for peace capable of acting against mass atrocities."

[58] Ibid. Statement by The Solomon Islands at the 99th Plenary Meeting, "We need to increase the legitimacy of the General Assembly, giving greater voice to its 192 members to oversee R2P implementation"; Statement by Venezuela at the 99th Plenary Meeting, "It should be stressed that if we hope to make the responsibility to protect a multilateral mechanism for collective action, we should do so through the General Assembly."

[59] Ibid. Statement by the Democratic People's Republic of Korea at the 100th Plenary Meeting "This is very complicated and sensitive, as it is based on the concept of humanitarian intervention"; Statement by Sudan at the 101st Plenary Meeting, "Some may argue that humanitarian intervention is not the same as the concept of the responsibility to protect. However, under close scrutiny, we find them to be two sides of the same coin"; Statement by South Korea at the 97th Plenary Meeting, "... the substance of R2P has nothing to do with so-called humanitarian intervention. R2P is distinctly different from humanitarian intervention, since it is based on collective action in accordance with the United Nations Charter, not on unilateral ones."

[60] Ibid. Statement by Ecuador at the 98th Plenary Meeting, "It is therefore legitimate to ask whether the Security Council ... should be the authority for military interventions for humanitarian protection purposes or whether deep comprehensive reform of the council should take place first"; Statement by New Zealand at the 97th Plenary Meeting, "Although New Zealand supports structural reform of the Security Council, we are concerned by suggestions that such changes are a prior condition for implementing the responsibility to protect."

[61] Ibid. Statement by Pakistan at the 98th Plenary Meeting, "R2P should not become a basis either for contravening the principles of non-interference and non-intervention or for questioning the national sovereignty and territorial integrity of any State"; Statement by Chile at the 98th Plenary Meeting, "The State's responsibility to protect is based on long-standing obligations arising from international law ..."

[62] Ibid. Statement by Cuba at the 99th Plenary Meeting, "The notion of the responsibility to protect does not exist as a legal obligation provided for in any instrument of international law or in the Charter of the United Nations"; Statement by Brazil at the 97th Plenary Meeting, "... it is a powerful political call for all States to abide by legal obligations already set forth in the Charter, in relevant human rights conventions and in international humanitarian law and other instruments."

[63] UNGA 2009c, para 1.

However, even though the resolution affirmed its consideration of R2P,[64] it did not define the scope of this consideration as per the request by the Secretary-General. In addition, the resolution did not address the other suggestions in the *Implementing R2P Report*.[65] The General Assembly has held three further formal debates on R2P, which took place in 2018, 2019 and 2021,[66] as well as several informal interactive dialogues between 2010 and 2017,[67] which provide an opportunity for Member States to reflect on the Secretary-General's report, share their governments' concerns and support for the doctrine, and identify steps taken to prevent and respond to atrocity crimes.[68]

4.3 The Pillars of R2P

According to the *Implementing R2P Report*, the doctrine is divided into three distinct pillars of responsibility. There is no set sequence in which these pillars are to be implemented and must therefore be ready for use at any point, both jointly and severally.[69] In a later report, the Secretary-General further notes in this context that there is never a situation where States would not have a responsibility to protect, and that it is the role of the international community to determine the best way to achieve the goals of R2P within the context of the three pillars, instead of determining when R2P should be implemented.[70]

---

[64] Ibid. para 2.

[65] Ryngaert and Cuyckens 2013, p. 122.

[66] UNGA 2018, 99th and 100th Plenary Meetings; UNGA 2019, 93rd–96th Plenary Meetings; United Nations UNGA 2021 64th–66th Plenary Meetings A/75/PV.64, A/75/PV.65, A/75/PV.66 (17–18 May 2021).

[67] United Nations General Assembly Sixty-fourth Session Informal Interactive Dialogue of the General Assembly "Early Warning, Assessment and the Responsibility to Protect (9 August 2010); Sixty-fifth Session Informal Interactive Dialogue on the Role of Regional and Sub-regional Arrangements in Implementing the Responsibility to Protect (12 July 2011); Sixty-fifth Session Informal Interactive Dialogue on "The Responsibility to Protect: Timely and Decisive Response (5 September 2012); Sixty-Sixth Session Informal Interactive Dialogue on the Report of the Secretary-General on the Responsibility to Protect: State Responsibility and Prevention (11 September 2013); Sixty-seventh Session Informal Interactive Dialogue on the Report of the Secretary-General on the responsibility to protect (8 September 2014); Sixty-eighth Session Informal Interactive Dialogue on the responsibility of States to protect their populations by preventing genocide, war crimes, ethnic cleansing and crimes against humanity (8 September 2015); Sixty-ninth Session Informal interactive dialogue of the General Assembly on the Report of the Secretary-General on the Responsibility to Protect: Mobilizing Collective Action: The Next Decade of the Responsibility to Protect (6 September 2016); Seventieth Session Informal interactive dialogue on the Report of the Secretary-General on the Responsibility to Protect: The responsibility to protect and accountability for prevention (6 September 2017).

[68] Schmidt 2016, pp. 271–272.

[69] UNGA 2009a, para 12.

[70] UNGA 2012, para 13.

4.3.1 Pillar One

The first pillar recalls the duty of States to protect its populations from genocide, war crimes, crimes against humanity and ethnic cleansing.[71] This pillar is rooted in the principle of State sovereignty, along with other pre-existing and continuous legal obligations of States towards their populations.[72] The Report emphasises that signing onto international instruments like the Rome Statute is a first step towards full implementation of the R2P doctrine.[73] The significance of R2P based crimes, and the obligation to address and prevent their commission within the framework of the Rome Statute is also noted.[74] The Report also notes the importance of States ratifying the Statute and assisting the Court in locating, arresting and surrendering persons responsible for committing or inciting R2P crimes.[75]

4.3.2 Pillar Two

The second pillar places a duty upon the international community of States to assist target States in meeting their protection responsibilities.[76] This pillar asserts that the international community should encourage and assist States in the exercise of R2P, build up capacities to protect populations from atrocity crimes, as well as preventing the commission of such crimes.[77] Assistance under pillar two can take many forms, which includes encouraging States to meet their responsibilities under pillar one, assisting in the exercise of this responsibility, building up protection capacities, and assisting States in the early detection and prevention of R2P-based crimes.[78] Assistance can also take the form of educational and training initiatives aimed at addressing human rights, as well as humanitarian standards and norms.[79] This pillar is also associated with developing strategies for capacity building and atrocity prevention.[80] These measures do not raise any legal questions and are merely measures of cooperation that can be offered to States.[81] Within the context of the ICC, Stahn identifies

[71] UNGA 2009a, para 11(a); De Beer and Tladi 2019, p. 224.

[72] Ibid. para 13.

[73] Ibid. para 17.

[74] Ibid. para 18.

[75] Ibid. para 19.

[76] Ibid. para 11(b); De Beer and Tladi 2019, p. 224.

[77] UNGA 2005b, paras 138–139.

[78] UNGA 2009a, para 28.

[79] UNGA 2009a, para 33.

[80] Ibid. para 44.

[81] Rodley 2016, p. 191.

that the second pillar provides additional authority to emphasise and strengthen the importance of domesticating ICC norms and procedures, while also linking the Court to development strategies.[82]

4.3.3 Pillar Three

Pillar Three of R2P places a responsibility upon States to respond collectively, in a timely and decisive manner, when a State fails to protect its populations from atrocity crimes.[83] While this pillar shares similarities with the controversial humanitarian intervention, in that it foresees that the use of force may be necessary to address and repress the commission of international crimes against populations, it is largely different as it operates within the scope of international frameworks associated with the prohibition of the use of force and therefore requires authorisation by the UN Security Council.[84] In the context of the situation in Libya, Security Council Resolution 1973, which authorised the use of force in Libya under Chapter VII of the UN Charter,[85] is recognised as a manifestation of R2P.[86] In its preamble, *Resolution 1973* makes a reference to R2P, Stating that the Libyan authorities held the responsibility to protect the Libyan population.[87] The intervention in Libya has also been deemed "the first full blown test" of R2P.[88]

For there to be successful implementation of the third pillar, early and flexible responses are needed that are aimed at addressing the specific needs of each situation.[89] While this pillar is often associated with the use of force authorised by the UN Security Council acting under Article 42 of the UN Charter, it can also include a range of non-coercive and non-violent measures that can be taken either through authorisation by the UN Secretary-General, or through regional or sub-regional arrangements that can be made without UN Authorisation.[90] These measures include negotiations, inquiries, mediation, conciliation, arbitration and judicial settlement.[91] In associating the third pillar with the ICC, the *Implementing R2P Report* indicates that these tools could assist in deterring decision makers from committing acts that would make them subject to prosecution by judicial bodies like the ICC.[92] In the *Timely and Decisive*

[82] Stahn 2015, p. 17.

[83] UNGA 2009a, para 11(c)

[84] De Beer and Tladi 2019, p. 224.

[85] UNSC 2011b, paras 1–4

[86] Deeks 2018, p. 758.

[87] UNSC 2011b, pre para 3.

[88] The Economist "The Lessons of Libya" (19 May 2011) available at https://www.economist.com/international/2011/05/19/the-lessons-of-libya (accessed 1 September 2020).

[89] UNGA 2009a, para 49.

[90] UNGA 2009a, para 51.

[91] Ramopoulos 2015, p. 10.

[92] UNGA 2009a, para 53.

Response report, the Secretary-General noted that the threat of referrals to the ICC could serve as a deterrent measure and that the engagement of the Court in response to the alleged commission of atrocities could contribute to the overall response to those crimes.[93]

4.3.4 Assessing the Implementation of the Three Pillars of R2P

At the 69th session of the UN General Assembly in 2015, the Secretary-General's annual report on R2P assessed the impact of the measures and initiatives that had been developed to implement R2P under the three pillars.[94] The report noted the improvement of the capacity of actors in identifying risk factors for atrocity crimes and in developing preventative and responsive strategies, while also identifying the need for more sustained and targeted action that addresses key sources of risk and the development of more effective mechanisms for the protection of populations.[95] The report assesses the range and impact of implementation efforts under each other the three pillars, including the actions taken by States, initiatives developed to assist States in the fulfilment of their protection responsibilities, as well as efforts by the international community to respond to atrocity situations with the help of various tools.[96]

The report also identifies various changes within the international landscape since the official recognition of R2P in 2005 that may influence efforts to promote and advance the doctrine. These changes include the rise in non-State armed groups and the increased access to information and communications technology.[97] The report concludes by setting out six priorities for advancing R2P over the next ten years: demonstrating political commitment to protecting at-risk communities; investing in atrocity prevention measures; ensuring timely and decisive response; preventing the recurrence of atrocity crimes; enhancing regional action; and strengthening focal point networks.[98]

---

[93] UNGA 2012, para 29.

[94] UNGA 2015.

[95] Ibid. para 17.

[96] Ibid. paras 18–44.

[97] UNGA 2015, paras 45–53.

[98] Ibid. paras 54–69.

4.4 R2P and the ICC

The Responsibility to Protect and the International Criminal Court have gained the status of two of the most prominent institutions tasked with enforcing and protecting international human rights.[99] The UN Secretary-General has highlighted that the ICC and R2P are tied together in a collective effort to address and prevent atrocity crimes.[100] The former Prosecutor of the ICC, highlighted the importance of the ICC within the framework of R2P, describing the Court as a "tool in the toolbox" in the implementation of R2P.[101] The ICC and R2P share the long-term goal of ending the commission of mass atrocity crimes within States, reaffirming State's obligations to protect their populations from atrocity crimes and ensuring that mechanisms are in place for the prosecution of such crimes.[102] States bear the additional responsibility to step in and take it upon themselves to execute the responsibilities to protect and prosecute in the situation where a State has failed to do so.[103]

In determining whether R2P could be used as a prism through which the ICC's frameworks for addressing non-cooperation could be strengthened and developed, it is necessary to undertake an investigation into the relationship between R2P and the ICC. This section will address how the ICC has been discussed in R2P-based literature, as well as investigate the similarities and conflicts between the two. The role of the ICC in the implementation of R2P's three pillars will be assessed, with particular focus on the issues that this relationship may encounter. In addition, this section will investigate how R2P can be implemented to improve and develop international criminal justice.

4.4.1 The ICC in R2P Texts

The ICC's role in the fight against atrocity crimes is addressed in many sections of the ICISS Report. The Report recognised the prevalence of many important institutions and mechanisms tasked with the protection of human rights as well as addressing issues relating to human security, which includes the ICC and the ad-hoc international criminal tribunals that preceded it.[104] The role of the Court in addressing modern demands and expectations, preventing atrocity crimes interacting with the UN Security Council and bringing those suspected of committing international crimes to

---

[99] Hehir and Lang 2015, p. 160.

[100] UNGA 2009a, para 18; UNGA 2012, para 29, "...the emergence of a system of international criminal justice has a positive influence on the development of the concept of R2P."

[101] Bensouda (2012) "The Role of the International Criminal Court under the Framework of the R2P" available at https://www.sam-network.org/video/the-role-of-the-international-criminal-court-under-the-framework-of-the-responsibility-to-protect (accessed 4 May 2020).

[102] Saba and Akbarzadeh 2020, p. 84.

[103] Ibid.

[104] ICISS 2001, para 1.14.

justice is all addressed in detail.[105] In the Implementing R2P Report, the ICC and the ad-hoc tribunals that preceded it are cited as important tools for implementing R2P, with the ICC being cited as a significant instrument for R2P practice.[106]

The role of the international community of States in addressing the failure to prevent the incitement and commission of atrocity crimes is also confirmed, emphasising that such acts must be referred to the ICC.[107] In addition, the 2012 Report of the Secretary-General recognised that the positive influence of an international criminal justice system, led by the ICC, was an important and positive development within the R2P doctrine.[108] In discussing the priorities to be achieved for the next ten years, the second Implementing R2P Report in 2015 cited the role of the ICC in strengthening atrocity prevention measures.[109]

4.4.2 *Overlaps and Differences Between the ICC and R2P*

The ICC and R2P are both relatively recent developments, which represent the efforts of the international community to prevent and stop serious international crimes, as well as enhance the mechanisms aimed at protecting human rights.[110] They show significant overlaps in terms of their shared historical development, their structure, and their goal to end mass atrocity crimes.[111] These overlaps indicate the potential for mutual supportiveness between them.

4.4.2.1 Similarities and Overlaps

The most notable similarity of the R2P and the ICC are that they both rely on the cooperation of States to function effectively.[112] This is highlighted in both the Rome Statute and in R2P literature.[113] In assessing the scope of the crimes covered, R2P and the ICC also overlap as they both are tasked with addressing war crimes,

[105] Ibid. paras 2.18, 2.19, 2.26, 3.30, 6.17 and 7.49.

[106] UNGA 2009a, paras 18–19.

[107] Ibid. para 54.

[108] UNGA 2012, para 29.

[109] UNGA 2015, para 66, "The International Criminal Court has a particularly important role to play, both by holding perpetrators of atrocity crimes to account and through the support it provides to national mechanisms under the principle of positive complementarity."

[110] Yejoon 2017, p. 71.

[111] Saba and Akbarzadeh 2020, p. 2.

[112] Turlan 2016 pp. 59–60.

[113] The Rome Statute of the International Criminal Court. (17 July 1998, 2187, UNTS 3, Entry into Force, 1 July 2002) [hereinafter Rome Statute/RS], Articles 86 and 87(5)(a); UNGA 2005b, para 138; UNGA 2009a, para 14, "The State ... remains the bedrock of the responsibility to protect..."

crimes against humanity and genocide.[114] R2P and the ICC complement each other in the fight against international atrocities. While R2P aims to prevent or stop the commission of atrocity crimes,[115] the ICC is tasked with punishing the perpetrators of such crimes.[116] The ICC has an additional prospective and deterrent function through its preliminary examinations, investigations, prosecutions, trials, and convictions.[117] R2P and the ICC also embrace the principle of complementarity, which assigns States with the primary responsibility to respond to the commission of atrocity crimes, while calling for international action in the event that a State is unable or unwilling to take action.[118] Under this principle, both frameworks aim to enhance or develop domestic capacities and mechanisms for addressing and preventing atrocity crimes.[119]

4.4.2.2 Differences and Conflicts

R2P and the ICC also exhibit several differences that may influence the interactions between them. These include differences in their institutional structures,[120] and the different ways in which they operate to achieve their related mandates.[121] The most important difference, however, is the distinction between R2P as a political norm, designed to strengthen the political will and capacity of States to prevent or halt the commission of atrocity crimes, and the ICC as a legal institution mandated to investigate and punish the commission of atrocities.[122] While R2P functionaries, such as the UN Security Council, can and are encouraged to invoke the ICC as a

---

[114] Ibid. Article 5(a)–(c); the ICC also has jurisdiction over the crime of aggression under Articles 5(d) and 8*bis* of the Rome Statute, the specifics of which have only been clarified recently; UNGA 2005b, para 138. The other crime within the scope of R2P is ethnic cleansing, which can be defined as the "forcible deportation of a population", falls under Article 7(1)(d) of the Rome Statute as a crime against humanity.

[115] Rosenberg 2009, p. 443, "R2P is a doctrine of prevention."

[116] Mills 2015, p. 87, The author also holds that this division of labour appears to make R2P and the ICC "ideal complements" in the fight against atrocity crimes; see also Saba and Akbarzadeh 2020, p. 2, where the authors describe R2P as a "policy norm" to gain the necessary political will to prevent or halt atrocity crimes, while the ICC is an "*ex post facto* mechanism" that is mandated to punish perpetrators after the commission of atrocity crimes.

[117] Holvoet and Mema 2015, p. 27; see also the preamble to the Rome Statute, which cites deterrence as one of the ICC's missions.

[118] Birdsall 2015, p. 55; see also: Yejoon 2017, p. 84, where the author confirms that for both frameworks to be authorised to handle an atrocity situation, it must be proven that a sovereign State is either unable or unwilling to carry out its primary responsibilities.

[119] Yejoon 2017, p. 85.

[120] Weerdesteijn and Hola 2020, p. 386, where the authors highlight that the ICC is a formal legal institution that functions in accordance with the letter of the law, while R2P is a political norm, with the responsibilities it promotes going above what is legally required of States.

[121] Ibid.

[122] Birdsall 2015, p. 55.

tool to assist in atrocity prevention,[123] the ICC does not benefit from a too close association with R2P as a political norm.[124] This is especially notable, considering that the Court is not supposed to be influenced by political considerations when making decisions.[125]

According to Birdsall, the ICC does not benefit from being too closely associated with R2P as it is not a powerful mechanism for stopping violence, as well as facing the risk of becoming too much of a political tool, influenced by various geopolitical struggles.[126] On the other hand, however, there also lies the argument that R2P's close association with the ICC may be harmful to its legitimacy as an international norm.[127] In this regard, Ralph highlights that an ICC indictment of government leaders, as was the case in the situation in Libya, can potentially link an R2P action to regime change, which can have an effect on the legitimacy of an intervention taken under R2P.[128]

4.4.2.3 An Analysis of the Similarities and Differences between R2P and the ICC

In analysing the similarities and differences between R2P and the ICC, two schools of thought on their relationship can be identified. The first school of thought suggests that, due to their differences, there should be minimal to no interaction between the two. This argument is based on the view that there is a need to separate the political influence of R2P from the ICC, a legal institution.[129] In this context, Stahn argues that it is dangerous to portray international criminal justice institutions like the ICC as tools for enforcing R2P, as may have the effect of blurring the distinction between international criminal justice and human rights instruments, as well as possibly facilitating international criminal justice as an instrument of war. Therefore, international criminal justice requires a certain degree of autonomy.[130] He then argues that interactions between the two should be limited to specific areas: alerting the international community of potential atrocity situations; developing international criminal law jurisprudence; and monitoring State compliance.[131] In addition, Tiemessen argues that the ICC should reject or limit investigations and prosecutions referred to it by the Security Council and States Parties as they reflect the political interests of the referring actors and may introduce an opportunity for the ICC to be considered a

---

123 Through the passing of resolutions that refer situations to the ICC under art 13(b) of the Rome Statute.

124 Schiff 2016, p. 302.

125 Weerdesteijn and Hola 2020, p. 387.

126 Birdsall 2015, p. 52.

127 Weerdesteijn and Hola 2020, p. 387.

128 Schiff 2016, p. 302, where the author describes the ICC's effects upon protection as "ambiguous".

129 Saba and Akbarzadeh 2020, p. 85.

130 Stahn 2015, p. 47.

131 Ibid. pp. 47–49.

political tool, which will undermine the ICC's legitimacy as an independent and impartial body.[132] These arguments suggest that minimal interactions or even full separation of the ICC and R2P is crucial for preserving their distinct identities.[133]

The second school of thought embraces the similarities between R2P and the ICC, calling for greater interaction between them. This view suggests that bringing the ICC within the R2P frameworks may have the effect of strengthening their shared goal of atrocity prevention.[134] This view is supported by the UN Secretary General and the ICC Prosecutor.[135] This can also be particularly illustrated by the combined invocation of R2P and the ICC in the context of the Libya situation.[136] These actions indicated the willingness of the Security Council to address and prevent the commission of atrocities in Libya.[137] The invocation of the ICC in this situation served to legitimise the interventions authorised by R2P and the final goal of regime change.[138]

Considering the above discussion, although the ICC may benefit from interacting more closely with R2P, these interactions have the potential to significantly affect the legitimacy of the ICC. Although bringing the ICC within the R2P toolbox may have the potential to put the Court's legitimacy at risk, a full separation of the two makes the work of the ICC impractical, considering that its effectiveness and enforcement of decisions are reliant on cooperation with States and other institutions, like the UN Security Council.[139] In order to promote a more balanced, effective and constructive

[132] Tiemessen 2014, p. 458.

[133] Saba and Akbarzadeh 2020, p. 85.

[134] Bellamy 2018, p. 287, where the author highlights that although R2P and international criminal justice are related, they are not equal to one another and must achieve their objectives independently of one another.

[135] UNGA 2012, para 29, where the UN Secretary-General highlights that the emergence of a system of international criminal justices has had a positive effect on the development of R2P; see also the speech by former ICC Prosecutor Bensouda at a conference held at the Stanley Foundation on "R2P: the Next Decade" (18 January 2012) available at https://www.youtube.com/watch?v=suJIXSsGzL0 (accessed 15 September 2020) "The Court, and international criminal justice in general, are part of the responsibility to protect".

[136] UNSC 2011a, pre para 9, "recalling the Libyan authorities' responsibility to protect its population", pre para 11, "stressing the need to hold to account those responsible for attacks"; para 4, "decides to refer the situation in the Libyan Arab Jamahiriya since 15 February to the Prosecutor of the International Criminal Court; UNSC 2011b, para 4; "Authorizes Member States … to take all necessary measures … to protect civilians and civilian populated areas under threat of attack …."

[137] Roth K (2011) The Security Council has at Last Lived up to its Duty (18 March 2011) available at https://www.hrw.org/news/2011/03/18/security-council-has-last-lived-its-duty (accessed 15 September 2020).

[138] Saba and Akbarzadeh 2020, p. 93.

[139] Ibid. p. 89, the authors also highlight that limiting the interactions between the ICC and the operationalisation of R2P through a body like the UN Security Council is not viable in practice, considering that the ICC and the Security Council are in close contact with each other as they usually deal with the same situations and crises.

approach to this interaction, it is essential to foster greater alignment and synergy between the ICC and the principles entrenched in R2P.[140]

4.4.3 The ICC Analysed through the Lens of the Three Pillars of R2P

In assessing the relationship between the ICC and R2P, one particular aspect of this relationship that has opened up much discussion is the role that the ICC plays in implementing the three pillars. Although the UN Secretary-General and the ICC Prosecutor have both identified the role that the ICC plays in implementing R2P,[141] there is a lack of clarity as to the proper role that the ICC plays regarding the implementation of the three pillars.[142] This next section seeks to investigate the extent to which the ICC can play a role in the implementation of each of the three pillars of R2P.

4.4.3.1 Pillar One

As pillar one of R2P concerns the primary responsibility of States to protect their populations from serious international crimes, it is crucial that States have effective frameworks in place to exercise this responsibility. According to the UN Secretary-General, signing onto an international agreement like the Rome Statute is one of the means through which States can implement R2P.[143] Ratification of the Rome Statute therefore has the effect of setting up the infrastructure needed to prosecute and punish the commission of atrocity crimes, therefore strengthening the rule of law. This ratification also has the effect of including several norms within the Statute into domestic legal frameworks, which can contribute to efforts to protect populations.[144]

However, merely ratifying the Statute is not sufficient for creating domestic legal frameworks for prosecuting atrocity crimes, as not all states have adjusted their

140 Stahn 2015, p. 44, identifies that there is a need for greater distance between the two, in order to preserve their autonomy, as well as improved connections between the two in specific areas of concern.

141 Bensouda (2012) "The Role of the International Criminal Court under the Framework of the R2P" available at https://www.sam-network.org/video/the-role-of-the-international-criminal-court-under-the-framework-of-the-responsibility-to-protect (accessed 4 May 2020); Speech by former ICC Prosecutor Bensouda at a conference held at the Stanley Foundation on "R2P: the Next Decade" (18 January 2012) available at https://www.youtube.com/watch?v=suJIXSsGzL0 (accessed 15 September 2020); UNGA 2009a, UNGA 2012, UNGA 2015.

142 Weerdesteijn and Hola 2020, pp. 379–380; the authors cite that most literature on this topic tends to either discuss the role of the ICC in implementing the three pillars in general, or places most of the focus on its role within the third pillar.

143 UNGA 2009a, para 17.

144 Weerdesteijn and Hola 2020, p. 388.

national laws to the requirements of the Statute. This includes a large disparity in the definitions of ICC crimes within domestic laws.[145] Therefore the legal frameworks that have been developed need to be enforced in practice. In order to deter individuals from committing atrocities, and therefore protecting populations, resources need to be dedicated to creating and building up the capacities needed to enforce existing laws and policies.[146] There may be broader positive implications associated with ratifying the Statute, which include the increased likelihood of ending civil wars and the facilitation of peace efforts.[147] On the other hand, ICC ratification and increased involvement in a target State may have the effect of extending the conflict by pursuing examinations and investigations that threaten the security of at-risk leaders.[148]

4.4.3.2 Pillar Two

As noted above, Pillar Two of R2P concerns the responsibility of the international community in assisting States in meeting their responsibilities under Pillar One. In linking the Rome Statute system with R2P, there is some, although little mention of the Court within the framework of this pillar. The *Implementing R2P Report* is silent on the link between the second pillar and the ICC, but does identify the need for programmes that are carefully targeted to build specific capacities within populations that would discourage the commission of serious international crimes.[149] In the 2014 report, the UN Secretary-General cites the ICC and other international criminal mechanisms as important actors for assisting States in protecting their populations from atrocity crimes.[150] According to Ainley, the ICC's strength lies in its capacity to encourage States to prosecute Rome Statute crimes domestically, in line with the principle of complementarity.[151] Under this pillar, the ICC is required to engage with the international community; consisting of other international institutions, NGO's and States Parties to expand its influence on international criminal justice.[152]

The preamble to the Rome Statute recognises that the effective prosecution of atrocity crimes must be ensured by taking measures at the national level and by enhancing international cooperation, and that the ICC is complementary to national

[145] Ibid. pp. 388–389

[146] Ibid. p. 389.

[147] Prorok 2017, p. 214, where the author notes that the ICC's influence on the outcomes of civil wars is greater when the Court is actually engaged in investigations or legal proceedings in a target State.

[148] Dancy and Montal 2017, p. 679, where the authors note that across all countries that the ICC has been involved in, there has been no substantial decrease in violence against civilians.

[149] UNGA 2009a, para 44.

[150] UNGA 2014, para 22, the Secretary-General also recognises that the ICC and other international criminal tribunals aim to assist States by sharing information, training national prosecutors and investigators, and fighting the impunity that allows for the commission of atrocity crimes.

[151] Ainley 2015, p. 48.

[152] Marshall 2010, p. 21.

criminal jurisdictions.[153] This dictates that as long as national criminal jurisdictions are willing and able to genuinely investigate and prosecute the matter which has come to the attention of the Court, the Court does not have jurisdiction.[154] In this sense, complementarity may strengthen the Courts' ability to support R2P based on the fact that the ICC, as a court of last resort, will not intervene in a situation if States enforce R2P themselves. Complementarity therefore has the effect of making the ICC less threatening to States by minimising its "intrusion" in the domestic affairs of States.[155]

In 2006, the Office of the Prosecutor released its Report on Prosecutorial Strategy,[156] which stated that the office had adopted a positive approach to complementarity, which encourages genuine national proceedings where possible, relies on national and international networks and participates in a system of international cooperation.[157] This positive complementarity sees the ICC, together with other organisations, assist States with weak judicial systems in building up their capacity to prosecute perpetrators of atrocity crimes.[158] However, the ICC itself does not directly engage in these capacity building initiatives,[159] as it is not a developmental agency.[160] Therefore, the extent to which the ICC is able to contribute to capacity building is limited. In 2014, the UN Secretary-General's annual report on R2P addressed the implementation of pillar two, citing the ICC and other international criminal mechanisms as important actors for assisting States in protecting their populations from atrocity crimes.[161]

4.4.3.3 Pillar Three

As noted above, Pillar Three places a responsibility on the international community in instances where States have failed to exercise their protection responsibilities

---

[153] RS, above n. 113, preamble, paras 4 and 10.

[154] Triffterer et al 2022, p. 14; see also RS, above n. 113, Article 17(1)(a) which recognises that a case is inadmissible before the Court where it is already being investigated or prosecuted by a State which has jurisdiction over it, unless the State is unwilling or unable to genuinely carry out the investigation or prosecution.

[155] Contarino and Negron Gonzales 2013, p. 418.

[156] ICC Office of the Prosecutor *Report on Prosecutorial Strategy* (16 September 2006).

[157] Ibid. para 2(a).

[158] Weerdesteijn and Hola 2020, p. 395.

[159] ICC Office of the Prosecutor *Prosecutorial Strategy 2009-2012* (1 February 2010) available at https://www.icc-cpi.int/Pages/item.aspx?name=otp-rep-strategy-2010 (accessed 1 November 2020) "… the Office will encourage genuine national proceedings where possible, including in situation countries, relying on its various networks of cooperation, but without involving the Office directly in capacity building or financial or technical assistance."

[160] Tillier 2013, p. 509.

[161] UNGA 2014 para 22, the Secretary-General also recognises that the ICC and other international criminal tribunals aim to assist States by sharing information, training national prosecutors and investigators, and fighting the impunity that allows for the commission of atrocity crimes.

towards their populations under the first pillar. R2P and the ICC have a shared goal in preventing the commission of atrocity crimes.[162] In particular, the preamble to the Rome Statute recognises deterrence as one of the aims of the Court.[163] The ICC is committed to ending impunity for atrocity crimes as a means to promote general prevention, which is aimed at upholding the application of international criminal law; as well as promoting deterrence, by signalling to the global community that the commission of atrocity crimes will not be ignored and unpunished.[164] Under the third pillar, the UN Security Council plays an important role in implementing and fulfilling the responsibility to protect, authorising the use of collective action in accordance with the UN Charter to respond to the commission of atrocity crimes.[165]

As already emphasised above, responses to atrocity crimes under the third pillar can consist of actions requiring the use of force under Article 42 of the UN Charter, as well as a range of non-coercive measures. In the context of the ICC, its interventions in the form of investigations and prosecutions could amount to non-military intervention under the third pillar.[166] As per the Rome Statute, the UN Security Council is authorised to refer a situation to the Court for investigation.[167] This includes situations in which the target State is not a State Party.[168] Alongside self-referrals and proprio motu referrals by the ICC Prosecutor,[169] referral by the UN Security Council assists in expanding the Court's preventative mandate within the R2P framework.[170] Within the context of the ICC's frameworks for non-cooperation, its decisions on non-cooperation and subsequent referrals to the Assembly of States Parties and the Security Council,[171] the procedures developed by the Assembly of States Parties for addressing non-cooperation,[172] as well as the measures available to the UN Security Council, could all constitute as actions under pillar three.

Although the ICC has a role to play in atrocity prevention as part of a variety of measures under the R2P toolbox, such a role will be limited and marginal,[173] as the primary mandate of the Court is to put an end to impunity for serious international

---

162 Holvoet and Mema 2015, p. 27

163 RS, above n 113, pre para 5, "... determined to put an end to impunity for the perpetrators of these crimes and thus to contribute to the prevention of such crimes."

164 Holvoet and Mema 2015, pp. 22–23.

165 UNGA 2005b, para 139; UNGA 2009a, para 49.

166 Yejoon 2017, p. 91.

167 RS, above n 113, Article 13(b).

168 Wenqi 2006 p. 89.

169 Articles 13(a) and (c) of the Rome Statute, above n. 113.

170 Holvoet and Mema 2015, pp. 23–24; see also Fehl 2015, pp. 47–48, where the author notes that criminal sanctions have been granted a prominent place within the non-military toolkit of R2P.

171 RS, above n. 113, Article 87(7).

172 ASP 2018a [Annex II Assembly Procedures relating to non-cooperation]; ASP 2018b [Annex III: Toolkit for the Implementation of the Informal Dimension of the Assembly Procedures relating to non-cooperation].

173 Holvoet and Mema 2015, p. 29.

crimes.[174] Broude notes that deterrence places a burden upon the Court, raising expectations that are unrealistic and counterproductive. In addition, most instances of crime prevention are reliant on processes that are beyond the mandate of the tribunal or court in question.[175] Therefore, the Court is encouraged to contribute to crime prevention by creating an environment that is consistent and credible, and does not tolerate the commission of serious international crimes.[176]

Although R2P has been internationally endorsed and recognised, there have been concerns surrounding its inconsistent implementation, the lack of political will within the UN and other organisations in implementing it, and the lack of specific guidelines for implementing the use of force under the third pillar.[177] In the context of the relationship between the Security Council and the ICC in the application of the third pillar, the manner in which the Security Council has interacted with the ICC has been labelled as inconsistent, as it has used its power to refer situations to the Court, but has not appropriately followed up on these situations, nor has it made an effort to assist the Court in prosecuting suspects. This failure of the Security Council in this regard has led to significant criticisms against the Court, as well as questions as to its credibility as an independent body.[178]

4.4.4 The Role of R2P in Strengthening the ICC

The ICC, and international criminal justice in general, are cited as an important tools for strengthening and implementing R2P.[179] According to Stahn, international criminal justice provides a strategy and language that is appealing to the enforcement of R2P, offering the doctrine a normative grounding in law.[180] In the context of the ICC, its jurisprudence has the effect of strengthening R2P through the clarification of certain legal aspects, such as the acts that constitute specific atrocity crimes.[181]

---

[174] Broude 2016, p. 196, the author also notes that although prevention is clearly embedded in the goals of the ICC, such a goal is secondary to the main goal. He also identifies that while the international community declares its willingness to see the prevention of serious international crimes, it does not expect the Court to actually achieve this goal, but instead only contribute to it.

[175] Broude 2016, p. 200; such measures for addressing non-cooperation include the development of educational and democratization initiatives, setting up early warning and surveillance systems and promoting the political will to intervene to bring atrocity crimes to an end.

[176] Ibid. p. 201.

[177] International Coalition for the Responsibility to Protect "Clarifying the Third Pillar of the Responsibility to Protect: Timely and Decisive Response" available at http://responsibilitytoprotect.org/Clarifying%20the%20Third%20Pillar.pdf (accessed 20 May 2020).

[178] Weerdesteijn and Hola 2020, p. 408; see also Bowman 2018, p. 268, where the author notes that the ICC continues to lose the confidence of its supporters who are frustrated by the uneven application of accountability while the Security Council does nothing to assist the Court in cooperation efforts.

[179] UNGA 2009a, paras 18–19; UNGA 2012, para 29; Contarino and Negron-Gonzales 2013, p. 411; Weerdesteijn and Hola 2020, p. 382.

[180] Stahn 2015, p. 17.

[181] Contarino and Negron-Gonzales 2013, p. 415

UN Member States have also emphasised the importance of the ICC in promoting the R2P doctrine, which includes the duty of States to ratify the Rome Statute and cooperate with the Court.[182] One can therefore determine from this, as well as from the above discussions, that R2P benefits from the work of the ICC in the fight against atrocity crimes.[183] In this regard, Megret holds that the ICC has become an essential part of R2P's effort to be seen as a concept that is broader and less controversial than humanitarian intervention.[184] Considering that this book aims to investigate how R2P can contribute to the development and strengthening of the ICC's non-cooperation frameworks, it is necessary to investigate how R2P can strengthen the Court and International Criminal Justice as a whole.

According to Megret, R2P can be invoked to assist in the improved operation of international criminal justice. In particular, increased involvement of the international community under R2P may have the effect of putting more pressure upon States to better cooperate with the Court.[185] Improving cooperation with the Court in this sense may also refer to improved remedies for addressing non-cooperation, which may have the effect of enhancing the efficiency of the Court and deterring instances of non-cooperation by increasing the reputational costs that may be associated with a failure to cooperate.[186] In addition, he holds that international involvement under R2P has led to a change in the way in which intervention is viewed by the international community from a political choice to a moral or legal duty to prevent and address the commission of atrocity crimes and protect the victims of such crimes.[187]

Considering that the ICC has a much firmer legal basis than R2P as it is a treaty-based instrument, R2P requires the support of other sources and institutions of international law to assist in strengthening its interactions and influence on the ICC, particularly with regards to preventing and addressing instances of non-cooperation.[188] Therefore, in order to investigate the potential for the increased involvement of R2P within the ICC, particularly issues relating to non-cooperation, it is necessary to identify and assess the bodies within the UN Charter system that have been given the primary role of promoting and implementing R2P throughout its three pillars.

---

[182] See e.g.: Statement by Sweden at the Informal Interactive Dialogue on the Responsibility to Protect (12 July 2011) "...we must acknowledge the link between prevention and accountability, and the closely related role of the International Criminal Court. As we have done before, we strongly urge the International Community to ratify the Rome Statute and to co-operate with the ICC"; Statement by Japan at the Informal Interactive Dialogue on the Responsibility to Protect (12 July 2011) "... universalization of the ICC through expanding its membership will play a crucial role for the prevention of the four serious crimes which the concept of the responsibility to protect is supposed to address.

[183] Schiff 2016 p. 302.

[184] Megret 2010 p. 15, available at https://papers.ssrn.com/sol3/papers.cfm?abstract_id=1933111 (accessed 24 March 2019).

[185] Megret 2010, p. 11; the author also notes that R2P can also assist the ICC by enhancing the political will of States to prosecute atrocity crimes.

[186] Jones 2016, p. 203.

[187] Megret 2010, p. 14.

[188] Ibid. p. 7.

4.5 R2P and the UN System

This section will assess the role of R2P within UN collective security frameworks, with specific focus on the role of the UN Security Council as the body tasked with the primary responsibility under the UN Charter to address matters relating to the maintenance of international peace and security. This section will also identify how the UN General Assembly can assist the Security Council in the maintenance of international peace and security.

4.5.1 The Security Council and R2P

The emergence of the R2P doctrine was partly influenced by the work of the UN Security Council. In particular, the Security Council's failure to respond to appropriately respond to various humanitarian crises is cited as one of the main reasons for the development of the doctrine.[189] Before the official adoption of R2P at the 2005 World Summit, the Security Council was already changing its stance towards protection obligations, evident in the adoption of various resolutions and agendas that encouraged the promotion of compliance with international humanitarian law; addressing issues relating to peacekeeping operations and humanitarian access; and improving responses to humanitarian emergencies.[190]

In 1999, the Security Council adopted Resolution 1265, which signalled its willingness to respond to attacks on civilians and adopted many elements that would later come to be associated with R2P.[191] In this Resolution, the Security Council expressed its willingness to respond to situations of armed conflict where civilians were being targeted and where humanitarian assistance to civilians was being deliberately obstructed.[192] The Resolution also called on Member States to ratify important human rights treaties and work towards ending the culture of impunity for atrocity crimes by prosecuting those responsible for such crimes.[193]

4.5.1.1 The Role of the Security Council in Implementing R2P

In the ICISS Report, it was highlighted that the UN Security Council held the primary responsibility under the UN Charter to address matters of the international peace and

[189] Gill 2013, p. 83 "There can be little doubt that the failures the Council in adequately responding to a number of major humanitarian crises in the closing decade of the last century were one of the main reasons for the development of the concept in the first place.

[190] Bellamy 2016, p. 252.

[191] UNSC 1999.

[192] Ibid. para 10.

[193] Ibid. paras 5–6.

security,[194] while also addressing the possible scenario where the Security Council failed to fulfil this role, requiring the need for alternative means for discharging R2P.[195] The Report identifies the UN General Assembly and its potential to step into a situation where the Security Council has failed to act appropriately, set up measures designed to mirror the structure of the UN Charter's Chapter VII powers, and hold the Security Council accountable for its actions.[196] The Report also recognised the role of regional organisations and their potential to pursue collective interventions should the Security Council fail to act, also noting that a number of organisations had developed mechanisms aimed at preventing, managing, and resolving conflict situations.[197] The Report also recognised the potential for these organisations for pursuing legitimate intervention strategies not requiring Security Council authorisation.[198]

At the 2005 World Summit, the Security Council was identified as bearing special responsibilities for the protection of populations,[199] and as such plays an important role in implementing the international community's timely and decisive R2P response to atrocity crimes.[200] The Security Council's leadership and engagement with implementing R2P is essential to the ultimate success or failure of R2P.[201] One of the weaknesses affecting R2P is the inconsistent manner in which the Security Council has implemented it. This is due to lack of consensus among the Council's Permanent members on how and in which situations R2P should be implemented.[202]

4.5.1.2 The Status and Application of R2P within the Security Council

Since its inception and acceptance within the international legal system, the responsibility to protect has seen rapid development.[203] According to Stahn, the development of R2P is part of a growing transformation of international law from a "state-and governing-elite-based system of rules into a normative framework designed to protect certain human and community interests.[204]" However, while the scope and structure of R2P is now clearly understood, its precise legal nature is not, with it being uncertain whether R2P is a concrete legal obligation, an example of soft law, an emerging

194 ICISS 2001, para 6.7.

195 Ibid. para 6.28.

196 Ibid. paras 6.29–6.35.

197 Ibid. paras 6.31 and 6.33.

198 Ibid. para 6.35.

199 UNGA 2005b para 139; see also UNSC 2006a, para 4, where the Security Council reaffirmed its role in implementing R2P.

200 Genser 2018, p. 431.

201 Ibid. p. 425.

202 Botte 2015, p. 1030.

203 Gill 2013, p. 86.

204 Stahn 2007, p. 101.

legal norm or a mere political concept.[205] States at the 2009 General Assembly debate on R2P had differing views on this topic, with some States not considering it a legal principle at all,[206] while others recognised it as a legal principle,[207] "a political commitment of the highest order,[208]" and an "emerging normative framework.[209]"

In assessing the place of R2P within the international legal system, the doctrine does not constitute a binding rule of international law, neither has it created new legal obligations.[210] However, it does reflect obligations present in already-existing legal texts,[211] especially in a number of conventions and human rights instruments that contain duties to protect populations from atrocity crimes and prevent the commission of such acts.[212] According to Stahn, none of the main documents which have illustrated R2P in depth can be regarded as binding international law under the classic sources of international law.[213] He notes that R2P is treated differently in each the documents associated with its creation, with largely different interpretations of the scope and meaning of the doctrine.[214] According to Peters, these documents employ ambiguous language to describe the binding force and the legal character of R2P.[215]

R2P itself has not been incorporated into international conventions, nor does it presently reflect a rule of customary international law. However, the references to and endorsement of R2P in UN Resolutions and reports by the UN Secretary-General do indicate that it has obtained the status of an important political principle and policy undertaking by key UN Organs and a large number of UN Member States.[216] One particular way in which the legal status of R2P can be confirmed within the international community is through its application and practice within the Security Council.[217] In the years that followed the 2005 World Summit, the Security Council

---

[205] Pandiaraj 2016, p. 801, where the author recognises that the degree of recognition that R2P has received over the years varied, leading to its normative and legal status being "heavily contested"; see also Peters 2011, p. 21.

[206] UNGA 2009b, Statement by China at the 98th Plenary Session, "… the responsibility to protect remains a concept and does not constitute a norm of international law."

[207] Ibid. Statement by Canada at the 97th Plenary Session, "… we have at our disposal a sophisticated normative legal framework based on international law."

[208] Ibid. Statement by Liechtenstein at the 97th Plenary Session.

[209] Ibid. Statement by Bangladesh at the 100th Plenary Session.

[210] Gill 2016, p. 86, where the author notes that R2P lacks both sufficient practice and *opinio juris* which would indicate that States consider it to be a binding rule of customary law.

[211] Ibid.

[212] Peters 2011, p. 22.

[213] Stahn 2007, p. 101; Article 38 of the Statute of the International Court of Justice 1945 identifies such sources as "international conventions", "international custom, as evidence of a general practice accepted as law", and "general principles of law".

[214] Ibid. p. 102.

[215] Peters 2011, p. 8.

[216] Gill 2013, p. 86.

[217] Eaton 2011, p. 801, "… the next time there is a humanitarian crisis, all eyes will fall on the Security Council to respond and responsibility to protect will likely be a central part of the discourse."

exercised much caution towards R2P, with mention of the doctrine in resolutions only occurring after lengthy political considerations.[218]

In more recent years, however, the Security Council has been more willing to include R2P in its resolutions and statements, with almost one hundred Security Council Resolutions and Statements making reference to R2P.[219] R2P is referred to in a wide variety of circumstances which indicates increased consensus that R2P is not only related to the use of force.[220] Although there seems to be an indication that R2P has gained more support within the Security Council, practice indicates that the implementation of R2P in atrocity situations has been inconsistent.[221]

According to Trahan, R2P places the Security Council under an increasingly emerging legal and moral obligation to act in the face of large-scale atrocity crimes, with referral to the ICC constituting a possible step to fulfil these obligations.[222] However, while R2P was developed in response to the failure of the Security Council to respond in an effective manner towards atrocity situations, it appears that the doctrine has been unable to encourage the Security Council to execute these obligations in an effective manner. Considering the deadlock and political considerations occurring within the Security Council affecting its relationship with the ICC, it is highly unlikely that other referrals to the ICC will come through such a referral mechanism any time soon.[223] This highlights the need for the Security Council's mandate under the UN Charter and R2P to be enhanced through the intervention of the General Assembly and the tools that have been developed to address Security Council inaction.

4.5.2 *The General Assembly and R2P*

The ICISS Report recognised that the Assembly plays a secondary, recommendatory role to that of the Security Council, as well as noting that interventions backed by the General Assembly had the potential to obtain much needed political and moral

---

[218] Bellamy 2016, p. 257; the author also notes that members were hostile towards R2P on the grounds that it constituted a potential challenge to State sovereignty.

[219] Global Centre for the Responsibility to Protect (2024) UN Security Council Resolutions and Presidential Statements Referencing R2P available at: https://www.globalr2p.org/resources/un-security-council-resolutions-and-presidential-statements-referencing-r2p/ (accessed 15 September 2024).

[220] Bellamy 2016, p. 262; the author also notes that the inclusion of R2P in Security Council resolutions and statements has become significantly less controversial than it was during the years following the 2005 World Summit.

[221] See Chap. 7 in the present book for case studies on how the Security Council has interacted with the ICC through the lens of R2P.

[222] Trahan 2013, p. 432.

[223] Bowman 2018, p. 264; see also O'Donohue (2014), The Security Council's Appalling Record of Referring Situations to the ICC, Justice in Conflict available at https://justiceinconflict.org/2014/05/23/the-security-councils-appalling-record-of-referring-situations-to-the-icc/ (accessed 21 May 2021).

support.[224] The Report also indicated its support for the General Assembly's use of the Uniting for Peace Resolution, which was developed to address the inconsistent use of the veto power.[225] The General Assembly served as the birthplace of R2P, as the forum through which the World Summit Outcome Document was adopted.[226] The role of the General Assembly is discussed in the Outcome Document, where it emphasised:

> *…the need for the General Assembly to continue consideration of the responsibility to protect populations from genocide, war crimes, ethnic cleansing and crimes against humanity and its implications, bearing in mind the principles of the Charter and international law.*[227]

The General Assembly's consideration of R2P was also encouraged in the *Implementing R2P Report,* identifying that the Assembly had a responsibility under the third pillar of R2P:

> *The General Assembly has an important role to play, even under pillar three. Its peace and security functions are addressed in Articles 11, 12, 14, and 15 of the Charter. Article 24 of the Charter confers on the Security Council 'primary', not total, responsibility for the maintenance of peace and security, and in some cases the perpetration of crimes relating to the responsibility to protect may not be deemed to pose a threat to international peace and security. Moreover, under the 'Uniting for peace' procedure, the Assembly can address such issues when the Council fails to exercise its responsibility with regard to international peace and security because of the lack of unanimity among its five permanent members. Even in such cases, however, Assembly decisions are not legally binding on the parties.*[228]

The report also drew attention of the General Assembly as the "world's premier inclusive political forum" and representing the "public expectations and shared responsibilities" of all UN Member States assembled in the Assembly, as opposed to the mere fifteen members of the Security Council.[229] The Secretary-General also urged the General Assembly to carefully consider the strategy for implementing R2P.[230] The UN Charter gives the General Assembly some leeway for recommending measures aimed at addressing an R2P situation, including the recommendation of forcible action.[231] However, this claim has been rejected by a number of UN Documents on various legal grounds.[232] In this regard, it is clear that the taking of binding sanctions is the duty of the Security Council as per Chapter VII of the UN Charter.[233] However,

---

224 ICISS 2001, para 6.7.

225 Ibid. para 6.29.

226 Schmidt 2016, p. 271.

227 UNGA 2005b para 139.

228 UNGA 2009a, para 63.

229 Ibid. paras 61 and 69.

230 Ibid. paras 69 and 71.

231 Ryngaert and Cuyckens 2013 p. 118.

232 UNGA 2004, para 203, where the UN Secretary-General recognised the responsibility of the Security Council in authorising military intervention as a last resort; UNGA 2005a, para 125, "the Charter gives full authority to the Security Council to use military force, including preventively, to preserve international peace and security".

233 UN Charter, above n. 6, Article 41.

given the representative character of the General Assembly and the higher legitimacy and recognition of its decisions,[234] it may still want to recommend sanctions in the event that the Security Council fails to fulfil its R2P obligations.[235]

4.5.2.1 Recognising R2P within the General Assembly

While the General Assembly has hosted extensive debates and sessions on R2P since 2009, these debates have not been able to deliver concrete results in terms of developing frameworks and measures for operationalising the responsibility to protect in various situations.[236] These sessions have however identified common themes which have emerged and influenced the advancement of R2P within the General Assembly, as well as informing how this responsibility is understood in the international system. Firstly, although States have agreed on the definition of R2P, the next step in this regard is to ensure effective implementation of the doctrine.[237]

The informal dialogues have in this regard identified that States have called for further clarity and focus in identifying R2P in practice, speaking out about the challenges arising from prevention and responses to atrocities, and developing measures aimed at overcoming such challenges.[238] The next theme that can be identified from these dialogues is agreement that R2P is rooted in prevention, with governments working to clarify the role of force and have constructive discussions on how to enhance protection capacities.[239] States also agreed that the three pillar system

[234] Evans 2008, p. 136. The author notes that if a decision were supported by a substantial majority of Member States it would provide a greater degree of legitimacy for a military intervention.

[235] Ryngaert and Cuyckens 2013, p. 119; UNGA 2009a, para 57.

[236] Ryngaert and Cuyckens 2013, p. 128.

[237] Schmidt 2016, p. 274; see also United Nations Deputy Secretary-General's remarks to General Assembly informal interactive dialogue on "Fulfilling our Collective Responsibility: International Assistance and the Responsibility to Protect" (8 September 2014) available at https://www.un.org/sg/en/content/dsg/statement/2014-09-08/deputy-secretary-generals-remarks-general-assembly-informal (accessed 21 November 2020) "Member States and the United Nations must now turn growing support for the Responsibility to Protect into more systematic implementation"; Statement by Barbados on Behalf of CARICOM at the Informal Interactive Dialogue on the Responsibility to Protect (12 July 2011) "CARICOM sincerely believes that the concept of the responsibility to protect deserves the further attention of the international community and looks forward to continuing engagement aimed at achieving its universal acceptance"; Statement by France at the Informal Interactive Dialogue on the Responsibility to Protect (5 September 2012) "The times of defining definitions has now passed."

[238] Schmidt 2016, p. 275; Statement by Germany at the Informal Interactive Dialogue on the Responsibility to Protect (12 July 2011) "The concrete task for us is to find out how regional organisations can further develop their cooperation and what role the EU can play in this respect;" Statement by France 2012 *ibid.* "The international community must react by using the whole panoply of instruments to its disposal, including Chapter VII and Invoking the International Criminal Court"; Statement by Cote d'Ivoire at the Informal Interactive Dialogue on the Responsibility to Protect (11 September 2013) "... prevention is at the heart of the principle of R2P."

[239] Statement by Germany 2011 "... the most important challenge ahead in further implementing RtoP is to work together between States and the international community early enough to prevent

provided for a constructive framework for understanding and implementing R2P principles.[240]

In this regard, the dialogues have provided a forum for discussing and understanding the scope of the pillars, and identifying the challenges that may arise when putting such action into operation.[241] These debates also noted that States continued to raise concerns on the potential misuse of R2P[242]; in that it can be manipulated to suit national interests, and that it is being selectively implemented.[243] In particular, States used the dialogue as a forum to debate the responses to specific situations and reflect on the impact these situations had on R2P.[244] These dialogues also increased

mass-atrocities and to provide protection"; Statement by Brazil at the Informal Interactive Dialogue on the Responsibility to Protect (11 September 2013) "… it is the emphasis on preventative measures, at both national and international levels, that strengthens institutional, political and economic capabilities of States…". See also the Statement by South Africa at the Informal Interactive Dialogue on the Responsibility to Protect (8 September 2015) where South Africa recommended that Member States to consider methods for more effective resourcing for implementing preventative measures.

240 Schmidt 2016, p. 276.

241 Statement by France at the Informal Interactive Dialogue on the Responsibility to Protect (5 September 2012) "The three pillars are equally important and without them the concept would be unbalanced and incomplete"; Statement by Ireland at the Informal Interactive Dialogue on the Responsibility to Protect (5 September 2012) "… we welcome the Secretary-General's examination in his report of the non-sequential, mutually supportive relationship between RtoP's three pillars, as well as his assessment that actions taken under an individual pillar may comprise elements of both prevention and response"; Statement by Egypt at the Informal Interactive Dialogue on the Responsibility to Protect (8 September 2015) "We believe that the three pillars should be sought in sequence and not simultaneously. In other words, we should move from one pillar to the other only after all efforts have been exhausted in the previous pillar." "… we call upon the Secretary-General to examine in greater depth the nexus between the three pillars, especially the parameters of the exhaustion of pillars I & II."

242 Schmidt 2016, p. 276.

243 Statement by Kenya at the Informal Interactive Dialogue on the Responsibility to Protect (12 July 2011) "It is imperative that the responsibility to protect is not applied in a discriminatory manner"; Statement by Syria at the Informal Interactive Dialogue on the Responsibility to Protect (6 September 2017) where Syria expressed its concerns with R2P, noting that Member States are misusing and politicising humanitarian principles, as well as applying R2P in an inconsistent and selective manner; Statement by Belarus at the Informal Interactive Dialogue on the Responsibility to Protect (6 September 2017) where Belarus noted that the legitimacy and implementation of R2P depends on the positions and interests of all States, which has led to double standards in the advancement and implementation of the doctrine; Statement by Israel at the Informal Interactive Dialogue on the Responsibility to Protect (6 September 2017) "… some UN Member States have a clear history of exploiting the ideals of this institution to further their own agenda and we must be vigilant to protect the views of this important doctrine from these attempts."

244 Statement by the USA at the Informal Interactive Dialogue on the Responsibility to Protect (5 September 2012) where the USA discussed the role it played with other UN Member States in protecting civilians in various situations, while also recognising that more work must be done to protect civilian populations in Syria; Statement by France 2012; "We cannot debate R2P without mentioning the drama being experienced by the Syrian people"; Statement by Georgia at the Informal Interactive Dialogue on the Responsibility to Protect (8 September 2014) "As a conflict affected country, Georgia is also in need of international oversight of the enforcement of the R2P and international involvement in the protection of civilians in the Russian occupied Georgian regions of Abkhazia and Tskhinvali"; Statement by Nigeria at the Informal Interactive Dialogue on the

the attention given to initiatives to restrain the use of the veto by the Security Council's permanent members in the face of atrocities.[245] States have also identified the need for more effective action by the Security Council to ensure accountability for measures implemented in the name of R2P.[246]

The Assembly has served as an important actor in condemning and addressing atrocity situations where the Security Council has been unable or unwilling to act. In addition, the General Assembly's resolutions have also provided a forum for Member States that are not members of the Security Council to express their concern with the Council's ineffective responses to atrocity crimes.[247] At the 80th meeting of the General Assembly in 2013,[248] States shared their views on the work of the Security Council in Syria.[249] In response to these views, General Assembly resolutions have since contained language that explicitly remind the Security Council of its primary responsibility for the maintenance of international peace and security, and to take action against serious violations and abuses of international humanitarian law and

---

Responsibility to Protect (8 September 2015) "The experiences of Cote d'Ivoire, Libya, Syria and South Sudan conveyed clear lessons that the cooperation of, and among Member States, as critically essential to the successful implementation of the Responsibility to Protect."

[245] Statement by Namibia at the Informal Interactive Dialogue on the Responsibility to Protect (8 September 2014) "... action or inaction by the Security Council is based on self-serving political considerations, which may hinder the effective implementation of the mandate of maintaining international peace and security. Calls for the reform of the Council, therefore, cannot be over stated;" Statement by Georgia 2014 "... we would like to raise our voice in calling upon the permanent members of the Security Council to agree to a voluntary restraint on the use of the veto in situations of genocide, war crimes, ethnic cleansing and crimes against humanity in order to make R2P implementation more effective and not dissuasive"; Statement by Poland at the Informal Interactive Dialogue on the Responsibility to Protect (6 September 2016) "Within the UN Framework, we proudly joined over half of the UN Member States and committed ourselves to the code of conduct on atrocity crimes, initiated by the ACT Group. We also endorsed the French-Mexican initiative to limit the use of veto by the permanent members of the Security Council"; Statement by Tanzania at the Informal Interactive Dialogue on the Responsibility to Protect (6 September 2016) "There must be a responsibility not to veto"; Statement by Botswana at the Informal Interactive Dialogue on the Responsibility to Protect (6 September 2017) where Botswana expressed its support of initiatives that had been adopted to strengthen atrocity crimes prevention such as the ACT Code of Conduct and the French and Mexican Initiative on Veto Restraint; Statement by the United Kingdom at the Informal Interactive Dialogue on the Responsibility to Protect (6 September 2017) "I just want to reiterate the UK's commitment to the responsibility to protect doctrine as a signatory of the ACT code of conduct and as a permanent member of the Security Council."

[246] Schmidt 2016, p. 277.

[247] Ibid. p. 279.

[248] UNGA 2013a, 80th Plenary Session.

[249] Ibid. Statement by South Africa, "The Council has clearly abdicated its responsibilities in the face of human calamity. Members of the Security Council seem to have given priority to their own national interests at the expense of the Syrian people"; Statement by Turkey, "Since dynamics within the Security Council prevent action by the body with the primary responsibility for the maintenance of international peace and security, the General Assembly should once again assume its responsibility to reflect the common sense of the international community"; Statement by Tanzania, which used this meeting to call on members of the Security Council to put aside their differences and agree on suitable courses of action to end the conflict in Syria.

international human rights law.[250] These resolutions have given States the opportunity to show to the broader international community that UN membership would not be affected by the decisions and politics of the Security Council.[251] As of 2024, the UN General Assembly has passed 38 resolutions making reference to R2P.[252]

In May 2021, the General Assembly adopted its first full resolution on the responsibility to protect since 2009.[253] Under this resolution, the General Assembly decided to include an item on R2P in its annual agenda, and formally requested that the Secretary-General reports annually on the topic.[254] This resolution was adopted with 115 States voting in favour, twenty eight abstaining and fifteen voting against.[255] Among the States that voted against the resolution included China, North Korea, Egypt, Russia, and Syria—States that are also not States Parties to the Rome Statute.[256]

Although this resolution illustrates UN Member States' growing willingness to implement and promote R2P,[257] such support of the doctrine varies among States and regional groups. There is therefore a need to strengthen State implementation of R2P through the application of measures available under the UN Charter to assist in strengthening the Security Council's protection mandate.

4.5.2.2 The Recommendatory Power of the General Assembly

Although the Security Council holds the primary responsibility under the UN Charter for the maintenance of international peace and security, it does not hold the exclusive responsibility for such matters.[258] In terms of the role of the General Assembly, the UN Charter gives the Assembly a general responsibility to address any matter

---

[250] UNGA 2013b, para 12.

[251] Schmidt 2016, p. 279.

[252] Global Centre for the Responsibility to Protect *R2P References in United Nations General Assembly Resolutions* (23 May 2024) available at: https://www.globalr2p.org/resources/un-general-assembly-resolutions-referencing-r2p-2/ (accessed 15 November 2024).

[253] UN General Assembly Seventy-fifth Session Resolution 75/277 [The responsibility to protect and the prevention of genocide, war crimes, ethnic cleansing, and crimes against humanity] A/RES/75/277 (18 May 2021).

[254] Ibid. paras 1 and 2.

[255] UNGA 2021 [The responsibility to protect and the prevention of genocide, war crimes, ethnic cleansing, and crimes against humanity], pp. 7–8.

[256] Ibid. p. 8.

[257] Global Centre for the Responsibility to Protect *Event Summary: UN General Assembly Debate on the Responsibility to Protect 2021* (18 May 2021) available at https://www.globalr2p.org/resources/unga-r2p-debate-2021/ (accessed 15 August 2021).

[258] Kenny 2016, p. 5; ICJ, Certain Expenses of the United Nations (Article 17, paragraph 2 of the Charter) (Advisory Opinion of 20 July 1962) ICJ Rep 151, p. 162; ICJ, Legal Consequences of the Construction of a Wall in the Occupied Palestinian Territory (Advisory Opinion of 9 July 2004) ICJ Rep 136, p. 148.

within the scope of UN Authority,[259] as well as a specific responsibility to make recommendations relating to the maintenance of international peace and security.[260]

As the most important purpose of the UN Charter is to maintain international peace and security through collective measures,[261] all UN Organs are required to engage in collective measures and not just the Security Council. In the *Certain Expenses of the United Nations* case, the ICJ observed that the UN Charter makes it clear that the UN General Assembly is also concerned with international peace and security. The Court also observed that the Assembly's power to recommend measures for the peaceful adjustment of a situation itself implies that some kind of action should be taken.[262] Therefore, the purpose of the UN in the maintenance of international peace and security provides the General Assembly with the power to recommend enforcement measures in the event of Security Council deadlock.[263]

In order to prevent conflict between the General Assembly and the Security Council, the Charter adds that the Assembly may not make any recommendations on disputes relating to matters of international peace and security unless the Security Council requests the Assembly to do so.[264] The General Assembly is also granted with a broad mandate to "recommend measures for the peaceful adjustment of any situation ... which it deems likely to impair the general welfare or friendly relations among nations.[265] This provision may have specific relevance for General Assembly action within the context of R2P taking into consideration that the adoption of measures aimed at protecting civilian populations have the effect of improving the general welfare among States.[266]

4.5.2.3 The Uniting for Peace Resolution

In the ICISS report, it was identified that a situation might arise where the Security Council would be unable or unwilling to perform its functions under the UN Charter. The report proposed that an alternative to Security Council action was obtaining the support of the General Assembly through the convening of an Emergency Special Session under the Uniting for Peace Resolution.[267]

The Uniting for Peace Resolution aims to address a situation where the Security Council is unable to come to a unanimous decision where the maintenance of international peace and security is under threat. This mechanism came about because of

---

259 UN Charter, above n 6, Article 10 of the UN Charter.

260 Ibid. Article 11.

261 Ibid. Article 1(1).

262 ICJ Certain Expenses of the United Nations (Advisory Opinion) ICJ Rep 151 (20 July 1962) p. 163.

263 Ramsden 2016, p. 283.

264 UN Charter, above n. 6 Article 12(1).

265 Ibid, Article 14.

266 Ryngaert and Cuyckens 2013, p. 117.

267 ICISS 2001, para 6.29.

a deadlocked Security Council during conflict in Korea in 1950. This deadlock was as a result of interference by the Soviet Union/Russia in exercising its veto power over a number of draft resolutions aimed at addressing the situation in Korea.[268] During this deadlock, the General Assembly met for its annual session where the USA submitted a request to include an item in the meeting's agenda titled "United Action for Peace", which aimed to enhance the role of the Assembly in preventing conflicts and restoring peace in the event of a Security Council deadlock arising from the use of the veto.[269]

The core of this resolution is part A, which reads:

> ... *if the Security Council, because of lack of unanimity of the permanent members, fails to exercise its primary responsibility for the maintenance of international peace and security in any case where there appears to be a threat to the peace, breach of the peace, or act of aggression, the General Assembly shall consider the matter immediately with a view to making appropriate recommendations to Members for collective measures, including in the case of a breach of the peace or act of aggression the use of armed force when necessary, to maintain or restore international peace and security. If not in session at the time, the General Assembly may meet in emergency special session within twenty-four hours of the request therefor. Such emergency* special *session shall be called if requested by the Security Council on the vote of any seven members, or by a majority of the Members of the United Nations...*[270]

This resolution is designed to allow the General Assembly to step into a situation where the Security Council has failed to reach consensus and set up measures designed to mirror the structure of Chapter VII of the UN Charter.[271] Resolution 377 therefore empowers the Assembly to consider any threat or breach of the peace and to recommend collective measures to Member States including the use of force following the breach of the peace or an act of aggression.[272] The Uniting for Peace Resolution was first adopted by a procedural vote by the Security Council in Resolution 119 to address the Suez Crisis of 1956. The resolution noted the lack of unanimity among the Security Council's permanent members and called for an emergency special session of the General Assembly to make appropriate recommendations.[273] The first emergency special session was held in November 1956 which saw the deployment of the first UN Emergency Force to supervise the cessation of hostilities in the region.[274] The Uniting for Peace Resolution has been implemented in ten other situations,[275] the most recent of which was implemented in March 2022 regarding the invasion of Ukraine by Russia.[276]

---

268 UNSC 1950a; UNSC 1950b.

269 Kenny 2016, p. 7.

270 UNGA 1950.

271 Carswell 2013, p. 459.

272 Kenny 2016, p. 8.

273 UNSC 1956.

274 UNGA 1956.

275 UNGA, Special Emergency Sessions, available at: https://www.un.org/en/ga/sessions/emergency.shtml (accessed 1 May 2022).

276 UNGA 2022a.

The ICISS recognised in its report that the mere possibility that action under this resolution can be taken is an important form of leverage that can be placed upon the Security Council to encourage it to act decisively and appropriately.[277] However, the fact that this resolution has only been used in a handful of situations illustrates the reluctance of UN Member States, particularly within the General Assembly, to challenge the authority of the permanent members of the Security Council.[278]

R2P texts have recognised that although the General Assembly is granted with the responsibility to address matters relating to the maintenance of international peace and security,[279] this responsibility is merely recommendatory and is not binding upon the Security Council.[280] However, although the decisions of the General Assembly are not binding, they may be authoritative.[281] This has led to concerns as to the legality of the Uniting for Peace Resolution, particularly with regards to the recommendation of coercive measures under Article 42 of the UN Charter.[282]

Objections to the Uniting for Peace Resolution include concerns as to the power that it gives the General Assembly, as well as the claim that its use is a violation of the UN Charter.[283] According to Ramsden, it can be argued that the Assembly could, in a single resolution, authoritatively interpret the scope of its implied powers, which could therefore grant the Assembly with legislative powers.[284] Noting that the UN Charter provides that the General Assembly cannot address a matter while it is still under consideration by the Security Council,[285] such a provision may also have the effect on barring any action by the General Assembly.[286] However, in the *Wall* advisory opinion, the ICJ observed from years of practice that the General Assembly and the Security Council may address in parallel the same situation.[287]

---

[277] ICISS 2001, para 6.30.

[278] Carswell 2013, p. 477; the author also notes that this reluctance is historically based on the fear of the economic and political consequences of challenging the authority of the permanent members.

[279] UN Charter, above n 6, Article 11.

[280] ICISS 2001, para 6.7; UNGA 2009a, para 63, "... Assembly decisions are not legally binding on the parties;" See also Ryngaert and Cuyckens 2013, p. 114, where the authors note that although decisions of the General Assembly are not binding, they may be authoritative.

[281] Ryngaert and Cuyckens 2013, p. 114; see also Koester 2015, pp. 394–395, where the author notes that a recommendation by the General Assembly may still carry some significant force as a strong Statement on the view of the majority of Member States or through a recommendation of actions such as economic sanctions.

[282] Ryngaert and Cuyckens 2013, p. 115, where the authors note that the General Assembly has recommended the enforcement of diplomatic and economic sanctions in R2P-like situations.

[283] UN General Assembly Fifth Session, Statement by Russia at the 301*st Plenary Meeting* A/PV.301 (2 November 1950) para 120.

[284] Ramsden 2016, p. 294.

[285] UN Charter, above n 6. Art 12.; however, see also Tladi 2019 p. 33, where the author notes that the general practice of the General Assembly in this context has been to consider and make recommendations on matters that are still on the Security Council's agenda.

[286] Ryngaert and Cuyckens 2013, p. 116.

[287] ICJ *Legal Consequences of the Construction of a Wall in the Occupied Palestinian Territory* (Advisory Opinion of 9 July 2004) ICJ Rep 136 p. 149; Ryngaert and Cuyckens 2013, p. 116, where

Another objection to the use of the Uniting for Peace Resolution is that it disrupts the balance of powers between the General Assembly and the Security Council whereby the General Assembly appears to take over the powers of the Security Council.[288] In addition, any action taken in opposition to the veto powers could have the effect of causing serious political tensions between States, including those holding a permanent seat on the Security Council.[289] There also lies the concern that the General Assembly's Influence may be undermined in instances where political bias and a lack of consensus in meetings leads to like-minded States acting collectively outside of the General Assembly to reach consensus.[290]

4.5.2.4 General Assembly Action in Reforming the Veto

The inaction of the Security Council in appropriately addressing the situation in Ukraine again highlighted the need for accountability among the permanent members in the use of the veto. In April 2022, the UN General Assembly adopted, without a vote, Resolution 76/262, mandating that the President of the General Assembly convenes a formal meeting within 10 working days of the casting of the veto by one or more permanent members of the Council, and hold a debate on the situation as to which the veto was cast, provided that the Assembly does not meet in an emergency special session on the same situation.[291]. The resolution also invited the Security Council, in accordance with Article 24(3) of the UN Charter, to submit a special report on the use of the veto in question, at least 72 hours before the discussion is to take place.[292] In addition, the resolution decided to include an item on the provisional agenda of the seventy-seventh session of the Assembly titled "Use of the veto".[293] The draft resolution was introduced by Liechtenstein as a result of two years of preparation by the State out of a growing concern at the inability of the

---

the authors observe that the General Assembly may work in parallel to the Security Council if It does not directly contradict Security Council Action.

[288] Melling and Dennett 2017, p. 300.

[289] Ibid. p. 304: see also Koester 2015, p. 395, where the author notes that any action taken in opposition to the veto may have the effect of weakening the authority of the Council as the body capable of authorising the use of force.

[290] Ramsden and Hamilton 2017, p. 900; see also UNSC 2013, where various States collectively called for the Security Council to act by referring the situation in Syria to the ICC.

[291] UNGA 2022b, para 1; see also United Nations Meetings Coverage "General Assembly Adopts Landmark Resolution Aimed at Holding Five Permanent Security Council Members Accountable for Use of Veto" GA/12417 (26 April 2022) available at: https://www.un.org/press/en/2022/ga12417.doc.htm.

[292] Ibid. para 3.

[293] Ibid. para 4; see also at para 5, "Also decides that, should a veto be cast by one or more permanent members of the Security Council during the remainder of the seventy-sixth session of the General Assembly, the President of the General Assembly shall convene a formal meeting of the Assembly, in accordance with paragraph 1 of the present resolution, under the agenda item entitled "Strengthening of the United Nations system"."

Security Council to carry out its work in accordance with its mandate under the UN Charter.[294]

The passing of this resolution garnered various reactions from member States, which were mostly positive, highlighting the need for formal responses to the use of the veto. For example, Mexico defended the resolution as an "important step forward in strengthening United Nations accountability", while Namibia emphasised their support of the resolution by identifying that African States attach great importance to Security Council reform to make it more "accessible, accountable, democratic, representative and effective, and to better reflect the current geopolitical reality".[295] While the reception to this resolution was mostly positive, some States had their reservations to its adoption. India voiced its concern with the text of the resolution citing it as a "piecemeal" reform. This was in reaction to a similar proposal by India and other pro-reform Member States in 2008, which was rejected on the basis that it was a "piecemeal initiative".[296] India also highlighted the lack of inclusivity in the manner that the resolution was proposed.[297] China held the view that the resolution gave the General Assembly a new mandate and is likely to cause procedural confusion and inconsistency in practice.[298] Russia also rejected the resolution, noting that without the veto, the Security Council would simply authorise questionable decisions imposed by a nominal majority that would not be possible to implement. In addition, Russia highlighted that the veto was not the problem, but instead the unwillingness of certain members of the Security Council to listen to others and achieve compromise, thus compelling the use of the veto.[299]

---

[294] United Nations Meetings Coverage "General Assembly Adopts Landmark Resolution Aimed at Holding Five Permanent Security Council Members Accountable for Use of Veto" GA/12417 (26 April 2022) available at: https://www.un.org/press/en/2022/ga12417.doc.htm, Statement by Liechtenstein.

[295] Ibid; see also the Statement by France where the delegation expressed their full commitment to reforming the Council into a body that is more representative of today's world, while preserving its executive and operational nature.

[296] Ibid. Statement by India, "It is therefore ironic that the same Member States who argued against "piecemeal" reform, are now supporting a piecemeal initiative which ignores the root cause of the problem."

[297] The Wire *'Piecemeal' Initiative Says India as UN General Assembly Adopts Resolution on Veto Reform* (26 April 2022) https://thewire.in/world/un-general-assembly-unsc-veto-power-reform (accessed 1 May 2022) "We have serious concerns about such 'take it or leave it' initiatives which do not make a genuine effort to take into account the perspectives and concerns of the wider membership."

[298] United Nations Meetings Coverage "General Assembly Adopts Landmark Resolution Aimed at Holding Five Permanent Security Council Members Accountable for Use of Veto" GA/12417 (26 April 2022) available at: https://www.un.org/press/en/2022/ga12417.doc.htm, Statement by China.

[299] United Nations Meetings Coverage "General Assembly Adopts Landmark Resolution Aimed at Holding Five Permanent Security Council Members Accountable for Use of Veto" GA/12417 (26 April 2022) available at: https://www.un.org/press/en/2022/ga12417.doc.htm, Statement by the Russian Federation.

4.6 Conclusion

Since its introduction, the responsibility to protect has transformed from a concept proposed by the ICISS into a common feature of international responses to genocide and mass atrocities.[300] International debate about this doctrine has adjusted its focus on the merits of the principle to discussions on its proper implementation.[301] In addition, organisations and States that once showed opposition towards R2P have started recognising and implementing it more.[302] Such statements by States considered hostile to the doctrine provide strong support for the idea that R2P should be regarded as a norm.[303]

The present chapter has identified mechanisms through which R2P can be utilised to address and prevent the commission of atrocity crimes. This chapter has also identified the potential for actions performed in the spirit of R2P to influence and strengthen the political will and capacities of States and international organisations in ensuring cooperation and holding States accountable for their failure or refusal to respond to requests of institutions like the ICC. In analysing the link between the ICC and R2P, this chapter has highlighted that these institutions share a goal in addressing and preventing the commission of atrocity crimes. Through the application of the three pillars of R2P, the ICC has an important role to play in the implementation of this doctrine by encouraging States to ratify its Statute, assisting in capacity building measures, and responding to and punishing R2P crimes that are within its jurisdiction. In turn, R2P and the principles entrenched within have a special role in strengthening the ICC in its protective mandate, particularly within the context of improved responses to instances of non-cooperation by States.

This chapter has also highlighted the importance of the UN Charter system as one of the primary mechanisms for the implementation and execution of the principles and duties entrenched within the doctrine. However, this chapter has also highlighted that R2P is not always implemented in an effective manner by these bodies, leading to situations where serious international crimes continue to be committed against populations without appropriate action. This highlights the need to identify the place of R2P through the lens of appropriate general international law frameworks that have been developed and are readily available for responding to and addressing the commission of serious international crimes.

---

[300] Bellamy and Dunne 2016, p. 12.

[301] United Nations Secretary-General *Press Release [Effective Prevention Requires Early, Active, Sustained Engagement, Stresses Secretary-General at Ministerial Round Table on 'Responsibility to Protect']* SG/SM/13838 (23 September 2011) available at https://www.un.org/press/en/2011/sgsm13838.doc.htm (accessed 5 December 2020) "...it is a sign of progress are now about how, not whether, to implement the responsibility to protect."

[302] Statement by China at the Informal Interactive Dialogue on the Responsibility to Protect (8 September 2014) where R2P is described by China as a "prudential norm" and that all States should establish relevant policies and mechanisms in implementing R2P.

[303] Bellamy and Dunne 2016, p. 12.

In observing the development of R2P over the years, one can conclude that it has not become a binding norm of international law; but instead, it would be more appropriate to speak of it as an international social, political, and moral norm comprising of various legal rules, as well as proposed rules and principles that have not yet attained the status of legally binding hard law.[304] According to Stahn, some of the features of R2P are well-embedded in contemporary international law, while other features are so new and innovative that it is premature to identify a crystallising practice.[305] Despite the lack of a legal status attached to R2P, endorsement of this doctrine may have the effect of making existing legal obligations more effective and bridge the legal gaps present in the application of protection obligations under international law.[306] Therefore, this book turns to determine whether R2P, along with the principles and obligations attached to it, can be complemented through the application of specific rules within general international law aimed at addressing and remedying the commission of serious breaches of international law.

References

Ainley K (2015) The Responsibility to Protect and the International Criminal Court: counteracting the crisis". International Affairs 91(1), 37–54.

Amneus D (2013) The coining and evolution of responsibility to protect: the protection responsibilities of the State. In: Zyberi G (ed) An Institutional Approach to the Responsibility to Protect. Cambridge University Press, Cambridge, pp. 3–32.

Assembly of States Parties (ASP) (2018a) Seventeenth Session Strengthening the International Criminal Court and the Assembly of States Parties. Parties Resolution ICC-ASP/17/Res.5 [Annex II Assembly Procedures Relating to Non-Cooperation].

Assembly of States Parties (ASP) (2018b) Seventeenth Session Report of the Bureau on non-cooperation [Annex: Toolkit for the Implementation of the Informal dimension of the Assembly procedures relating to non-cooperation]. ICC-ASP/17/31. Annex III.

Bellamy AJ (2016) UN Security Council. In: Bellamy AJ, Dunne T (eds) The Oxford Handbook on the Responsibility to Protect, 1st edn. Oxford University Press, Oxford, pp. 249–268.

Bellamy AJ (2018) Responsibility to Protect: Justice and Responsibility—Related but Not Synonymous. In: Waterlow J, Schuhmacher J (eds) War Crimes Trials and Investigations; A Multi-Disciplinary Introduction. Palgrave Macmillan, Cham, pp. 263–299.

Bellamy AJ, Dunne T (2016) R2P in Theory and Practice. In: Bellamy AJ, Dunne T (eds) The Oxford Handbook on the Responsibility to Protect, 1st edn. Oxford University Press, Oxford, pp. 3–16.

Benjamin BN (1992) Unilateral Humanitarian Intervention: Legalizing the Use of Force to Prevent Human Rights Atrocities. Fordham International Law Journal 16(1), 120–158.

Birdsall A (2015) The Responsibility to Prosecute and the ICC: A Problematic Relationship? Criminal Law Forum 26; 51–72.

Botte A (2015) Redefining the Responsibility to Protect Concept as a Response to International Crimes. The International Journal of Human Rights 19(8), 1029–1043.

---

304 Amneus 2013, p. 13.

305 Stahn 2007, p. 110.

306 Amneus 2013, p. 14.

Bowman K (2018) The International Criminal Court and the Security Council: The Power of Politics and the Undermining of Justice. In: Nicholson J (ed) Strengthening the Validity of International Criminal Tribunals. Brill Nijhoff, Leiden, pp. 245–270.
Breau S (2018) The ECOWAS Intervention in Sierra Leone. In: Ruys T, Corten O (eds) The Use of Force in International Law: A Case Based Approach. Oxford University Press, New York, pp. 527–540.
Broude T (2016) The Court Should Avoid all Considerations of Deterrence and Instead Focus on Creating a Credible and Legitimate Normative Environment in Which Serious Crimes are Not Tolerated. In: Steinberg RH (ed) Contemporary Issues Facing the International Criminal Court. Koninklijke Brill NV, Leiden, pp. 194–201.
Carswell AJ (2013) Unblocking the UN Security Council: The Uniting for Peace Resolution. Journal of Conflict and Security Law 18(3) 453–480.
Contarino M, Negron-Gonzales M (2013) The International Criminal Court. In: Zyberi G (ed) An Institutional Approach to the Responsibility to Protect. Cambridge University Press, Cambridge, pp. 411–436.
Dancy G, Montal F (2017) From Law Versus Politics to Law in Politics: A Pragmatist Assessment of the ICC's Impact. American University International Law Review 32(3), 645–705.
De Beer AC, Tladi D (2019) The Use of Force against Syria in Response to the Alleged Chemical Weapons by Syria: A Return to Humanitarian Intervention? Zeitschrift fur auslandisches offentliches Recht und Völkerrecht 79(2) 205–239.
Deeks A (2018) The NATO Intervention in Libya—2011. In: Ruys T, Corten O (eds) The Use of Force in International Law: A Case Based Approach. Oxford University Press, New York, pp. 749–759.
Eaton J (2011) An Emerging Norm—Determining the Meaning and Legal Status of the Responsibility to Protect. Michigan Journal of International Law 32(4), pp. 765–804.
Evans G (2008) The Responsibility to Protect: Ending Mass Atrocity Crimes Once and For All. The Brookings Institution, Washington DC 2008.
Fehl C (2015) Probing the Responsibility to Protect's Civilian Dimension: What Can Non-Military Sanctions Achieve? In: Fiott D, Koops J (eds) The Responsibility to Protect and the Third Pillar: Legitimacy and Operationalization. Palgrave Macmillan, London, pp. 39–57.
Franchini D, Tzanakopoulos A (2018) The Kosovo Crisis—1999. In: Ruys T, Corten O (eds) The Use of Force in International Law: A Case Based Approach. Oxford University Press, New York, pp. 594–662.
Genser J (2018) The United Nations Security Council's Implementation of the Responsibility to Protect: A Review of Past Interventions and Recommendations for Improvement. Chicago Journal of International Law 18(2), 419–500.
Gill TD (2013) The Security Council. In: Zyberi G (ed) An Institutional Approach to the Responsibility to Protect. Cambridge University Press, Cambridge, pp. 83–108.
Gulati G, Khosa I (2013) Humanitarian Intervention: To Protect State Sovereignty. Denver Journal of International Law and Policy. 41(3) 397–416.
Hehir A (2019) Hollow Norms and the Responsibility to Protect. Springer International Publishing, Cham.
Hehir A, Lang A (2015) The Impact of the Security Council on the Efficacy of the International Criminal Court and the Responsibility to Protect. Criminal Law Forum 26, 153–179.
Holvoet M, Meman M 2015 The International Criminal Court and the Responsibility to Protect. In: Fiott D, Koops J (eds) The Responsibility to Protect and the Third Pillar: Legitimacy and Operationalization. Palgrave Macmillan, London, pp. 21–38.
Hurd I (2011) Is Humanitarian Intervention Legal? The Rule of Law in an Incoherent World. Ethics and International Affairs 25(3), 293–313.
ICISS (2001) The Responsibility to Protect: Report of the International Commission on Intervention and State Sovereignty, available at: https://www.globalr2p.org/resources/the-responsibility-to-protect-report-of-the-international-commission-on-intervention-and-state-sovereignty-2001/ (accessed 15 July 2020).

Jones A (2016) Non-cooperation and the Efficiency of the International Criminal Court. In: Bekou O, Birkett DJ (eds) Cooperation and the International Criminal Court: Perspectives from Theory and Practice. Brill, Leiden, pp. 185–209.

Kenny C (2016) Responsibility to Recommend: The Role of the UN General Assembly in the Maintenance of International Peace and Security. Journal on the Use of Force and International Law 3(1), pp. 3–36.

Kritsiotis D (1998) Reappraising Policy Objections to Humanitarian Intervention. Michigan Journal of International Law 19(4), 1005–1050.

Koester C (2015) Looking Beyond R2P for an Answer to Inaction in the Security Council. Florida Journal of International Law, 27(3) 377–398.

Marshall KA (2010) Prevention and Complementarity in the International Criminal Court: A Positive Approach. Human Rights Brief 17(2), 21–26.

Megret F (2010) ICC, R2P and the International Community's Evolving Interventionist Toolkit SSRN, 1–36. Available at https://papers.ssrn.com/sol3/papers.cfm?abstract_id=1933111 (accessed 24 March 2019).

Melling G, Dennett A (2017) The Security Council veto and Syria: responding to mass atrocities through the 'Uniting for Peace' resolution. Indian Journal of International Law 57(3–4) 285–307.

Merriam JJ (2001) Kosovo and the Law of Humanitarian Intervention. Case Western Reserve Journal of International Law 33(1) 111–154.

Mills K (2015) R2P and the ICC: At Odds or in Sync? Criminal Law Forum 26, 73–99.

Pandiaraj S (2016) Sovereignty as Responsibility: Reflections on the Legal Status of the Doctrine of Responsibility to Protect. Chinese Journal of International Law, 15(4), 795–815.

Peters A (2011) The Security Council's Responsibility to Protect. International Organizations Law Review 8, 15–54.

Prorok AK (2017) The (In)compatibility of Peace and Justice? The International Criminal Court and Civil Conflict Termination. International Organization, 71(2), 213–243.

Ramopoulos T (2015) International Law and the Application of the Third Pillar Approach. In: Fiott D, Koops J (eds) The Responsibility to Protect and the Third Pillar: Legitimacy and Operationalization. Palgrave Macmillan.

Ramsden M (2016) 'Uniting for Peace' and Humanitarian Intervention: The Authorising Function of the UN General Assembly. Washington Law Review 25(2), 267–305.

Ramsden M, Hamilton T (2017) Uniting Against Impunity: The UN General Assembly as a Catalyst for Action at the ICC. International and Comparative Law Quarterly 66, 893–921.

Rodley N (2016) R2P and International Law: A Paradigm Shift In: Bellamy AJ, Dunne T (eds) The Oxford Handbook on the Responsibility to Protect, 1st edn. Oxford University Press, Oxford, pp. 186–207.

Rosenberg SP (2009) Responsibility to Protect: A Framework for Prevention. Global Responsibility to Protect 1, 442–477.

Ryngaert C, Cuyckens H (2013) The General Assembly. In: Zyberi G (ed) An Institutional Approach to the Responsibility to Protect. Cambridge University Press, Cambridge, pp. 109–129.

Saba A, Akbarzadeh S (2020) The ICC and R2P: Complementary or Contradictory? International Peacekeeping, 28(1), 84–109.

Schiff BN (2016) Can the International Criminal Court contribute to the Responsibility to Protect? International Relations 30(3), 298–313.

Schmidt M (2016) UN General Assembly. In: Bellamy AJ, Dunne T (eds) The Oxford Handbook on the Responsibility to Protect, 1st edn. Oxford University Press, Oxford, pp. 269–287.

Stahn C (2007) The Responsibility to Protect: Political Rhetoric or Emerging Legal Norm? American Journal of International Law 101(1), 99–120.

Stahn C (2015) Marital Stress or Grounds for Divorce? Re-thinking the Relationship between R2P and International Criminal Justice. Criminal Law Forum 26, 13–50.

Thakur R (2016) Rwanda, Kosovo and the International Commission on Intervention and State Sovereignty. In: Bellamy AJ, Dunne T (eds) The Oxford Handbook on the Responsibility to Protect, 1st edn. Oxford University Press, Oxford, pp. 94–113.

Thakur R, Weiss T (2009). R2P: From Idea to Norm—and Action? Global Responsibility to Protect, 1(1), 22–53.
Tiemessen A (2014) The International Criminal Court and the Politics of Prosecutions. The International Journal of Human Rights 18(4–5), 444–461.
Tillier J (2013) The ICC Prosecutor and Positive Complementarity: Strengthening the Rule of Law. International Criminal Law Review 13(3), 507–591.
Tladi D (2019) The Use of Force in Self-Defence against Non-State Actors, Decline of Collective Security and the Rise of Unilateralism: Whiter International Law? In: O'Connell ME, Tams CJ, Tladi D (eds) Self-Defence Against Non-State Actors. Cambridge University Press, New York, pp. 14–8.
Trahan J (2013) The Relationship Between the International Criminal Court and the UN Security Council: Parameters and Best Practices. Criminal Law Forum 24, 417–473.
Triffterer O, Bergsmo M, Ambos K (2022) Preamble. In: Ambos K (ed) Rome Statute of the International Criminal Court: Article-by-Article Commentary. Beck/Nomos/Hart, Munich, pp. 1–17.
Turlan P (2016) The International Criminal Court Cooperation Regime—A Practical Perspective from the Office of the Prosecutor. In: Bekou O, Birkett DJ (eds) Cooperation and the International Criminal Court: Perspectives from Theory and Practice. Brill, Leiden, pp. 58–79.
UN General Assembly (UNGA) (1950) Fifth Session. Resolution 377 A [Uniting for Peace] A/RES/377.
UN General Assembly (UNGA) (1956) First Emergency Special Session Middle East: Resolutions Adopted by the General Assembly during its 1st emergency special session [Resolutions 997-1002] A_3354 (ES- I).
UN General Assembly (UNGA) (2004) Fifty-Ninth Session. Report of the High-level Panel on Threats, Challenges and Change [A more secure world: our shared responsibility] A/59/565.
UN General Assembly (UNGA) (2005a) Fifty-Ninth Session. Report of the Secretary General [In larger freedom: towards development, security, and human rights for all] A/59/2005.
UN General Assembly (UNGA) (2005b) Sixtieth Session. World Summit Outcome Document. Resolution A/RES/60/1.
UN General Assembly (UNGA) (2009a) Sixty-Third Session. Report of the Secretary-General: [Implementing the Responsibility to Protect] A/63/677.
UN General Assembly (UNGA) (2009b) Sixty-third Session. 97th-101st Plenary Meetings A/63/PV.97; A/63/PV.98; A/63/PV.99; A/63/PV.100; A/63/PV.101.
UN General Assembly (UNGA) (2009c) Sixty-Third Session. Resolution 63/308 [The Responsibility to Protect] A/Res/63/308.
UN General Assembly (UNGA) (2012) Sixty-sixth Session. Report of the Secretary General [Responsibility to protect timely and decisive response] A/66/874.
UN General Assembly (UNGA) (2013a) Sixty-Seventh Session. 80th Plenary Session A/67/PV.80.
UN General Assembly (UNGA) (2013b) Sixty-Eighth Session. Resolution 68/182 [Situation of human rights in the Syrian Arab Republic] A/RES/68/182.
UN General Assembly (UNGA) (2014) Sixty-eighth Session. Report of the Secretary General [Fulfilling our collective responsibility: international assistance and the responsibility to protect] A/68/947.
UN General Assembly (UNGA) (2015) Sixty-Ninth Session. Report of the Secretary-General [A Vital and Enduring Commitment: Implementing the Responsibility to Protect] A/69/981.
UN General Assembly (UNGA) (2018) Seventy-second Session. 99th & 100th Plenary Meetings A/72/PV.99 & A/72/PV.100.
UN General Assembly (UNGA) (2019) Seventy-third Session. 93rd-96th Plenary Meetings A/73/PV.93; A/73/PV.94; A/73/PV.95; A/73/PV.96.
UN General Assembly (UNGA) (2021) Seventy-fifth Session. 64th–66th Plenary Meetings A/75/PV.64; A/75/PV.65; A/75/PV.66.
UN General Assembly (UNGA) (2022a) Eleventh Emergency Session. Resolution ES-11 [Aggression Against Ukraine] A/ES-11/L.1.

UN General Assembly (2022b) Seventy-sixth Session. Resolution 76/262 [Standing Mandate for a General Assembly debate when a veto is cast in the Security Council] A/76/L.52.

UN General Assembly (UNGA) (2024) Seventy-eight Session. Report of the Secretary General [Responsibility to Protect: The Commitment to Prevent and Protect Populations from Atrocity Crimes] A/78/901.

UN Security Council (UNGA) (1950a) Draft Resolution [The Complaint of Aggression upon the Republic of Korea] UN Doc S/1653.

UN Security Council (UNGA) (1950b) Joint Draft Resolution [Complaint of Aggression upon the Republic of Korea] UN Doc S/1894.

UN Security Council (UNSC) (1956) Resolution 119 [Complaint by Egypt against France and the United Kingdom] S/Res/119.

UN Security Council (UNSC) (1999) Resolution 1265 [The Protection of civilians in armed conflict] S/RES/1265.

UN Security Council (UNSC) (2006a) Resolution 1674 [on protection of civilians in armed conflict] S/RES/1674.

UN Security Council (UNSC) (2006b) Resolution 1706 [on expansion of the mandate of the UN Mission in Sudan to support the implementation of the Darfur Peace Agreement] S/RES/1706.

UN Security Council (UNSC) (2011a) Resolution 1970 [Peace and Security in Africa] S/RES/1970.

UN Security Council (UNSC) (2011b) Resolution 1973 [On the Situation in the Libyan Arab Jamahiriya] S/RES/1973(2011) (17 March 2011) paras 1-4.

UN Security Council (UNSC) (2013) Sixty-seventh Session The situation in the Middle East [Letter dated 14 January from the Charge d'affaires ai of the Permanent Mission of Switzerland to the United Nations addressed to the Secretary-General] A/67/694-S/2013/19.

Weerdesteijn M, Hola B (2020) Tool in the R2P Toolbox? Analysing the Role of the International Criminal Court in the Three Pillars of the Responsibility to Protect. Criminal Law Forum 31, 377–414.

Weiss TG (2016) R2P Precedents and Prospects. In: Bellamy AJ, Dunne T (eds) The Oxford Handbook on the Responsibility to Protect, 1st edn. Oxford University Press, Oxford, pp. 56–73.

Wenqi Z (2006) On Co-operation by States not Party to the International Criminal Court. International Review of the Red Cross 88(861): 87–110.

Yejoon R (2017) The Role of the International Criminal Court in Implementing the Responsibility to Protect. Florida Journal of International Law, 29(0) 69–98.

Chapter 5
General International Law as a Tool for Strengthening ICC Responses to Non-cooperation Through the Lens of R2P

Contents

5.1 Introduction 126
5.2 Non-cooperation and R2P Analysed Through the Lens of State Responsibility 127
 5.2.1 Identifying an Internationally Wrongful Act 127
 5.2.2 The Consequences of a Breach of an International Obligation 128
 5.2.3 Recipients of the Obligations of Cessation, Non-repetition, and Reparation 130
 5.2.4 Non-cooperation with the ICC as an Internationally Wrongful Act 130
5.3 Non-cooperation as a Breach of a Peremptory Norm of General International Law 131
 5.3.1 Identifying Peremptory Norms 132
 5.3.2 Obligations Under Peremptory Norms 135
5.4 Individual State Obligations to Protect Peremptory Norms 141
 5.4.1 Legal Bases for Individual Responses to Breaches of Peremptory Norms 141
 5.4.2 Specific Individual Responses to Breaches of Peremptory Norms 142
 5.4.3 Analysing the use of Individual Responses to Non-cooperation 149
5.5 Conclusion 150
References 151

Abstract This chapter seeks to examine the role played by general international law in strengthening the ICC's responses to non-cooperation, using R2P as a framework. Acknowledging that the Court's traditional remedies for responding to non-cooperation are a part of a broader strategy, this chapter explores how mechanisms beyond the ICC's cooperation provisions could provide for more effective solutions. Building on the previous chapter's analysis of R2P, this chapter investigates specific rules and principles of general international law, particularly those developed by the International Law Commission (ILC) for addressing breaches of international obligations. The chapter identifies how R2P aligns with the rules on State Responsibility and the principles attached to peremptory norms of general international law, examining whether these tools can assist in strengthening or complementing existing remedies for responding to non-cooperation. By analysing obligations under R2P, State responsibilities and obligations *erga omnes*, this chapter also seeks to identify ways in which States could collectively or individually respond to instances of non-cooperation. It also explores the potential for States to invoke remedies independently when institutional frameworks under the Assembly of States Parties or the UN Security Council are ineffective.

M. L. Jacobs, *The Consequences of Non-cooperation with the International Criminal Court*, International Criminal Justice Series 37,
https://doi.org/10.1007/978-94-6265-675-8_5

Keywords General International Law · Peremptory Norms · State Responsibility · ICC · R2P · Non-cooperation

5.1 Introduction

In searching for effective remedies for responding to and preventing non-cooperation, the ICC has recognised that referrals of a finding of non-cooperation were but one of many tools available as a method of last resort, or as part of a strategy for the promotion of cooperation and remedying non-cooperation.[1] This is a recognition that there exist under international law other mechanisms, outside the scope of the ICC's cooperation frameworks, that may be more effective in addressing a State's failure to cooperate.[2]

As the previous chapter identified the application of R2P as a tool to enhance the ICC's mandate, as well as the role played by the UN collective security system in recognising and implementing the doctrine, this chapter turns to analyse how R2P fits in with specific rules and principles of general international law that have been extensively developed to address and remedy breaches of specific obligations under international law. This chapter will look to the International Law Commission's work on State Responsibility, as well as its work on Peremptory Norms of General International Law. This investigation shall be done with a view to identifying whether R2P, together with these international law frameworks, can assist in developing improved responses to instances of non-cooperation. While the ILC has not been a significant actor in the development of R2P,[3] some subjects within the Commission's programme of work are relevant to the idea of a collective responsibility to protect populations from atrocity crimes. Such topics, which will be addressed below, include the rules on State Responsibility,[4] as well as Peremptory Norms of General International Law.[5]

This chapter will first analyse the role of R2P through the lens of State responsibility. This section will begin by identifying the rules within these articles that are relevant to the obligations required of States under R2P. This will be followed by the identification of specific remedies within these frameworks relevant to the failure to cooperate with the ICC. This will be followed by an analysis of non-cooperation with

---

[1] ICC, Prosecutor v Uhuru Muigai Kenyatta [Judgment on the Prosecutor's appeal against Trial Chamber V(B)'s "Decision on Prosecution's application for a finding of non-compliance under Article 87(7) of the Statute"] 19 August 2015, ICC-01/09-02/11-1032, para 51.

[2] Sluiter and Talontsi 2016, p. 103.

[3] Pronto 2013, p. 179.

[4] International Law Commission, Articles on the Responsibility of States for Internationally Wrongful Acts (2001) A/RES/56/10.

[5] ILC Seventy-Third Session Report of the International Law Commission [Chapter IV(E): Peremptory Norms of General International Law: Text of the Draft Conclusions and Legal Consequences of Peremptory Norms of General International Law (jus cogens)] A/77/10 (18 April–3 June and 4 July–5 August 2022).

the ICC through the lens of the rules relating to peremptory norms of general international law. In addition, this section will identify the obligations entrenched in the Rome Statute and R2P as obligations *erga omnes.* Finally, this chapter will identify whether States can implement specific remedies under the rules of State responsibility to respond to instances of non-cooperation on their own initiative should institutionalised frameworks under the Assembly of States Parties and the UN Security Council be ineffective. The overall discussion will also include an analysis of relevant case law before international tribunals.

5.2 Non-cooperation and R2P Analysed Through the Lens of State Responsibility

Developed in 2001, the ILC's Articles on State Responsibility are considered an important part of international law, forming a unified regime of responsibility applicable to the breach of international obligations by States.[6] Together with the Rome Statute and the Responsibility to Protect, these rules on State Responsibility reflect the efforts of the larger international community in developing stronger frameworks for fighting impunity for breaches of international law, particularly where the maintenance of international peace and security is at stake. While R2P and the Rome Statute are not discussed in the text of the Articles, nor in its commentaries, the rules on State responsibility do appear to share some similarities with these frameworks, which will be analysed below.

5.2.1 Identifying an Internationally Wrongful Act

The basic principle underlying the Articles on State Responsibility is that every internationally wrongful act of a State entails the international responsibility of that State.[7] Furthermore, an internationally wrongful act of a State is present when conduct consisting of an act or omission is attributable to the State under international law and constitutes a breach of an international obligation of that State.[8] The legal consequences that follow the commission of an internationally wrongful act do not have an effect on the duty of the responsible State to perform the obligation

[6] Creutz K "The Tenacity of the Articles on State Responsibility as a General and Residual Framework: An Appraisal" (5 August 2021) EJIL:Talk! available at: https://www.ejiltalk.org/the-tenacity-of-the-articles-on-state-responsibility-as-a-general-and-residual-framework-an-appraisal/ (accessed 29 October 2022).

[7] Article 1 of the Articles on State Responsibility; see also Crawford 2002, p. 77, at para 1.

[8] Article 2 of the Articles on State Responsibility.

breached.[9] Instead, a new legal relationship is established between the parties to assist in repairing the relationship affected by the wrongful act.[10]

5.2.2 *The Consequences of a Breach of an International Obligation*

Following the breach of an international obligation, several consequences await States responsible for such breaches. These consequences may take the form of ceasing the wrongful act and making assurances of non-repetition of the act, as well as obligations to make reparations for the damage caused by the wrongful act. These consequences will be analysed below.

5.2.2.1 The Obligations of Cessation and Assurances of Non-repetition

As a first step, the responsible State is placed under an obligation to cease the wrongful act, followed by an obligation to offer assurances of non-repetition of that act if the circumstances so require.[11] The obligation of cessation aims to put an end to the violation of international law, and protects the interests of both the injured State or States, as well as the interests of the international community as a whole in preserving and relying on the rule of law.[12] With regard to the obligation to offer assurances and guarantees of non-repetition, such an obligation is concerned with restoration of confidence in a continuing relationship between the responsible State and the injured State or States.[13]

---

[9] Article 29 of the Articles on State Responsibility; See also: ICJ, ICJ, Legal Consequences Arising from the Policies and Practices of Israel in the Occupied Palestinian Territory, including East Jerusalem (Advisory Opinion of 19 July 2024), General List No. 186 in the Occupied Palestinian Territory, including East Jerusalem (Advisory Opinion of 19 July 2024) 2024, General List No. 186, para 267.

[10] Crawford 2002, p. 194, at para 2.

[11] Articles 30(a) and (b) of the Articles on State Responsibility; See also: ICJ, ICJ, Legal Consequences Arising from the Policies and Practices of Israel in the Occupied Palestinian Territory, including East Jerusalem (Advisory Opinion of 19 July 2024), General List No. 186 in the Occupied Palestinian Territory, including East Jerusalem (Advisory Opinion of 19 July 2024), General List No. 186, para 268, for examples of the obligation of cessation highlighted by the Court.

[12] Crawford 2002, p. 197, at para 5.

[13] Ibid. p. 198, at para 9, where the commentary also notes that such assurances are most sought when the injured State has reason to believe that the mere restoration of the pre-existing situation is not enough.

5.2.2.2 Obligations to Make Reparations

The State responsible for the internationally wrongful act is also placed under an obligation to make full reparations for the injury caused by the act, be it material or sentimental injury.[14] Reparation may refer to three specific acts: namely restitution, compensation, and satisfaction.[15]

Restitution places an obligation upon the responsible State to re-establish the situation that existed prior to the commission of the wrongful act, to the extent that it is materially possible and proportionate.[16] Restitution may take the form of either material restoration, juridical restoration, or a combination of both. Material restitution may refer to the return of territory, persons, or property;[17] while juridical restitution refers to the modification of a legal situation through the revocation or amendment of a provision enacted in a violation of a rule of international law, the rescinding or reconsideration of an administrative or judicial measure unlawfully adopted in respect of a person or property of a foreigner, or a requirement that steps be taken for the termination of a treaty.[18]

Compensation places an obligation upon the responsible State to compensate the injured State for any financially assessable damage not repaired through restitution.[19] This form of reparation is the most commonly sought-after remedy in international practice.[20] In addition, an international court or tribunal which has jurisdiction with respect to a claim of State responsibility has the power to award compensation for the damage suffered.[21] Satisfaction places an obligation upon the responsible State to

[14] Article 35 of the Articles on State Responsibility.

[15] ICJ, ICJ, Legal Consequences Arising from the Policies and Practices of Israel in the Occupied Palestinian Territory, including East Jerusalem (Advisory Opinion of 19 July 2024), General List No. 186 in the Occupied Palestinian Territory, including East Jerusalem (Advisory Opinion of 19 July 2024), General List No. 186, para 269.

[16] Article 35 of the Articles on State Responsibility.

[17] ICJ, Legal Consequences Arising from the Policies and Practices of Israel in the Occupied Palestinian Territory, including East Jerusalem (Advisory Opinion of 19 July 2024), General List No. 186 in the Occupied Palestinian Territory, including East Jerusalem (Advisory Opinion of 19 July 2024), General List No. 186, para 270, where the Court highlights that restitution includes an obligation on Israel to return land and other immovable property, assets, and cultural property taken from Palestinians.

[18] Crawford 2002, p. 213, at para 5; see also ICJ, Legal Consequences Arising from the Policies and Practices of Israel in the Occupied Palestinian Territory, including East Jerusalem (Advisory Opinion of 19 July 2024), General List No. 186, para 268, where the Court highlighted that this obligation involves repealing all legislation and measures adopted for the creation or maintenance of the unlawful situation in Palestine.

[19] Article 36 of the Articles on State Responsibility; ICJ, Legal Consequences Arising from the Policies and Practices of Israel in the Occupied Palestinian Territory, including East Jerusalem (Advisory Opinion of 19 July 2024), General List No. 186, para 271.

[20] ICJ, Case Concerning the Gabcikovo-Nagymaros Project [Hungary v Slovakia] Judgment of 25 September 1997 ICJ Rep. 1997 7, p. 81 at para 152, "... it is a well-established rule of international law that an injured State is entitled to obtain compensation from the State which has committed an internationally wrongful act..."

[21] Crawford 2002, p. 218, at para 2.

make reparations for an injury that cannot be repaired through restitution or compensation.[22] Acts such as acknowledgement of breach, an expression of regret, a formal apology or another appropriate modality are the forms through which Satisfaction may materialise.[23] Satisfaction may not be out of proportion to the injury and may not take a form that humiliates the responsible State.[24]

5.2.3 Recipients of the Obligations of Cessation, Non-repetition, and Reparation

The remedies available under the rules of State responsibility identified above may be owed to a State, a group of States, or the international community as a whole, depending on the context of the obligation and the circumstances surrounding the breach.[25] There also lies the possibility that these obligations may be owed to any person or entity other than a State.[26] While the Articles do not explicitly deal with the possibility of the invocation of responsibility by non-State entities, this provision merely recognises that it may be possible through some procedure where a non-State entity may invoke the responsibility of a State on its own initiative without the involvement of other States.[27] Therefore such a provision opens up the possibility that the ICC may be owed these obligations following situation of non-cooperation by a State Party.

5.2.4 Non-cooperation with the ICC as an Internationally Wrongful Act

According to Kress and Prost, the failure to comply with a request by the ICC, contrary to the provisions of the Rome Statute, reflects the language of the Articles on State Responsibility, and therefore constitutes a breach of an international obligation.[28] The failure of a State to comply with the obligations required of it by the Court has a negative effect on the on the proper functioning of the Court as it extends

---

[22] Article 37(1) of the Articles on State Responsibility; see also Crawford 2002, p. 231 at para 3, where commentary notes that injuries requiring satisfaction are usually of a symbolic character.

[23] Article 37(2) of the Articles on State Responsibility; see also Crawford 2002, p. 233, at para 5, where the commentary notes that assurances or guarantees of non-repetition may also amount to a form of satisfaction. In addition, the appropriate mode of satisfaction will be determined with regard to the circumstances of each case.

[24] Article 37(3) of the Articles on State Responsibility.

[25] Article 33(1) of the Articles on State Responsibility.

[26] Article 33(2) of the Articles on State Responsibility.

[27] Crawford 2002, p. 210, at para 4.

[28] Kress and Prost 2022, p. 2475.

the length of proceedings, leading to its inability to render swift justice for victims of serious international crimes and a negative view of the Court among the international community.[29]

In addition, the third pillar of R2P places a collective responsibility upon States to respond to a State's failure to effectively protect against and prevent the commission of serious atrocity crimes.[30] According to Rosenberg, the obligations under R2P consist of the collective obligations of the international community of States and the national obligations of individual States.[31] She notes that while these obligations are independent of each other, there is a link between them, in that R2P relies on peaceful, coordinated actions taken by the international community as a whole followed by coercive measures through the Security Council should these peaceful means fail.[32] Therefore, where a State has failed to cooperate with the ICC's requests to arrest and surrender persons for prosecution, such a failure not only constitutes a breach of an obligation under the rules of State responsibility, but also constitutes a breach of the obligations required of States under pillar three of R2P.

5.3 Non-cooperation as a Breach of a Peremptory Norm of General International Law

This chapter now turns to the responsibility of States for a serious breach of an obligation arising under a peremptory norm of general international law, as recognised under the Articles on State Responsibility.[33] Such a breach is considered serious where it involves a gross or systematic failure by the responsible State to fulfil such obligations.[34] Such rules relating to peremptory norms of general international law have been expanded upon through the creation of the Draft Conclusions on Peremptory Norms of General International Law, the content of which mirrors the text of the Articles on State Responsibility. In establishing more effective frameworks for addressing non-cooperation through the lens of R2P, this section looks to identify the failure to cooperate with the ICC and the obligations under R2P as breaches of peremptory norms.

29 Jones 2016, pp. 193–194.

30 UNGA 2009, para 11(c).

31 Rosenberg 2009, p. 448.

32 Ibid. pp. 448–449.

33 Article 40(1) of the Articles on State Responsibility.

34 Article 40(2) of the Articles on State Responsibility.

5.3.1 Identifying Peremptory Norms

The Draft Conclusions on Peremptory Norms of General International Law define a peremptory norm as:

> *a norm accepted and recognized by the international community of States as a whole as a norm from which no derogation is permitted and which can be modified only by a subsequent norm of general international law having the same character.*[35]

The legal bases for peremptory norms can be found in customary international law,[36] as well as treaty provisions and general principles of law.[37] Commentary notes that customary international law is the most common basis for the emergence of peremptory norms of general international law, while treaty provisions and general principles of law may form the basis of peremptory norms to the extent that they can be regarded as norms of general international law.[38]

For a norm to be identified as peremptory, there must be evidence that such a norm is accepted and recognised by the international community of States.[39] Such acceptance and recognition must be from a large and representative majority of States.[40] Forms of evidence of acceptance and recognition include public Statements made on behalf of States, government legal opinions, diplomatic correspondence, legislative acts, court decisions, treaty provisions and resolutions.[41] Other means of identifying the peremptory character of a norm of general international law include decisions of international courts and tribunals;[42] as well as the works of expert bodies established by States or international organisations and the teachings of the most qualified legal writers.[43]

---

[35] Text of the Draft Conclusions and Legal Consequences of Peremptory Norms of General International Law (jus cogens)] above n. 5, Conclusion 3.

[36] Ibid. Conclusion 5(1).

[37] Ibid. Conclusion 5(2).

[38] Ibid. Commentary on Conclusion 5, para 7, where it is noted that while there is little practice to support the emergence of peremptory norms from treaties and general principles, there remains a possibility that these sources of international law can form the basis of peremptory norms.

[39] Ibid. Conclusion 6(2).

[40] Ibid. Conclusion 7(2) ibid.; this conclusion also recognises that acceptance and recognition by all States is not required for a norm to be considered peremptory.

[41] Ibid. Conclusion 8(2) ibid.; see also commentary on this conclusion, at para 3, which recognises that this list of forms of evidence of acceptance and recognition is not a closed list.

[42] Ibid. Conclusion 9(1).

[43] Ibid. Conclusion 9(2).

5.3.1.1 The Obligation to Protect Peremptory Norms

Peremptory Norms of general international law give rise to obligations owed to the international community, to which all States have a legal interest.[44] Such obligations are referred to as *erga omnes* obligations. According to the *Institut de Droit International,* an obligation *erga omnes* is defined as:

> *an obligation under international law that a State owes in any given case to the international community, in view of its common values and its concern for compliance, so that a breach of that obligation enables all States to take action.*[45]

Obligations *erga omnes* were first defined by the ICJ in the *Barcelona Traction* case, where a distinction was made between the obligations of a State towards the international community as a whole, and obligations towards another State in the field of diplomatic protection.[46] The Court held in this instance that such obligations derive from various fields of international law, such as the prohibition of acts of aggression and genocide, as well as the recognition of principles and rules concerning the protection of basic human rights.[47] Obligations *Erga Omnes* have been increasingly referred to and reaffirmed in international case law, which suggests that the protection of fundamental values of the international community has become an important aspect in the adjudication of cases before the ICJ.[48]

Erga omnes obligations can be strengthened through the application of such provisions in treaty provisions. In such an instance, such an obligation can therefore overlap with an obligation *erga omnes partes.*[49] Obligations *erga omnes partes* are defined by the Institut De Droit International as:

[44] Text of the Draft Conclusions and Legal Consequences of Peremptory Norms of General International Law (jus cogens)] above n. 5, Conclusion 17(1).

[45] Institut De Droit International Fifth Commission Resolution [Obligations Erga Omnes in International Law] 27 August 2005 Article 1(a).

[46] ICJ, Case Concerning the Barcelona Traction, Light and Power Company, Limited [Belgium v Spain] Second Phase Judgment of 5 February 1970. ICJ Rep 1970 3, para 33.

[47] Ibid. para 34.

[48] Tanaka 2021, p. 2; ICJ Case Concerning East Timor [Portugal v Australia) Judgment of 30 June 1995. ICJ Rep 1995 90, para 29, where the court recognised the obligation to protect the right of self-determination had the character of Erga Omnes; ICJ, Legality of the Threat or Use of Nuclear Weapons (Advisory Opinion of 8 July 1996), ICJ Rep 1996 226, para 79, where the Court highlighted that respect for the rules of international humanitarian law are fundamental to the respect of the human person and are to be observed by all States whether or not they have ratified the conventions that contain them, because they constitute "intransgressible principles of international customary law"; ICJ, Application of the Convention on the Prevention and Punishment of the Crime of Genocide (Bosnia and Herzegovina v Serbia and Montenegro) Judgment of 11 July 1996 (Preliminary Objections) ICJ Rep. 1996 595, para 31; ICJ, Legal Consequences of the Construction of a Wall in the Occupied Palestinian Territory (Advisory Opinion of 9 July 2004) ICJ Rep 2004 136, para 155; ICJ Questions Relating to the Obligation to Prosecute or Extradite (Belgium v Senegal) Judgment of 20 July 2012 ICJ Rep. 2012 422, para 68; ICJ Application of the Convention on the Prevention and Punishment of the Crime of Genocide (Croatia v Serbia) Judgment of 3 February 2015 ICJ Rep 2015 3, para 87.

[49] Tanaka 2021, p. 6.

> *an obligation under a multilateral treaty that a State party to the treaty owes in any given case to all the other States Parties to the same treaty, in view of their common values and concern for compliance, so that a breach of that obligation enables all these States to take action.*[50]

In the case of Gambia v Myanmar, the ICJ held that any State Party to the Genocide Convention, including States not specifically affected by the breach, may invoke the responsibility of another State party with a view to ascertaining the alleged failure to comply with its obligations *erga omnes partes* and to bring such a failure to end.[51]

However, the *erga omnes* character of peremptory norms does not itself create obligations for third States, instead the legal consequences of obligations on third States are established by practice and the legal decisions of international courts and tribunals, with the help of the International Law Commission.[52] According to the ILC Articles, any State or institution other than an injured State is entitled to invoke the responsibility of another State if the obligation breached is owed to a group of States, including that State, as is established for the protection of a collective interest of the group.[53] This argument is in line with the ICTY Appeals Chamber judgment in the *Blaskic case*, where it was held that each UN Member State has a legal interest in seeking compliance by any other Member State with the orders and requests of the International Tribunal, which may also include a collective response through other intergovernmental organisations.[54] The Appeals Chamber also determined that such collective action may take the form of political or moral condemnation, a request to cease the breach, or the imposition of economic or diplomatic sanctions.[55]

5.3.1.2 Identifying Peremptory Norms within the Scope of the Rome Statute and R2P

The Conclusions on Peremptory Norms identified a number of norms in international law that have attained peremptory status, and has published a non-exhaustive list of such norms, taking into consideration the possible existence or subsequent emergence of other peremptory norms.[56] Such norms include the prohibition of aggression, the

---

[50] Article 1(b) of the Resolution on Obligations Erga Omnes.

[51] ICJ Application of the Convention on the Prevention and Punishment of the Crime of Genocide [The Gambia v Myanmar) Request for Provisional Measures (Order of 23 January 2020) ICJ Rep 2020 3, para 41.

[52] International Law Commission Seventieth Session Third Report on Peremptory Norms of General International Law (jus cogens) by Dire Tladi, Special Rapporteur A/CN.4/714 (12 February 2018) para 110.

[53] Article 48 of the Articles on State Responsibility.

[54] ICTY, Prosecutor v Tihomir Blaskic [Appeals Chamber: Judgment on the request of the Republic of Croatia for review of the decision of Trial Chamber II of 18 July] 29 October 1997, IT-95-14-AR108 bis, para 36.

[55] Ibid. para 36(ii).

[56] Text of the Draft Conclusions and Legal Consequences of Peremptory Norms of General International Law (jus cogens)] above n. 5, Conclusion 23.

prohibition of genocide, the prohibition of crimes against humanity, and recognition of the basic rules of international humanitarian law.[57] In the context of the Rome Statute and the *World Summit Outcome Document,* the duty of States to prevent and prosecute the crimes recognised in these texts are peremptory norms.[58] States Parties to the Rome Statute are therefore, as under an obligation to ensure that States comply with their cooperation duties under the Statute, as well as work together to ensure that these breaches are responded to and addressed in a timely and effective manner.

5.3.2 *Obligations Under Peremptory Norms*

Under the Conclusions on Peremptory Norms, a serious breach of peremptory norms places States under the obligation to lawfully bring to an end any serious breaches,[59] as well as not recognise or sustain an unlawful situation arising from such a breach.[60] In addition, the ILC proclaims the breach of an obligation arising under a peremptory norm is serious if it involves a gross or systematic failure by the responsible State to fulfil that obligation.[61] The enforcement of these obligations encompasses a variety of measures aimed to ensure that breaches of the law are identified, responded to, and prevented.[62] Such measures include a wide variety of enforcement mechanisms, predominantly through various institutionalized means. Such institutionalised frameworks have been developed in more recent times to accommodate the direct protection or enforcement of community interests.[63]

5.3.2.1 The Obligation to Bring Serious Breaches to an End

The obligation to bring to an end serious breaches of peremptory norms builds on the general obligation to cooperate under international law and is recognised under various sources of international law.[64] According to Crawford, such cooperation is carried out under frameworks developed by international organisations, such as the Rome Statute and the UN Charter, in response to grave breaches of international

[57] Annex to the Conclusions on Peremptory Norms.

[58] The Rome Statute of the International Criminal Court. (17 July 1998, 2187, UNTS 3, Entry into Force, 1 July 2002) [hereinafter Rome Statute/RS], art 5; UNGA 2005, para 138.

[59] Text of the Draft Conclusions and Legal Consequences of Peremptory Norms of General International Law (jus cogens)] above n. 5, Conclusion 19(1).

[60] Ibid. Conclusion 19(2).

[61] Ibid. Conclusion 19(3).

[62] Tams 2011, p. 381.

[63] Ibid. p. 382.

[64] Text of the Draft Conclusions and Legal Consequences of Peremptory Norms of General International Law (jus cogens)] above n. 5, Commentary on Conclusion 19, para 2.

law. Such frameworks are often the only way in which effective remedies for such breaches can be provided for.[65]

The ICJ has recognised in several cases that in executing this obligation, States must cooperate with the United Nations to bring to an end the breach of obligations arising from a peremptory norm of general international law.[66] In addition, it is also recognised that the UN General Assembly and the Security Council are empowered to consider what further action is required to bring an illegal situation to an end.[67] This obligation to cooperate to bring serious breaches to an end may also be implemented through non-institutionalised forms of cooperation, such as *ad hoc* arrangements by a group of States acting together to end such a breach.[68]

The ILC's commentary also notes that the obligations of States to act collectively to end serious breaches of peremptory norms have particular consequences for cooperation within UN organs and other international organisations. In the face of such breaches, international organisations are therefore required to act within their mandates, and when permitted to do so under international law to bring those breaches to an end.[69] Therefore, where an international organisation has the discretion to act, this obligation to cooperate places a duty on the members of those organisations to act with a view to the organisation exercising that discretion in a manner to bring those breaches to an end.[70]

Therefore, in the context of the frameworks for cooperation in the Rome Statute and R2P, States are therefore placed under an obligation to ensure that the cooperation duties under the Rome Statute are complied with, as well as cooperate to ensure that

---

[65] Crawford 2002, p. 149, at para 3.

[66] ICJ Legal Consequences of the Separation of the Chagos Archipelago from Mauritius in 1965 Advisory Opinion of 25 February 2019 ICJ Rep. 2019 95, pp. 139–140 at para 182; see also: ICJ, Legal Consequences of the Construction of a Wall in the Occupied Palestinian Territory (Advisory Opinion of 9 July 2004) ICJ Rep 2004 136, p. 200 at para 159, where the ICJ held that one of the obligations arising from the breach of such obligations was an obligation on other States, while respecting the UN Charter and international law, to ensure that any impediment arising from such breaches are brought to an end.

[67] ICJ, Legal Consequences of the Construction of a Wall in the Occupied Palestinian Territory (Advisory Opinion of 9 July 2004) ICJ Rep 2004 136, para 160.

[68] Text of the Draft Conclusions and Legal Consequences of Peremptory Norms of General International Law (jus cogens)] above n. 5, Commentary on Conclusion 19 supra, note 5, para 10; Commentary also notes that such measures should be consistent with international law; see also: ICJ, Legal Consequences of the Construction of a Wall in the Occupied Palestinian Territory (Advisory Opinion of 9 July 2004) ICJ Rep 2004 p. 200 at para 159.

[69] ICJ, Legal Consequences Arising from the Policies and Practices of Israel in the Occupied Palestinian Territory, including East Jerusalem (Advisory Opinion of 19 July 2024), General List No. 186, para 281.

[70] Text of the Draft Conclusions and Legal Consequences of Peremptory Norms of General International Law (jus cogens)] above n. 5, Commentary on Conclusion 19 supra, note 5, para 10; Commentary also notes that such measures should be consistent with international law.

any breaches in the execution of the Rome Statute's mandate are responded to and addressed in a timely and effective manner. The failure to bring these breaches to a result in consequences against that State or group of States either through judicial decisions and referrals, or through measures under the UN Charter.[71]

5.3.2.2 Obligations of Non-recognition and Non-assistance

In protecting peremptory norms, States are under an obligation not to contribute to violations of international law.[72] Unlike the obligation to bring breaches to an end, the duties of non-recognition and non-assistance are negative duties that require States from acting in a manner that may result in the continuation of an ongoing breach of a peremptory norm.[73] Noting that peremptory norms can be regarded as a subset of *erga omnes* obligations, Tanaka argues that in appropriate circumstances, the obligations of non-recognition and non-assistance arise as legal consequence of an *erga omnes* obligation.[74]

The obligations of non-recognition and non-assistance relate to situations that are ongoing and require urgent resolution. Such situations include those relating to the territorial acquisition brought about by the use of force, or the denial by a State of the right to self-determination.[75] Therefore, such an obligation will not have much effect in situations of non-territorial and non-status-based violations of peremptory norms, such as genocide and breaches of the rules of humanitarian law, if those acts have already been committed.[76] In the context of the ICC, non-recognition may take the form of States discouraging non-cooperation and addressing potential or ongoing instances of non-cooperation during public meetings, either within the context of sessions of the Assembly of States Parties, or during debates or discussions within UN forums.

---

[71] Text of the Draft Conclusions and Legal Consequences of Peremptory Norms of General International Law (jus cogens)] above n. 5, Commentary on Conclusion 19 supra, note 5, para 10; Commentary also notes that such measures should be consistent with international law, Conclusion 19(4); Articles 87(5)(b) and 87(7) of the Rome Statute supra, note 56; Chapter VII of the UN Charter supra, note 15; Articles 36(1), 36(2)(c) and 36(2)(d) of the Statute of the International Court of Justice 1945.

[72] Brilmayer and Tesfalidet 2011, p. 8.

[73] Text of the Draft Conclusions and Legal Consequences of Peremptory Norms of General International Law (jus cogens)] above n. 5, Commentary on Conclusion 19 supra, note 5, para 10; Commentary also notes that such measures should be consistent with international law, Commentary on Conclusion 19, para 12.

[74] Tanaka 2021, p. 13; see also Article 5(b) of the Resolution on Obligations Erga Omnes, which provides that should a widely acknowledged grave breach of an erga omnes obligation occur, all States to which the obligation is owed shall not recognise the situation created by the breach as lawful.

[75] Ibid. p. 14; ICJ, Legal Consequences Arising from the Policies and Practices of Israel in the Occupied Palestinian Territory, including East Jerusalem (Advisory Opinion of 19 July 2024), General List No. 186, para 230.

[76] Aust 2021, p. 247.

The obligation of non-recognition is recognised in various court decisions and UN Resolutions, and is identified as part of customary international law.[77] For example, in the *South West Africa* advisory opinion, the *Wall* advisory opinion, and the recent *Israel* advisory opinion, the ICJ has held that all States are under an obligation not to recognise an illegal situation resulting from the breach of an obligation widely recognised as having peremptory character.[78] This obligation is also recognised in ICC case law, where the Trial Chamber recognised the duty of non-recognition as a general principle of law.[79]

However, international practice has been inconsistent in specifying what is required of States fulfilling this obligation.[80] On the one hand it appears that tribunals and UN Organs have been reluctant to provide general rules for the content of this obligation.[81] This is illustrated in the *Wall* advisory opinion, where very little guidance was given with regard to the content of this obligation as a result of uncertainty surrounding the practical effects of non-recognition.[82] On the other hand, there have been efforts to clarify the content of this obligation. The ICJ in the *Namibia* advisory opinion specified various obligations that arose from the obligation of non-recognition, including abstaining from entering into treaty relations with South Africa in all cases where the South African Government purports to act on behalf of or concerning Namibia; abstaining from invoking or applying existing bilateral treaties or provisions concluded on behalf of Namibia involving intergovernmental cooperation; abstaining from sending diplomatic or special missions to South Africa; abstaining from sending consular agents to Namibia and withdrawing agents already there; and abstaining from entering into any relationship or dealings with South Africa on behalf of or concerning Namibia which may entrench

[77] Text of the Draft Conclusions and Legal Consequences of Peremptory Norms of General International Law (jus cogens)] above n. 5, Commentary on Conclusion 19 paras 13–14.

[78] ICJ, Legal Consequences for States of the Continued Presence of South Africa in Namibia (Southwest Africa) notwithstanding Security Council Resolution 276 (1970) (Advisory Opinion of 1971) ICJ Rep 16, at para 119, where the Court held that UN Member States were under an obligation to recognize the illegality and invalidity of South Africa's continued presence in Namibia, as well as refrain from lending any support or assistance to South Africa with reference to its occupation of Namibia, para 159; ICJ, Legal Consequences Arising from the Policies and Practices of Israel in the Occupied Palestinian Territory, including East Jerusalem (Advisory Opinion of 19 July 2024), General List No. 186, para 279.

[79] ICC, Prosecutor v Bosco Ntaganda [Second Decision on the Defense's challenge to the jurisdiction of the Court in respect of Counts 6 and 9] 9 January 2017, ICC-01/04-02/06-1707, para 53.

[80] Aust 2021, p. 248.

[81] Kontorovich 2015, pp. 589–590.

[82] ICJ, Legal Consequences of the Construction of a Wall in the Occupied Palestinian Territory (Advisory Opinion of 9 July 2004) [Separate Opinion of Judge Kooimans] ICJ Rep. 2004 232, para 44, where it was held that the duty of non-recognition is an obligation without real substance.

its authority over that territory.[83] Such obligations were also specified in the recent advisory opinion on Israel's presence in the occupied Palestinian territories.[84]

Practice within the UN also highlights that the obligation of non-recognition, although recognised, is not expressly referred to or implemented appropriately by States.[85] Following the Russian annexation of Crimea in 2014, the General Assembly adopted a resolution which affirmed the territorial integrity of Ukraine and called upon States and international organisations not to recognise the altered status of this annexed territory and to refrain from any action or dealing that might be interpreted as recognition of the altered status.[86] According to Aust, debates by States before and after the vote highlighted that very few States actually expressly referred to non-recognition in their statements.[87]

5.3.2.3 The Protection of Peremptory Norms Analysed Through the Lens of R2P

While there is a duty upon States to bring grave breaches of peremptory norms to an end, there are divided views as to whether such an obligation forms part of existing international law. On the one hand, there lies an argument against the existence of a positive duty to cooperate to end serious breaches of peremptory norms. According to Hakimi, the rules on State responsibility do not identify the conduct that satisfies a duty to cooperate or address a failure to cooperate.[88] Commentary suggests that these Articles do not prescribe the form that cooperation should take because of the diverse circumstances involved. In addition, although the ILC recognised that cooperation may not be associated with a specific institution, it is assumed that most cooperation will occur through an international organisation.[89]

---

[83] ICJ, Legal Consequences for States of the Continued Presence of South Africa in Namibia (Southwest Africa) notwithstanding Security Council Resolution 276 (1970) (Advisory Opinion of 1971) ICJ Rep 16, paras 122–124.

[84] ICJ, Legal Consequences Arising from the Policies and Practices of Israel in the Occupied Palestinian Territory, including East Jerusalem (Advisory Opinion of 19 July 2024), General List No. 186 Advisory Opinion, supra, note. 75, para 278.

[85] Aust 2021, p. 249.

[86] UNGA 2014, para 6.

[87] Aust 2021, p. 249; the author also notes that statements made in the debates appeared to not convey a clear sense of understanding of their obligations not to recognize.

[88] Hakimi 2014, p. 255.

[89] Crawford 2002, p. 249 at para 2, where it is also noted that non-institutionalised cooperation is also envisaged.

The opposite view holds that the duty to cooperate is part of existing law,[90] with several international human rights treaties recognising this duty in their preambles.[91] However, since these references are found in the preambular paragraphs of the treaties, which indicate what the particular treaty would like to achieve, these references to cooperation may be better understood as a goal of States, rather than a duty.[92] Several international tribunals have also recognised this obligation to cooperate to end breaches of peremptory norms as part of existing international law. An example of this is the judgment of the ICJ in the *Bosnia-Serbia Genocide Case,* where the Court determined that the Genocide Convention places States under an obligation to try to avert genocidal conduct in and by third States.[93] However, the Court also held that the duty to prevent genocide requires different measures of each State, depending on that State's specific tools and frameworks for averting crises.[94]

Other cases in various tribunals, including the ICC, have identified various duties in these articles as part of international law.[95] In this regard Hakimi holds the view that R2P should offer a framework for obligating and holding States responsible for certain acts. Under this framework, each State has multiple duties relating to R2P, whereby responsibility for one or more duties should attach to that State or group of States that have specific ties to a situation.[96]

---

[90] Bird 2011, p. 887.

[91] Convention on the Prevention and Punishment of the Crime of Genocide A/Res.260 (III) 1948, "... in order to liberate mankind from such an odious scourge, international co-operation is required;" International Covenant on Civil and Political Rights 1966, "Considering the obligation of States under the Charter of the United Nations to promote universal respect for the observance of human rights and freedoms"; African Charter on Human and Peoples' Rights OAU Doc.CAB/Leg/67/3 rev.5 (1982) "Reaffirming the pledge ... to coordinate and intensify their cooperation and efforts to achieve a better life for the peoples of Africa and to promote international cooperation...."

[92] Bird 2011, p. 887.

[93] ICJ Application of the Convention on the Prevention and Punishment of the Crime of Genocide (Bosnia and Herzegovina v Serbia and Montenegro) Judgment, 26 February 2007, ICJ Rep 2007 43, para 438, "... for a State to be held responsible for breaching its obligation of prevention, it does not need to be proven that the State definitely had the power to prevent the genocide; it is sufficient that it had the means to do so and that it manifestly refrained from using them."

[94] Ibid. para 430, "... the obligation of States parties is rather to employ all means reasonably available to them, so as to prevent genocide so far as possible"; see also Hakimi 2014, p. 256, who recognises that a State that does not have any mechanisms available for addressing such situations may not have to act at all.

[95] European Court of Human Rights, Guzelyurtlu and Others v Cyprus and Turkey, 29 January 2019, 36925/07, paras 157–158, where the Court recognised articles 40 and 41 of the ILC Articles as relevant international law; ICC, Prosecutor v Bosco Ntaganda [Second Decision on the Defence's challenge to the jurisdiction of the Court in respect of Counts 6 and 9] 9 January 2017, ICC-01/04-02/06-1707, para 53, where the Court emphasised that there is a duty not to recognise situations as lawful created by certain breaches of international law.

[96] Hakimi 2014, p. 259.

5.4 Individual State Obligations to Protect Peremptory Norms

Should institutionalised frameworks, such as the Assembly of States Parties and the UN Security Council, be unable to address the failure to cooperate in an effective manner, there lies the question whether general international law provides for a situation where States may act on their own initiative to such instances of non-cooperation. According to Kress and Prost, it is uncertain whether and to what extent a State Party may react individually to the failure to cooperate.[97] It is therefore necessary to analyse how States can respond to non-cooperation in their individual capacities, through the lens of the third pillar of R2P and the Rome Statute system, under the basic rules of general international law.

5.4.1 Legal Bases for Individual Responses to Breaches of Peremptory Norms

Although R2P places a collective duty upon the international community of States to put an end to and prevent the commission of atrocity crimes, this doctrine also places a duty upon States to take steps to ensure that they do not contribute to the proliferation of mass atrocities. The collective obligation of the international community to take coordinated action to assist States in their protective mandates also implies individual State responsibility to take reasonable steps in preventing atrocity crimes.[98] In addition, while international law does not prohibit the application of unilateral measures to bring serious breaches of peremptory norms to an end if such measures are consistent with international law, the conclusions on peremptory norms do place emphasis on the use of collective measures in response to such breaches.[99]

Under R2P's third pillar, there is a collective responsibility to respond to a State's failure to effectively protect against and prevent the commission of atrocity crimes.[100] While this pillar implies resort to military action by the international community of States following a failure to exercise its primary protection responsibilities,[101] R2P does not expand the rights of States to interfere in a coercive manner in the domestic affairs of other States.[102]

---

[97] Kress and Prost 2022, p. 2490.

[98] Rosenberg 2009, pp. 449–450, where the author notes that this duty suggests at minimum that individual States should refrain from acting in a way that supports the actions of other States in the commission of atrocity crimes.

[99] Text of the Draft Conclusions and Legal Consequences of Peremptory Norms of General International Law (jus cogens)] above n. 5, Commentary on Conclusion 19 para 7.

[100] UNGA 2009, para 11(c).

[101] Ramopoulos 2015, p. 10; the author also notes that the third pillar can also be associated with a range of less coercive measures not requiring the use of force.

[102] Bellamy and Reike 2011, p. 96.

While the obligation to cooperate with the ICC may span throughout all three pillars of R2P, the focus in this book remains concerned with how R2P can strengthen responses to non-cooperation with the ICC. Therefore, this section will not focus on the primary responsibility to protect described under the first pillar, nor capacity building structures under the second pillar, but instead will establish how timely and decisive response frameworks under the third pillar can be used within the context of responses to non-cooperation conducted by States on their own initiative on an individual level. In establishing a duty upon States to individually respond to instances of non-cooperation, this section will investigate how such a duty is recognised through the lens of the remedies contained within the rules of State responsibility and peremptory norms of general international law.

5.4.2 Specific Individual Responses to Breaches of Peremptory Norms

As already noted above, peremptory norms give rise to obligations which are owed to the international community, in which all States have a legal interest. Where a State commits a breach of such an obligation, all the States to which the obligation is owed are entitled to claim cessation of the wrongful act plus performance of the obligation of reparation in the interest of the State, entity or individual which is specifically affected by the breach. Where there is a jurisdictional link between the State committing the wrongful act and a State to which the obligation is owed, that State has standing to bring a claim to an international tribunal in relation to a dispute concerning compliance with that obligation.[103] There also lies the option of a State to resort to countermeasures in order to place pressure on a responsible State to perform its obligations under international law. These remedies will be analysed below, together with an investigation into the appropriateness of their implementation within the framework of the Rome Statute system and R2P.

5.4.2.1 Resort to Judicial Settlement

Under the rules of State responsibility, an injured State is entitled to invoke the responsibility of another State if the obligation directly injures that State or the act is of a nature that will radically change the position of all other States to which that obligation is owed.[104] Invoking this responsibility may be interpreted as presenting a claim before an international tribunal, such as the International Court of Justice.[105] According to Tams, public interest claims before international courts and tribunals or other judicial bodies may be the least problematic form of enforcement action for

[103] Article 3 of the Resolution on Obligations Erga Omnes.

[104] Article 42 of the Articles on State Responsibility.

[105] Crawford 2002, para 7.

States.[106] Although most instances of judicial settlement ,will be conducted through the ICJ,[107] other tribunals may also be relied upon to settle disputes between States.[108]

The ICJ has jurisdiction over all cases referred to it by States. This includes all matters within the framework of the UN Charter, as well as other treaties and conventions in force.[109] States Parties to the ICJ Statute may at any time declare that they recognise the jurisdiction of the Court in various legal disputes. Among such disputes includes those relating to the nature or extent of reparations to be made for the breach of an international obligation.[110] The ILC Articles also recognises the right of any State other than the injured State to invoke the responsibility of another State where the obligation breached is owed to a group of States and is established for the collective interest of that group,[111] or that the obligation breached is owed to the international community as a whole.[112]

As non-cooperation with the ICC is cited as the breach of an international obligation and therefore an internationally wrongful act that gives rise to the international responsibility of that State,[113] one can therefore argue that in the instance where non-cooperation has occurred and neither the Assembly of States Parties, nor the UN Security Council are able to address and remedy such non-cooperation, a State Party to the Rome Statute may then be able to approach the ICJ or a related tribunal and invoke a claim against the non-cooperating State on the basis of such a failure to cooperate being categorised as a breach of an *erga omnes* obligation.

Case law has identified that States not directly injured by an alleged breach of erga omnes obligations may have standing to approach an appropriate tribunal in certain circumstances. In the Namibia advisory opinion, the ICJ held that the provisions of certain international instruments of a humanitarian character, as well as court decisions may entitle States to uphold some general principle even if the breach in question has not affected that State's material interests.[114] In the *Barcelona Traction*

---

[106] Tams 2011, p. 383, the author also notes that compared to other forms of enforcement, legal proceedings before international courts present the least risk of abuse.

[107] De Wet 2013, p. 12, where the author recognises that the ICJ has substantive jurisdiction over the whole field of international law which makes it better suited to settling disputes than other specialised international judicial bodies; see also article 92 of the Charter of the United Nations 1945 which recognises that the ICJ is the principal judicial organ of the United Nations.

[108] Ibid. Article 95.

[109] Article 36(1) of the Statute of the International Court of Justice 1945.

[110] Ibid. Article 36(2)(d).

[111] Article 48(1)(a) of the Articles on State Responsibility

[112] Article 48(1)(b) of the Articles on State Responsibility; see also Crawford 2002, p. 276 at para 1, where it is noted that article 48 is complementary to the rules contained in article 42 discussed above.

[113] Kress and Prost 2022, p. 2475.

[114] ICJ, Legal Consequences for States of the Continued Presence of South Africa in Namibia (Southwest Africa) notwithstanding Security Council Resolution 276 (1970) (Advisory Opinion of 1971) ICJ Rep 16, p. 54 at para 44; see also Tanaka 2018, p. 531, where the author notes that the Court suggests that even though no material damage may exist, a State may be entitled to invoke the responsibility of a wrongdoing State if such rights are vested by treaty or customary law.

case, the ICJ ruled that in order to bring a claim in respect of the breach of obligations arising from another State, a State must establish that its rights were violated.[115]

More recent case law appears to accept that third States may have standing under certain instances. The first instance is where a treaty contains a clause that allows any State Party to a treaty to submit a dispute concerning the interpretation or application of a treaty to an international court such as the ICJ. Where an *erga omnes* obligation is contained in the treaty and the dispute concerns the interpretation or application of that obligation, any State Party to that treaty has standing before the court in question by virtue of that clause.[116] This can be illustrated in the dispute between South Africa and Israel concerning allegations of Genocide.[117] The ICJ observed that all States Parties to the Genocide Convention had a common interest to ensure the prevention, suppression and punishment of genocide, by committing themselves to fulfilling the obligations contained in the Convention. Such a common interest has the implication that any State Party to the Genocide Convention may invoke the responsibility of another State Party, including through the institution of proceedings before the Court, with a view to determining the alleged failure to comply with its *obligations erga omnes partes* under the Convention, and to bringing that failure to an end.[118]

The second instance is where the clause identified above is not provided within the treaty in question. In this case, a question arises as to whether a not directly injured State Party to the treaty has standing before an international court or tribunal in response to an alleged breach of an *erga omnes* obligation, even though there is no express clause within that treaty that recognises such standing.[119] In the *Whaling in the Antarctic* judgment, the standing of Australia before the Court in relation to the wrongful conduct of Japan under the Whaling Convention was accepted on the basis that Australia had invoked Japan's *erga omnes* obligations.[120] According to Tanaka, this case appears to suggest that there is some scope to argue that the standing of a non-injured State in response to the breach of *erga omnes* obligations in international law may be accepted if there is a consensual basis for the Court's jurisdiction over that matter.[121] This confirms that States that have not been directly injured by a

---

[115] ICJ, Case Concerning the Barcelona Traction, Light and Power Company, Limited [Belgium v Spain] Second Phase Judgment of 5 February 1970. ICJ Rep 1970, para 35.

[116] Tanaka 2021, p. 21.

[117] ICJ, Case Concerning the Application of the Convention on the Prevention and Punishment of the Crime of Genocide in the Gaza Strip [South Africa v Israel] Request for the Indication of Provisional Measures (Order of 26 January 2024) General List. No. 192.

[118] Ibid. para 33.

[119] Tanaka 2021, p. 22.

[120] ICJ Whaling in the Antarctic (Australia v Japan; New Zealand intervening) Judgment of 31 March 2014 ICJ Rep 2014 para 239.

[121] Tanaka 2021, p. 23; however, the author does note that this view has not been tested in jurisprudence.

wrongful act can have standing to invoke the responsibility of a breach of an *erga omnes* obligation before an international court or tribunal if that court or tribunal can establish jurisdiction.[122]

5.4.2.2 Resort to Countermeasures

According to Kress and Prost, an alternative response to non-cooperation could take the form of the adoption of individual countermeasures against a non-cooperating State as a last resort.[123] Countermeasures against a responsible State are limited to acts such as the non-performance for the time being of international obligations of the State taking the measures towards the responsible State.[124] According to commentary, countermeasures may take the form of the non-performance of a single obligation or the non-performance of several obligations simultaneously.[125] In the event that countermeasures are adopted, such a measure would only be resorted to when all other reasonable options for addressing an internationally wrongful act are exhausted.[126]

According to Crawford, the use of countermeasures is not entirely lawful, and should only be resorted to should all other measures fail to induce cessation or reparation.[127] Case law has also confirmed that countermeasures are contrary to international law, but are however justified by a violation of international law allegedly committed by the responsible State against which such measures are directed.[128] A State is therefore required first call upon the responsible State to fulfil its duties;[129] then formally notify the responsible State of the decision to take countermeasures, as well as the need to offer to negotiate.[130] Countermeasures may not be taken and must be suspended if already taken if the internationally wrongful act has ceased.[131] Considering that countermeasures are a mechanism for exerting pressure on the

[122] Ibid. p. 24; see also Article 3 of the Resolution on Obligations Erga Omnes, which notes that where there is a jurisdictional link between the State committing the wrongful act and a State to which the obligation is owed, that State has standing to bring a claim to an international tribunal in relation to a dispute concerning compliance with that obligation.

[123] Kress and Prost 2022, p. 2491.

[124] Article 49(2) of the Articles on State Responsibility.

[125] Crawford 2002, p. 285, para 6.

[126] Kress and Prost 2022, p. 2491.

[127] Crawford 2019, p. 809; see also: ICJ, Case Concerning the Gabcikovo-Nagymaros Project [Hungary v Slovakia] Judgment of 25 September 1997 ICJ Rep. 1997 7, para 84, where the ICJ notes that the injured State must have called upon the State committing the wrongful act to cease the wrongful act or make reparation for such act before resorting to countermeasures.

[128] Case Concerning Air Service Agreement of 27 March 1946 between the United States of America and France (9 December 1978) Reports of International Arbitral Awards XVIII 417 p. 444 at para 84.

[129] Article 52(1)(a) of the Articles on State Responsibility.

[130] Ibid. Article 52(1)(b). However, see also Article 52(2), which recognises the right of an injured State to take urgent countermeasures that are necessary to preserve its rights.

[131] Ibid. Article 52(3)(a).

responsible State in the absence of a judicial decision, they cannot be taken while a dispute is pending before an international tribunal.[132] In addition, recourse to countermeasures runs the risk of giving rise to a further reaction, thereby causing an escalation which will lead to a worsening of the conflict. Such measures must therefore be used in moderation and accompanied by a genuine effort at resolving the dispute.[133]

The use of countermeasures are also restricted by conditions placed upon directly injured States as per the Articles on State Responsibility.[134] In relation to this is the provision within the ILC articles where any derogation from a peremptory norm of general international law is prohibited when using countermeasures.[135] Therefore, a State taking countermeasures against a State committing an act of genocide cannot counter such an act with another act of genocide.[136] In addition, such circumstances cannot justify or excuse a breach of a State's obligations under a peremptory rule of general international law.[137] Therefore, countermeasures that are contradictory to obligations *erga omnes* are not permitted in international law.[138] In addition, countermeasures must be proportional to the injury suffered by the alleged breach.[139]

Other challenges in the implementation of third-party countermeasures are also identified. Firstly, the fact that countermeasures are not a mandatory action highlights that there is no guarantee that such measures will be taken by an adequate number of States in a timely and effective manner.[140] This effectiveness may also be reflected by the political will and capacities of States, with more powerful States being able to take effective countermeasures; while smaller States being unable to take as effective measures against such wrongful acts.[141] There also lies the fear that triggering countermeasures may lead to abuse by States. Therefore, careful consideration must be given to whether the duty to protect community interests reflected in *erga omnes*

---

[132] Article 52(3)(b) of the Articles on State Responsibility; see also Case Concerning Air Service Agreement of 27 March 1946 between the United States of America and France (9 December 1978) Reports of International Arbitral Awards XVIII 417 at para 80.

[133] Case Concerning Air Service Agreement of 27 March 1946 between the United States of America and France (9 December 1978) Reports of International Arbitral Awards XVIII 417, p. 445 at para 91; see also Tams 2011, p. 392, where the author notes that States employ countermeasures cautiously.

[134] Tanaka 2021, p. 19.

[135] Article 26 of the Articles on State Responsibility.

[136] Crawford 2002, p. 188 at para 4.

[137] Ibid. para 6.

[138] Tanaka 2021, p. 20.

[139] ICJ, Case Concerning the Gabcikovo-Nagymaros Project [Hungary v Slovakia] Judgment of 25 September 1997 ICJ Rep. 1997 7, para 85, where the ICJ affirmed that countermeasures must be equal to the injury suffered, taking into consideration the rights in question.

[140] Tanaka 2021, p. 18.

[141] Koskenniemi 2001, p. 343; the author also notes that in the case of smaller States, they may be heavily reliant on other States for aid, including the State responsible for the internationally wrongful act, which may make that State less likely to adopt effective countermeasures for fear of reprisals after the fact.

obligations should be entrusted to individual States acting on their own assessment of what is legal.[142]

The general rule with regards to the use of countermeasures is that States directly injured by a breach of an international obligation are entitled to the full range of legal remedies available under the Articles on State responsibility.[143] This includes the right to take countermeasures following a breach of an international obligation in order to induce a responsible State to comply with its obligations under part II of the Articles on State Responsibility.[144] While States other than the injured State have the right to invoke the responsibility of another State in order to protect the collective interests of a group or the international community as a whole,[145] the right to use Countermeasures does not extend to them in the same way. There does however lie the possibility of States not directly affected or injured by a breach of *erga omnes* obligations can be entitled to take countermeasures in response to such breaches. Such countermeasures are referred to as third-party countermeasures.[146]

However, the current state of positive international law regarding third-party countermeasures remains uncertain. This is recognised within the Articles on State Responsibility where commentary observes that State practice with regards to third party countermeasures is sparse and involves a limited number of States. As a result, there is no clearly recognised entitlement of States to take countermeasures in the collective interest.[147] However, the Institut de Droit International has a contrasting view in its resolution on *Erga Omnes* which proclaims that should a widely acknowledged grave breach of an *erga omnes* obligation occur, all States to which the obligation is owed are entitled to non-forcible countermeasures under conditions similar to those applying to a State that is directly affected by a breach.[148]

Although the Articles on State Responsibility do not expressly recognise the use of countermeasures by third States, it does provide for the right of third States to take lawful measures against a responsible State to ensure cessation of a breach and reparation in the interest of an injured State or of the beneficiaries of the obligation breached.[149] Commentary on this provision highlights that lawful measures are prescribed, rather than countermeasures so as to not prejudice any position

[142] Crawford 2019, pp. 810–811, where the author notes that although there is broad agreement that the mechanisms and institutions for collective reactions to violations of erga omnes obligations must be developed and improved, it is uncertain whether it is appropriate to entrust the protection of collective interests to individual States that are acting on the basis of their own understanding of international legality.

[143] Article 42 of the Articles on State Responsibility.

[144] Ibid. Article 49(1).

[145] Ibid. Articles 48(1)(a)-(b).

[146] Tanaka 2021, p. 16.

[147] Crawford 2002, p. 305 at para 6; commentary also recognises that it is not appropriate to include a provision within the ILC articles which permits third States to take countermeasures to induce a responsible State to comply with its obligations. Questions relating to the development of the obligation was therefore left to the further development of international law.

[148] Article 5(c) of the Resolution on Obligations Erga Omnes.

[149] Article 54 of the Articles on State Responsibility.

concerning measures taken by States other than the injured State in response to breaches of obligations for the protection of the collective interest or those owed to the international community as a whole.[150] According to De Wet, the inclusion of this provision suggests that while the ILC Articles are generally concerned with the rights of injured States, international customary and treaty law may still provide for the use of countermeasures by non-injured States in the case of violations of *erga omnes* obligations.[151]

In the Wall Advisory Opinion, the ICJ emphasised the importance of positive obligations of States in taking lawful measures to bring violations of erga omnes obligations to an end. The Court also urged States to adopt measures beyond the obligation of non-recognition.[152] Other examples of third-party countermeasures include the freezing of funds and non-performance of bilateral agreements by States in response to human rights violations in Kosovo in 1998;[153] the freezing of assets and travel restrictions on members of the Zimbabwean government in response to human rights violations from 2003 onwards;[154] and sanctions against Russia in response to the annexation of the Crimea in 2014.[155]

According to Tanaka, restricting the use of countermeasures only to injured States based on bilateralism is contradictory to the *erga omnes* nature of relevant obligations that all States have an interest in. As there is no centralised framework to secure compliance with *erga omnes* obligations among States, there appears to be some scope that argues that a decentralised response by any member of the international community against infringements of these obligations should be a necessary alternative in the international legal system. However, the effectiveness of such measures may be compromised by a lack of coordination between States.[156]

As has already been highlighted above, the failure of a State to cooperate with the ICC amounts to a breach of an obligation arising out of an international treaty, which therefore entails international responsibility for the State concerned. Therefore, the adoption of countermeasures in response to instances of non-cooperation, should not be ruled out as an available option to States. However, it may be difficult to determine a rational basis upon which such action could be taken, considering that

---

150 Crawford 2002, p. 305 at para 7.

151 De Wet 2013, p. 11.

152 ICJ, Legal Consequences of the Construction of a Wall in the Occupied Palestinian Territory (Advisory Opinion of 9 July 2004) ICJ Rep 2004, pp. 159–160.

153 Bird 2011, p. 897, where such acts included the freezing of Yugoslav funds and flight bans.

154 Ramjathan-Keogh K "SALC Policy Brief: The Imposition of International Sanctions on Zimbabwe" (18 July 2019) Southern Africa Litigation Centre available at: https://www.southernafricalitigationcentre.org/2019/07/18/salc-policy-brief-the-imposition-of-international-sanctions-on-zimbabwe/ (accessed 1 May 2022) which identifies a number of sanctions against Zimbabwe by the USA from 2003 to 2008, and EU Sanctions since 2002.

155 Aslund 2019, pp. 14–15; such sanctions included travel bans and asset freezes on individuals and companies accused of undermining democracy, misappropriating Ukrainian property, and violating human rights; and various economic sanctions covering trade of oil, finance and sharing of defence technology.

156 Tanaka 2021, pp. 17–18.

the right to take such measures is generally confined to a State injured by such an act. In addition, considering that the use of countermeasures is a radical response to instances of non-cooperation, it has not been used by States to encourage or force cooperation. It is therefore uncertain whether such a remedy would be effective in practice as a finding of State responsibility would not automatically assist in securing cooperation with the Court.[157]

5.4.3 Analysing the use of Individual Responses to Non-cooperation

According to Bekou, it is not entirely clear whether a State may engage in individual actions against another State in the event of institutional failure, considering that the combined effect given to existing non-cooperation remedies, as contained in the Rome Statute and under the third pillar of R2P appear to prioritise collective responses to non-cooperation over individual responses.[158] In the *Blaskic Appeal Judgment* the appeals chamber held that as the principles of the UN Charter and the spirit of the ICTY Statute aim to limit the risks of arbitrariness and conflict as far as possible, collective or joint action taken through an intergovernmental organisation is preferred and prioritised.[159] Regardless, it may still be possible for individual State actions to be utilised under certain circumstances. According to Brilmayer and Tesfalidet, international law does make provision for the appropriateness of third State obligations in that these States are under a legal obligation not to contribute to another State's violation of international law, such as a failure or refusal to cooperate with the requests of the ICC. Such an obligation is satisfied where the third State is not involved at all in the legal dispute or is involved on the side of the victim or injured State.[160] There are two views regarding the appropriateness of such actions.

Firstly, a State Party to the Rome Statute cannot individually go beyond the recommendations of the Assembly of States Parties against a non-cooperating State. According to this view, individual countermeasures would be excluded as a possible remedy against a non-cooperating State in the absence of action or recommendations by the Assembly.[161] Therefore although the international community may take measures against the violation of international law, such an obligation to take action

[157] Bekou 2019, pp. 926–927.

[158] Ibid. p. 926.

[159] ICTY, Prosecutor v Tihomir Blaskic [Appeals Chamber: Judgment on the request of the Republic of Croatia for review of the decision of Trial Chamber II of 18 July] 29 October 1997, IT-95-14-AR108 bis, para 36; the Appeals Chamber also emphasises that such action may only be taken after a judicial finding has been made by the International Tribunal, and that such action may take the form of political or moral condemnation, a collective request to cease the breach, or the imposition of economic or diplomatic sanctions.

[160] Brilmayer and Tesfalidet 2011, p. 6.

[161] Bekou 2019, p. 927.

arises from the fact that a body like the Assembly of States Parties or the UN Security Council requested that action be taken.[162] As a consequence, Part IX of the Rome Statute would be construed as a partly self-contained regime as to the legal consequences following the commission of the internationally wrongful act.[163]

The alternative view holds that in the event that an institution like the Assembly of States Parties or the UN Security Council fails to mobilise an appropriate response against a non-cooperating State, general customary international law would apply, allowing States to respond to non-cooperation on their own initiative.[164] This view is in line with the cooperation regime envisaged by the First Additional Protocol to the Geneva Conventions, which proclaims that States may act jointly or individually in cooperation with the United Nations and the UN Charter.[165] Therefore, in evaluating the potential for States to act on their own initiative in response to instances of non-cooperation, it is highly unlikely that a decentralised response to the failure to cooperate can be achieved. This is due to the collective nature of international cooperation represented within the Rome Statute, the three pillars of R2P, and the UN Charter. If individual State responses to non-cooperation can be made a reality, consideration should be made regarding principles of fairness and good faith when operationalising such responses to a breach of an international obligation.

5.5 Conclusion

In this chapter, the role of specific frameworks under general international law for strengthening the ICC's responses to non-cooperation by States was analysed through the lens of its relationship with the cooperation frameworks under the Rome Statute and the principles and obligations entrenched in the Responsibility to Protect. This analysis was conducted with a view to establishing whether these frameworks could assist in strengthening the tools available to the institutions tasked by the ICC to address non-cooperation, namely the Assembly of States Parties and the UN Security Council. In conducting this analysis, this chapter observed the following:

Firstly, as non-cooperation with the requests of the ICC is a breach of that specific treaty, such a breach can therefore be considered an internationally wrongful act, which entails the international responsibility of the non-cooperating State. When conducting this observation, there lies the question whether the frameworks under State Responsibility, together with the application of R2P, can be applied as additional tools to assist the Court and its associated bodies in responding to instances of non-cooperation.

---

[162] Brilmayer and Tesfalidet 2011, p. 6.

[163] Kress and Prost 2022, p. 2490.

[164] Ibid. p. 2491.

[165] Article 89 of the Protocol Additional to the Geneva Conventions of 12 August 1949 and relating to the Protection of Victims of International Armed Conflicts (Protocol I) of 8 June 1977.

Secondly, this chapter identified that the prevention and prosecution of crimes entrenched in the Rome Statute and under R2P are examples of peremptory norms of general international law. The protection of such norms therefore gives rise to obligations *erga omnes,* which are obligations owed to the international community, in which all States have a legal interest. These obligations are further strengthened through their application in multilateral treaties as obligations *erga omnes partes.* In protecting peremptory norms, States are therefore under an obligation to lawfully end the breach of such norms, as well as not recognise or sustain an unlawful situation caused by a breach. Therefore, the application of the conclusions on peremptory norms to the cooperation obligations under the Rome Statute can help strengthen the Court's ability to ensure States cooperate with its requests, as well as in responding to instances of non-cooperation that have been communicated to it.

Finally, this chapter analysed whether States could respond on their own initiative to instances of non-cooperation through the application of remedies identified within the rules on State responsibility. In conducting this analysis, it was concluded that even though there lies the possibility that States could respond to non-cooperation without the application of institutionalised frameworks, the collective nature of the obligations under the Rome Statute, the UN Charter, and the responsibility to protect suggests that such decentralised responses to breaches of international law are discouraged. As a result, reliance on remedies developed through the ICC Assembly of States Parties and the UN Security Council are preferred. However, as it has been identified in a previous chapter, neither the Assembly of States Parties, nor the Security Council have addressed instances of non-cooperation in an effective manner with the current frameworks at their disposal.

This chapter therefore argues that the application of the principles entrenched within R2P, the rules on State responsibility and peremptory norms of general international law can enhance the ability of these bodies to respond to non-cooperation more effectively. This book therefore turns to analyse how R2P, along with the rules on general international law identified above, can be applied within the frameworks developed by the Assembly of States Parties and the UN Security Council to ensure a more effective regime for responding to instances of non-cooperation. The chapter to follow will begin this analysis by investigating how R2P, together with the identified rules of general international law, can assist the Assembly of States Parties in developing and strengthening its frameworks for responding to non-cooperation.

References

Aslund A (2019) Western Economic Sanctions on Russia over Ukraine, 2014-2019. CESifo Forum 20(4) 14–18, available at: https://www.cesifo.org/de/publikationen/2020/aufsatz-zeitschrift/western-economic-sanctions-russia-over-ukraine-2014-2019 (accessed 20 September 2022).

Aust HP (2021) Legal Consequences of Serious Breaches of Peremptory Norms in the Law of State Responsibility. In: Tladi D (ed) Peremptory Norms of General International Law (Jus Cogens) Disquisitions and Disputations. Koninklijke Brill Nijhoff, Leiden, pp. 227–256.

Bekou O (2019) Dealing with Non-cooperation at the ICC: Towards a More Holistic Approach. International Criminal Law Review 19(6): 911–937.

Bellamy AJ, Reike R (2011) The Responsibility to Protect and International Law. In: Bellamy AJ, Davies SE, Glanville L (eds) The Responsibility to Protect and International Law. Martinus Nijhoff, Leiden, pp. 81–101.

Bird A (2011) Third State Responsibility for Human Rights Violations. European Journal of International Law 21(4), 883–900.

Brilmayer L, Tesfalidet IY (2011) Third State Obligations and the Enforcement of International Law. International Law and Politics 44(1) 1–53.

Crawford J (2002) The International Law Commission's Articles on State Responsibility: Introduction, Text and Commentaries. Cambridge University Press, Cambridge.

Crawford J (2019) Brownlie's Principles of Public International Law, 9th edn. Oxford University Press, Oxford.

De Wet E (2013) Invoking Obligations Erga Omnes in the Twenty-first Century: Progressive Developments Since Barcelona Traction. South African Yearbook of International Law, 38, 2–19.

Hakimi M (2014) Toward a Legal Theory on the Responsibility to Protect. Yale Journal of International Law 39(2) 247–280.

Jones A (2016) Non-cooperation and the Efficiency of the International Criminal Court. In: Bekou O, Birkett DJ (eds) Cooperation and the International Criminal Court: Perspectives from Theory and Practice. Brill, Leiden, pp 185–209.

Kontorovich E (2015) Economic Dealings with Occupied Territories. Columbia Journal of Transnational Law 53, 584–637.

Koskenniemi M (2001) Solidarity Measures: State Responsibility as a New International Order? British Yearbook of International Law 72(1), 337–356.

Kress C, Prost K (2022) International Cooperation and Judicial Assistance. In: Ambos K (ed) Rome Statute of the International Criminal Court: Article-by-Article Commentary. Beck/Nomos/Hart: Munich, pp 2452–2701.

Pronto AP (2013) The International Law Commission. In: Zyberi G (ed) An Institutional Approach to the Responsibility to Protect. Cambridge University Press, Cambridge, pp 179–196.

Ramopoulos T (2015) International Law and the Application of the Third Pillar Approach. In: Fiott D, Koops J (eds) The Responsibility to Protect and the Third Pillar: Legitimacy and Operationalization. Palgrave Macmillan, London, pp 4–20.

Rosenberg SP (2009) Responsibility to Protect: A Framework for Prevention. Global Responsibility to Protect 1, 442–477.

Sluiter G, Talontsi S (2016) Credible and Authoritative Enforcement of State Cooperation with the International Criminal Court. In: Bekou O, Birkett DJ (eds) Cooperation and the International Criminal Court: Perspectives from Theory and Practice. Brill, Leiden, pp. 80–113.

Tams CJ (2011) Individual States as Guardians of Community Interests. In: Fastenrath U, Geiger R, Khan D, Paulus A, von Schorlemer S, Vedder C (eds) From Bilateralism to Community Interest; Essays in Honour of Bruno Simma. Oxford University Press, Oxford, pp. 379–405.

Tanaka Y (2018) Reflections on Locus Standi in Response to a Breach of Obligations Erga Omnes Partes: A Comparative Analysis of the Whaling in the Antarctic and South China Sea Cases. The Law & Practice of International Courts and Tribunals, 17(3), 527–554.

Tanaka Y (2021) The Legal Consequences of Obligations Erga Omnes in International Law. 68 Netherlands International Law Review 68, 1–33.

UN General Assembly (UNGA) (2005) Sixtieth Session. World Summit Outcome Document. Resolution A/RES/60/1.

UN General Assembly (UNGA) (2009) Sixty-Third Session. Report of the Secretary-General: [Implementing the Responsibility to Protect] A/63/677.

UN General Assembly (UNGA) (2014) Sixty-eighth Session Resolution 68/262 [Territorial Integrity of Ukraine] A/RES/68/262.

Chapter 6
The Responsibility to Protect and General International Law as Tools for Strengthening the Assembly of States Parties

Contents

6.1 Introduction 154
6.2 Pillar Two of R2P as a Tool for Enhancing the Assembly of States Parties' Cooperation Frameworks 155
6.2.1 Complementarity as a Tool under the Second Pillar of R2P 155
6.2.2 Promoting Positive Complementarity 158
6.2.3 Strengthening Complementarity Activities through the Secretariat of the Assembly 162
6.3 Pillar Three of R2P as a Tool for Strengthening the Assembly's Responses to Non-cooperation 166
6.4 Developing Remedies for Strengthening the Assembly's Responses to Non-cooperation 168
6.4.1 Approaching the ICJ 169
6.4.2 Warnings 172
6.4.3 Administrative Fines 173
6.4.4 Loss of Participation Rights in Assembly Decisions 174
6.4.5 Analysing the Adoption of Additional Remedies for Addressing Non-cooperation 178
6.5 Conclusion 179
References 180

Abstract This chapter explores how R2P and general international law can strengthen the Assembly of States Parties' responses to non-cooperation by States. The Assembly of States Parties has consistently emphasised the responsibility of States to protect populations from atrocity crimes. Despite this commitment, the Assembly's existing frameworks for addressing non-cooperation have not been fully effective, often relying on non-coercive measures that have failed to hold States accountable for their failure to cooperate or otherwise prevent future breaches of obligations under the Rome Statute. This chapter therefore seeks to assess how the Assembly of States Parties can effectively utilise the principles contained in the three pillars of R2P, as well as the tools present in general international law, to strengthen its mechanisms for responding to non-cooperation that has been referred to it by a Court decision.

M. L. Jacobs, *The Consequences of Non-cooperation with the International Criminal Court*, International Criminal Justice Series 37,
https://doi.org/10.1007/978-94-6265-675-8_6

Keywords Assembly of States Parties · Rome Statute · R2P · Non-cooperation · General International Law · Remedies · State Responsibility · United Nations · ICJ · ICC · Complementarity

6.1 Introduction

Following the official recognition of R2P at the 2005 World Summit,[1] the Assembly of States Parties acknowledged R2P for the first time at its fourth annual session in December 2005. In the preambular paragraphs of its resolution on Strengthening the International Criminal Court and the Assembly of States Parties, the Assembly recognised:

> *that each individual State has the responsibility to protect its population from genocide, war crimes, and crimes against humanity, that the conscience of humanity continues to be deeply shocked by unimaginable atrocities in various parts of the world, and that the need to prevent the most serious crimes of concern to the international community, and to put an end to the impunity of the perpetrators of such crimes, is now widely acknowledged...*[2]

This paragraph mirrors paragraph 138 of the 2005 World Summit Outcome Document and highlights ICC States Parties' commitment to protecting populations from atrocity crimes, and in addressing and punishing such crimes.

These resolutions are important sources for recording developments within the mandate of the Court. In the context of cooperation obligations, one can observe that the law on cooperation has seen much development, which is particularly notable within the frameworks for responding to instances of non-cooperation. However, these resolutions also indicate that non-cooperation is increasingly problematic as the years progress and additional frameworks are introduced to counter the failure to cooperate. The adoption of these various procedures, soft action, and dialogue; although useful to the extent that these actions provide evidence of swift responses to non-cooperation; have not been successful in holding responsible States accountable or preventing future instances of non-cooperation.[3]

Assembly of States Parties has developed a range of frameworks and mechanisms for addressing non-cooperation,[4] as well as various reports, press releases and other documents published during its annual sessions.[5] However, the Assembly has yet to use these measures effectively to respond to instances of non-cooperation that

[1] UNGA 2005, paras 138 and 139.

[2] ASP 2005, pre para 1.

[3] Bekou 2019, pp. 929–930.

[4] ASP 2018a [Annex II Assembly Procedures relating to non-cooperation]; ASP 2018b [Annex: Toolkit for the Implementation of the Informal Dimension of the Assembly Procedures relating to non-cooperation]

[5] Assembly of States Parties *Non-cooperation available at* https://asp.icc-cpi.int/en_menus/asp/non-cooperation/pages/default.aspx (accessed 4 April 2020).

have been communicated to it.[6] In previous chapters, it was identified that the ICC and R2P are complementary to each other in the fight against impunity for serious international crimes, and that the application of R2P to the Court's cooperation frameworks can assist in developing more effective responses to instances of non-cooperation.[7] In addition, this book has also identified that the application of specific aspects of general international law, namely State responsibility for internationally wrongful acts and peremptory norms of general international law can further enhance and complement such frameworks.[8]

Therefore, this present chapter will assess how the Assembly of States Parties can enhance its frameworks for responding to non-cooperation, through the application of the principles and tools available under the responsibility to protect and general international law. This chapter will begin the investigation by analysing the Assembly's relationship with the second pillar of R2P, in building up the capacities of States in responding to breaches of international law through the application of the Rome Statute's Complementarity principle. This will be followed by an analysis into the application of the third pillar of R2P, and frameworks entrenched in general international law, to the Assembly's tools for responding to non-cooperation. This section will also identify specific remedies recognised in general international law that could be implemented to enhance or otherwise complement the Assembly's responses to instances of non-cooperation.

6.2 Pillar Two of R2P as a Tool for Enhancing the Assembly of States Parties' Cooperation Frameworks

As has already been noted in Chap. 2, the Assembly of States Parties needs to be strengthened to enable it to be better equipped to address and remedy instances of non-cooperation referred to it by the ICC Chambers. This section will identify the how the work of the Assembly of States Parties links with principles entrenched within the second pillar of R2P, with a view to strengthening State capacities to respond to cooperation obligations in an effective manner.

6.2.1 *Complementarity as a Tool under the Second Pillar of R2P*

To prevent instances of non-cooperation from occurring, there need to be effective measures in place for States to assist them in executing their cooperation obligations. In analysing the development of such frameworks, the application of the tools

[6] Ambach 2022, p. 2783.

[7] See Chap. 4 in the present book.

[8] See Chap. 5 in the present book.

available under the second pillar of R2P may assist the Assembly of States Parties in building up the national capacities of States to cooperate with the Court under the complementarity principle.

6.2.1.1 The Assembly's Role in Capacity Building

In the context of the ICC and its relationship with the second pillar, the UN Secretary-General has cited the Court as an important actor for assisting States in protecting populations from atrocity crimes.[9] Closer interactions are therefore needed between the ICC and pillar two of R2P in order to ensure effective capacity building strategies.[10]

According to Bekou, the key to complying with the Rome Statute's cooperation obligations is for States to enact domestic legislation that implements such provisions.[11] However, there is a gap between international and national justice systems due to the fact that the successful implementation of the complementarity principle is reliant on the political will and capacities of States to respond to atrocity crimes.[12] Apart from the lack of political will, other hurdles to implementation of domestic legislation complimentary to the Rome Statute include the type of legal system a State follows, and potential conflicts with national constitutions and already-existing domestic provisions.[13]

Capacity building activities by the ICC have focused on those States that have been unable to genuinely investigate and prosecute serious international crimes.[14] Such activities have included support for the implementation of legislation; rule of law activities, including activities associated with cooperation between the Court and specialized international and regional organisations; identification of donor States; and open dialogue between parties on how to promote positive complementarity.[15] In ensuring the effective creation and dissemination of information to the public, the ICC has set up various outreach programmes which aim to explain to communities that are the focus of ICC prosecutions the role and functions of the Court. These outreach programmes include information sessions and training programmes.[16]

In assessing the role that capacity building plays in ensuring States can cooperate with the ICC and ensuring there are appropriate measures in place for responding

---

[9] UNGA 2014, para 22.

[10] Saba and Akbarzadeh 2020, p. 97.

[11] Bekou 2019, p. 932; the author also notes that reviewing existing national legal frameworks, examining their compatibility with the Rome Statute, and putting the procedures in place to enable execution of ICC cooperation requests is essential for the Court's success.

[12] Behrmann 2016, p. 313.

[13] Case Matrix Network *Implementing the Rome Statute of the International Criminal Court* (September 2017) available at https://www.legal-tools.org/doc/e05157/pdf/ (accessed 31 May 2021).

[14] Ambach 2022, p. 2786.

[15] ASP 2014, paras 34 and 39.

[16] Saxon 2015, p. 130.

to instances of non-cooperation, attention should be placed on the role of the rule of law in building up these capacities. Under the UN System, the rule of law refers to a principle of governance in which all persons, institutions, entities, and States are accountable to laws that are publicly promulgated, equally enforced, and independently adjudicated; and which are consistent with human rights norms and standards. The rule of law requires measures that ensure adherence to principles of supremacy, equality, accountability, and fairness in the application of the law, separation of powers, participation in decision-making, legal certainty, avoidance of arbitrariness, and legal and procedural transparency.[17]

At the 2005 World Summit, Member States recognised the need for "universal adherence to and implementation of the rule of law at both the national and international levels" and reaffirmed their commitment to "an international order based on the rule of law and international law.[18]" The rule of law was included in the agenda of the General Assembly at the Sixty First Session in 2006,[19] and continues to be an agenda item in the Sixth Committee.[20] At the 70th session of the General Assembly, States emphasised the vital role played by the ICC in the fight against impunity for serious international crimes, in accordance with the principle of complementarity. Also expressed was the view that complementarity was of utmost importance, as well as the emphasis on the primary responsibility of States to investigate and prosecute violations of international law. Delegations also encouraged States to consider ratifying to the Rome Statute. The importance of nationally owned transitional justice mechanisms to strengthen the rule of law was also emphasised.[21]

6.2.1.2 The Role of the Assembly in Promoting Complementarity

In assessing the Assembly's role in promoting complementarity, the Kampala Review Conference, and the resolution that emerged from it, empowered the Assembly with the authority to provide for the exchange of information between the Court, States Parties, and other parties related to the strengthening of domestic jurisdictions.[22]

The Assembly has three roles to play in promoting complementarity. Firstly, and most importantly, the Assembly has an educational role to play by highlighting to other bodies that complementarity should be prioritised. The Assembly's strength

[17] United Nations and the Rule of Law *What is the Rule of Law,* available at https://www.un.org/ruleoflaw/what-is-the-rule-of-law/ (accessed 20 December 2021).

[18] UNGA 2005, para 134.

[19] UNGA 2006a, See also UNGA 2006b, para 5.

[20] United Nations Sixth Committee. *The Rule of Law at the National and International Levels (Agenda Item 82),* available at https://www.un.org/en/ga/sixth/69/rule_of_law.shtml (accessed 20 December 2021).

[21] UN General Assembly Sixth Committee Seventieth Session. *The Rule of Law at National and International Levels,* available at: https://www.un.org/en/ga/sixth/71/rule_of_law.shtml (accessed 20 December 2021).

[22] Review Conference of the International Criminal Court *Resolution on Complementarity* RC/Res.1 (8 June 2010) para 9.

in this regard is its member's knowledge of and commitment to the principle of accountability for atrocity crimes.[23] The next function the Assembly performs is to convene with relevant actors in order to address complementarity effectively.[24] The last function that the Assembly is tasked with is improving the distribution and sharing of information among the various actors engaged in addressing complementarity.[25] It is therefore important for the Assembly of States Parties to assist States in implementing the Rome Statute at a national level in order to ensure enhanced cooperation between States and the Court as well as to ensure that States are deterred from deciding to not comply with cooperation requests.[26]

6.2.2 *Promoting Positive Complementarity*

The concept of positive complementarity is particularly important for the Assembly for building up the domestic capacities of States to prosecute ICC crimes. Positive complementarity recognises that the ICC can, and should, assist national governments to prosecute atrocity crimes.

Positive complementarity allows the court to encourage domestic jurisdictions to fulfil their own obligations to prosecute international crimes.[27] This would allow the court to undertake prosecutions only in the situation where there a State has no available domestic alternatives, thereby avoiding the situation where the Court is overwhelmed with cases.[28] According to former ICC Prosecutor Moreno-Ocampo, the absence of trials before the ICC, as a result of effectively functioning national institutions, would be a major success for the Court.[29] Positive complementarity

---

[23] Goldston (2011), *Complementarity and the ASP: Opportunities for Impact [Presentation to the Hague Working Group on the Rule of Law]*, available at https://www.justiceinitiative.org/publications/complementarity-and-assembly-state-parties-opportunities-impact (accessed 5 January 2021) p. 5. There are a number of reasons as to why complementarity is important in this context, including the fact that accountability for atrocity crimes is the law, which needs to be emphasised; that the Court needs the help of domestic legal systems to function effectively; and it can assist in promoting development of the rule of law, as well as ensure that law reform is possible.

[24] Goldston (2011), above n. 23, p. 6. Emphasis is placed in this regard on the extensive programmes that have been put in place aimed at promoting the rule of law and complementarity.

[25] Ibid; a freer flow of information would make it easier discuss complementarity in various fora where appropriate.

[26] Phillipe 2006, p. 397.

[27] Burke-White 2016, pp. 208-209.

[28] Tillier 2013, p. 508, where the author emphasises that the Role of the Court is not to open as many investigations as possible, but instead should favour national proceedings.

[29] ICC Office of the Prosecutor *Informal expert paper [The Principle of Complementarity in Practice}* ICC-01/04-01/07-1008-AnxA (30 March 2003) p. 3.

assumes that States would prefer to avoid proceedings before the ICC, as the costs of such proceedings are higher those before domestic courts.[30]

In addition, positive complementarity assumes that States do not want their citizens brought before the ICC, and that States would prefer to conduct criminal proceedings against their own citizens in order to avoid ICC proceedings.[31] At the resumed eighth session of the Assembly of States Parties in 2010, the Report of the Bureau on stocktaking: Complementarity, the Bureau of the Assembly of States Parties identified that positive complementarity could take many forms, including technical assistance, capacity building, the development of physical infrastructure and assistance with legislation.[32] In identifying the role of the ICC in these activities, the Report noted that such interventions should not result in additional resources for the Court, nor should the court become a development organisation or implementing agency.[33]

6.2.2.1 Benefits and Challenges of Positive Complementarity

According to Burke-White, positive complementarity would allow the Court to encourage national judiciaries to fulfil their own obligations under international law to prosecute international crimes, including the Geneva Conventions and the Genocide Convention.[34] Such activity could include communicating with States in which atrocities may be occurring; establishing legal and judicial training and cooperation mechanisms in order to strengthen a weak domestic justice system, and monitoring the progress of such mechanisms.[35] In addition, the Court can also utilise publicity and outreach mechanisms to increase the reputational costs for States that fail to undertake genuine prosecutions on their own. Such publicity can take the form of statements to the UN Security Council, the Assembly of States Parties, or other organisations that will condemn States for failing to prosecute atrocity crimes.[36]

The Court must however be cautious in promoting and encouraging domestic prosecution of atrocity crimes. Noting that the ICC is a legal body within an international system that is dominated by political considerations, it must work at recognising and

[30] Burke-White and Slaughter 2006, p. 341, where the authors note that there are political benefits and incentives associated with adjudicating matters domestically rather than through an international tribunal where domestic officials have little to no control over proceedings.

[31] Burke-White 2016, p. 208, where the author notes that ICC intervention into otherwise exclusively domestic criminal processes imposes considerable sovereignty costs upon national governments that States may seek to avoid by choosing to investigate and prosecute these matters themselves.

[32] ASP 2010a, paras 16–17.

[33] Ibid., para 42.

[34] Burke-White 2016, p. 207; See also Marshall 2010, p. 22, where the author notes that positive complementarity places the ICC under a duty to act to enhance the ability of States to undertake genuine investigations and prosecutions of serious international crimes.

[35] Ibid.

[36] Ibid., p. 209, where the author notes that statements to such bodies can have a significant influence on the reputational costs that the States in question may face for failing to act.

embracing the political context of its mandate and actions, while at the same time avoid being influenced by these political considerations.[37] This may include identifying and acting on diplomatic opportunities for encouraging prosecutions or arrests by domestic authorities, delaying prosecutions during politically sensitive moments until such time that the Court can be guaranteed support from national governments to complete investigations and arrests, or simply engaging or bargaining with national governments that have the resources necessary to allow the Court to carry out its mandate.[38]

6.2.2.2 Enhancing the Promotion of Positive Complementarity

The 2010 Report of the Bureau on Complementarity proposed recommendations for enhancing the complementarity principle through the application of positive complementarity at the national level.[39] In establishing the role that the Assembly should play, the report recommended:

> *The Assembly should establish a designated function within the Secretariat of the Assembly of States Parties, within existing resources, tasked with facilitating the exchange of information between the Court, States Parties, signatory States, international organizations, civil society and other stakeholders, aimed at strengthening domestic jurisdictions. The Secretariat should provide an update on progress in this regard to the Assembly of States Parties.*[40]

The Role of the Assembly of States Parties in strengthening positive complementarity was further emphasised in other international fora. A particularly notable forum was the Greentree process, a series of three meetings co-hosted by the International Centre for Transitional Justice, Denmark, and South Africa.

6.2.2.3 The Greentree Meetings

The first Greentree Meeting was held in October 2010, with it aiming to build up the momentum created at the Kampala Review Conference and to bring together high-level actors in international justice, rule of law assistance and the development sector to explore how to implement the concept of complementarity.[41] Among the subjects addressed at this meeting was the consideration of employing other mechanisms

---

[37] Burke-White 2016, p. 210, where the author notes that encouraging or threatening national governments with the possibility of international prosecution runs the risk that the Court is viewed as political.

[38] Ibid., pp. 210–211.

[39] ASP 2010a, para 54.

[40] Ibid., para 54(e).

[41] International Centre for Transitional Justice *Meeting Summary of the Retreat on "Complementarity after Kampala: The Way Forward"* (19 November 2010) available at https://www.ictj.org/sites/default/files/ICTJ-Global-Complementarity-Greentree-2010-English.pdf (accessed 15 March 2022) para 3.

and institutions that could strengthen complementarity, such as the Assembly of States Parties. Participants at the meeting identified that while the Assembly was an appropriate forum for strengthening complementarity, it was also handicapped by a lack of adequate financial resources and human capacity which heavily limited its role in this regard.[42]

The second meeting was held in December 2011 under the theme of Supporting complementarity at the national level: An integrated approach to the rule of law.[43]" Among the various topics considered in this meeting was the role that the ICC and the Assembly of States Parties could play in strengthening national capacities. While it was identified that these bodies had limited capacities and resources to strengthen the domestic capacities of States, participants did highlight several ways in which they could be of assistance. The report highlighted that a mechanism had been created within the Assembly to facilitate the exchange of information between the Court, States, civil society, and other stakeholders. The report also acknowledged that individual States could play a more active role in capacity building, with it being suggested that Assembly States pooled resources to pursue accountability for serious crimes.[44]

A third Greentree meeting, themed "Supporting complementarity at the national level: From theory to practice", was held in October 2012, organised in close consultation with the Assembly of States Parties.[45] The meeting focused on discussions surrounding the challenges and difficulties faced by States in the promotion of accountability in national jurisdictions.[46] Such challenges included a lack of infrastructure and financial resources, limited human resources and a lack of adequate training of staff.[47] The participants of the meeting recognised that in response to the issue of political will, it was necessary to adopt measures that assisted in strengthening the political will of States. Such measures included reinforcing the independence of the judiciary and prosecutors, encouraging stakeholders to provide development assistance to strengthen capacity and independence and offer political support.[48]

---

[42] Ibid., para 16.

[43] International Centre for Transitional Justice *Synthesis Report on "Supporting Complementarity at the National level: An Integrated Approach to Rule of Law"* (7–9 December 2011) available at: https://www.ictj.org/sites/default/files/ICTJ-Global-Greentree-Two-Synthesis-Report-2011.pdf (accessed 15 March 2022).

[44] Ibid., para 10.

[45] International Centre for Transitional Justice *Synthesis Report on "Supporting Complementarity at the National Level: From Theory to Practice"* (25–26 October 2012) available at: https://www.ictj.org/sites/default/files/ICTJ-Report-Greentree-III-Synthesis-ENG-2012.pdf (accessed 15 March 2022).

[46] Ibid., para 5; these challenges were analysed through cases studies on the experiences in Colombia, the Democratic Republic of the Congo, Guatemala and the Ivory Coast. The experiences in these States were highlighted with a view to looking at experiences in different contexts where assistance was being provided to national prosecutions.

[47] Meeting Summary Greentree *III* above n. 46, para 7; it was also identified that the lack of political will and difficulties concerning the prioritisation of cases were common to these situations and challenges.

[48] Ibid., para 8.

Participants also identified the various mechanisms designed to facilitate and strengthen national responses to international crimes in these regions.[49] In identifying the role played by the ICC, the meeting recognised that the Court will only deal with a small number of cases and that the primary responsibility to address atrocity crimes lies with States. In this regard, participants at the meeting identified that the ICC may be able to cooperate with domestic authorities through the provision of information and evidence, as well as through the sharing of best practices.[50] This meeting concluded by suggesting that stakeholders form an informal group to discuss the way forward on the issue of resources for assistance to support efforts towards complementarity.[51]

6.2.2.4 The Significance of Greentree for Positive Complementarity

The Greentree meetings placed much emphasis on the intervention of the international community and other stakeholders in building up the domestic criminal law capacities of States to enhance their ability to investigate and prosecute Rome Statute crimes within their territories and courts. According to Owuor, these meetings provided a valuable forum for the clarifying the link between international criminal justice and developmental agencies to promote and strengthen positive complementarity.[52] These meetings also highlighted the important role that bodies within the ICC have in developing the positive complementarity concept, particularly the Assembly of States Parties, particularly with its potential to pool resources from member states to assist in capacity building initiatives.

6.2.3 Strengthening Complementarity Activities through the Secretariat of the Assembly

The Secretariat of the Assembly of States Parties was established under Article 112 of the Rome Statute, which provides that:

> *The Assembly may establish such subsidiary bodies as may be necessary, including an independent oversight mechanism for inspection, evaluation and investigation of the Court, in order to enhance its efficiency and economy.*[53]

---

[49] Ibid., paras 14–18.

[50] Ibid., para 20.

[51] Ibid., para 24.

[52] Owuor 2017 p. 186.

[53] Rome Statute of the International Criminal Court. (17 July 1998, 2187, UNTS 3, Entry into Force, 1 July 2002) [hereinafter Rome Statute/RS], Article 112(4).

The Secretariat was established as a result of the adoption of a resolution at the second session of the Assembly in 2003.[54] Under the Annex to the resolution, the Secretariat functions to provide the Assembly and its subsidiary bodies with

> *...independent substantive servicing as well as administrative and technical assistance in the discharge of their responsibilities under the Rome Statute, where applicable by means of pooling with resources available with the Court...*[55]

These duties are further emphasised under the Rules of Procedure of the Assembly of States Parties,[56] in which specific functions were contemplated and assigned for the Secretariat:

> *... shall receive, translate, reproduce and distribute documents, reports and decisions of the Assembly, Bureau and other subsidiary bodies that may be established by the Assembly; interpret speeches made at the meetings ....; and generally, perform all other work which the Assembly or Bureau may require.*[57]

Such work required by the Assembly or Bureau may therefore also include the overseeing of positive complementarity assignments and projects.[58] This provision highlights that that the Secretariat has been entrusted with a wide range of responsibilities which may be difficult to implement, considering the limited number of resources available.

6.2.3.1 The Role of the Secretariat in Promoting Positive Complementarity

At the Kampala Review Conference, States Parties requested the Secretariat to use its existing resources to assist in the exchange of information between the Court, States Parties, and other stakeholders in order to strengthen domestic jurisdictions.[59] At the tenth session of the Assembly of States Parties, the Secretariat was mandated to work on the promotion of complementarity under two levels.

The first level, referred to as the "general level" requires the Secretariat to set up an information base relating to complementarity events; identify main complementarity actors and their roles; facilitate contacts between donor States, organisations, civil society and recipient States; and give designated actors the ability to share information. The other level, a case specific level, the Secretariat is required to adopt a proactive role of sharing and exchanging information between complementarity stakeholders within international criminal law and the donor community. Such a

---

[54] ASP 2003.

[55] Ibid., Annex, Rule 4.

[56] ASP 2002.

[57] Ibid., Rule 37.

[58] Owuor 2017, p. 226.

[59] ASP 2010b, para 10.

role would place the Secretariat at the centre of the coordination of the activities of stakeholders tasked with the implementation of positive complementarity.[60]

6.2.3.2 Limitations of the Secretariat in Fulfilling its Complementarity Mandate

Several limiting factors on the side of the Secretariat have rendered the mandate in implementing the policy of positive complementarity relatively ineffective. The most notable in this regard is the limited financial and operational resources available to the Secretariat in the form of the limited budgetary allocation from the Assembly, as well as its sharing of resources and infrastructure with the ICC.[61] Another limiting factor is the structuring of the Secretariat. While it is part of the Court structure, the Secretariat should ideally be an independent body as critics of the Court may withhold their support for the Secretariat and its programmes if perceived to be operating under the Court.[62]

The issue of constrained resources is further reinforced is that the Secretariat is funded through the budget of the ICC and has no income of its own and may not receive voluntary contributions from States or international organisations unless expressly allowed by the Assembly of States Parties.[63] The extensive mandate of the Secretariat is also another factor that may affect its role in promoting and implementing positive complementarity. As the Secretariat is tasked with assisting in multiple aspects of the mandate of the Assembly, it must stretch its limited resources in the coordination of other activities, which in turn this is disadvantageous to its work on positive complementarity. In this regard, there is also a limited number of staff available to the Secretariat for the proper performance of positive complementary activities.[64]

6.2.3.3 Strengthening the Secretariat's Positive Complementarity Mandate

As it currently stands, the Secretariat of the Assembly of States Parties does not have the tools available to it for the proper and effective implementation of positive complementarity programmes, with it being tasked to perform a variety of functions within the ICC with very limited financial, physical, and human resources. In this

[60] Owuor 2017, p. 231.

[61] Ibid., p. 232; see also ASP 2003, pre para 5, where it is provided that the Secretariat is attached to the registry to the Court and operates under the full authority of the Assembly.

[62] Ibid., p. 234.

[63] ASP 2003, Annex, Rule 9.

[64] Owuor 2017, pp. 235–236; the author identifies that an independent body with a large number of staff tasked with the specialised function of coordinating positive complementarity activities would be a preferable alternative to the current system.

regard, Owuor proposes that the current system in which activities coordinated by the Secretariat are restructured; or alternatively, an additional body with a degree of independence is set up which deals specifically with positive complementarity.[65]

Owuor recognises the need for a body with a sufficient level of independence to fund its own programmes and maintain flexibility in the implementation of specific frameworks and activities. This new body would exist independently of the ICC, its registry, and the office of the prosecutor, which will ease concerns of bias and undue influence.[66] Additionally, this proposed independent body with specialisation in positive complementarity, would have the advantage of being able to concentrate only on positive complementarity projects. This specialisation would introduce efficiency in and effective control of projects and policies relating to positive complementarity. However, the Secretariat could also be structured to cater for positive complementarity in a manner that would not require the development of a separate independent body. Considering that the Secretariat was established by way of a resolution, rather than through lengthy amendment or drafting procedures, another resolution could be swiftly passed to allow for the restructuring of the Assembly Secretariat.[67]

Considering that the recognition of new institutions for implementing international law principles is subject to the political will and considerations of the international community, any proposed independent body that is tasked with better operationalising positive complementarity would generate greater acceptance and reach among States Parties if seen to have its own budget financed through Member State contributions rather than through the budget of the ICC itself. The establishment of a new body tasked with operationalising positive complementary would be given a greater degree of independence and acceptance in realising its mandate may be possible if recognised within the Rome Statute.[68]

6.2.3.4 Challenges in Implementation

The above proposals for the better operationalisation of positive complementarity do however lie with their own risks. Most notably, effecting such change within the structure of the ICC and the Assembly of States Parties requires an elaborate legal process in which amendments to the Rome Statute are debated and negotiated among members of the Assembly. Such an amendment process is long-winded and requires a majority vote of States Parties at an Assembly meeting.[69] Owuor submits in this regard that the debate and process of amending the Rome Statute to introduce provisions for the establishment of a new body for addressing positive complementarity

[65] Ibid., pp. 238–239.

[66] Ibid., pp. 239–240.

[67] Owuor 2017, p. 241.

[68] Ibid., p. 142.

[69] RS, above n 53, Article 121(2); see also Article 121(3) which provides that where consensus cannot be reached over a proposed amendment, such amendment requires a two/thirds majority vote in favour of the proposal by States Parties.

would take up a lot of time, and such a process would not be acceptable to many States that were involved in the original drafting negotiations.[70]

Should the Assembly authorise the establishment of this new body, another problem lies with the financial implications of such a task. Although this body would be financially independent, its budget would still be sourced from the Assembly which would imply that it would still be subject to the financial constraints that the Secretariat currently faces.[71] Another concern lies with the degree of acceptance of such a body. In this regard, the widespread acceptance of an independent body may not necessarily be important for the proper functioning of a body tasked with implementing positive complementarity, but rather the ability of such a body in delivering and coordinating activities involved in the process of realising the goals of positive complementarity. Therefore, taking these concerns into consideration, an alternative suggestion is for the Secretariat to be restructured in a manner that positive complementarity is prioritised and adequate of resources are allocated in order to achieve its objectives.[72]

6.3 Pillar Three of R2P as a Tool for Strengthening the Assembly's Responses to Non-cooperation

Under the third pillar of R2P, the referral of situations to the ICC, as well as the investigation and prosecution of atrocity crimes, are all tools through which R2P can be implemented.[73] In addition, the ICC's responses to non-cooperation and referrals to the Assembly of States Parties are tools for the proper implementation of the third pillar. The *Assembly Procedures Relating to Non-cooperation* and the *Toolkit for the implementation of the Informal Dimension of the Assembly Procedures Relating to Non-cooperation* are examples of the various responses to non-cooperation available to the Assembly. These responses can be divided into two forms of compliance mechanisms which can be associated with interventions under pillar three of R2P.

The first set of compliance mechanisms are punitive mechanisms. Such mechanisms aim to punish or shame a State into compliance following a breach of a duty or obligation to cooperate and enables the application of sanctions regimes and formal determinations of non-compliance. This compliance mechanism is usually operated according to specific legal rules and is the subject of considerable legal debates.[74] The

[70] Owuor 2017, pp. 239–240, where the author notes that such a process "would take years"; and at 242 where the establishment of such a body would be a "long, drawn out process"; RS, above n 53, Article 121(4), which provides that an amendment will enter into force for all States Parties one year after seven eighths of States have deposited instruments of ratification or acceptance with the UN Secretary-General.

[71] Owuor 2017, p. 240.

[72] Ibid., p. 242.

[73] UNGA 2009, para 53.

[74] Hunter 2016, p. 368.

formal responses to non-cooperation found in the *Assembly Procedures Relating to Non-cooperation* and the various steps that must be taken to implement such procedures can be associated with this compliance mechanism as well as actions under pillar three.[75]

The second set of compliance mechanisms, known as managerial mechanisms, aim to prevent instances of non-cooperation or encourage compliance with cooperation obligations before a breach is realised. These mechanisms function by addressing the challenges faced by States in complying with the requests of a specific regime through support systems such as professional networks and transparency actions. These mechanisms are usually not contained in binding legal instruments and more commonly fall under softer policy initiatives.[76] The informal responses to non-cooperation found in the Assembly Procedures,[77] as well as the various resources and templates contained in the Bureau Toolkit,[78] can be seen as interventions under managerial mechanisms as well as interventions under the third pillar.

While the Assembly has set up several procedures that contribute to the effective implementation of responses to non-cooperation, this book has identified that these measures have not been sufficient and additional tools under general international law are needed to fill the gap and assist in developing a stricter sanctions mechanism.[79] In the previous chapter, it was identified that the failure of a State to cooperate with the ICC amounts to an internationally wrongful act entailing the international responsibility of that State; and that the remedies available under the Articles on State Responsibility and the Conclusions on Peremptory Norms can be applied to situations of non-cooperation before the ICC.

In recognising the collective nature of the obligation to bring breaches of peremptory norms to an end,[80] the ILC's commentary notes that other international organisations may also adopt measures consistent with international law, and within their mandate to bring such breaches to an end.[81] In this regard, the Assembly is therefore required, as per the conclusions on peremptory norms, to act within its mandate to assist in bringing breaches of peremptory norms to an end. Alongside the obligation to bring breaches to an end, the Assembly can also address instances of non-cooperation

---

[75] ASP 2018a, paras 14(a)–(g)

[76] Hunter 2016, p. 368.

[77] ASP 2018a, paras 18, 20 and 22.

[78] ASP 2018b, paras 11–27 (obtaining and sharing of information relating to the travel of ICC suspects); paras 28–42 (preventing instances of non-cooperation); paras 43–47 (promoting awareness of issues relating to non-cooperation).

[79] Babaian 2018, p. 97.

[80] ILC Seventy-Third Session Report of the International Law Commission [Chapter IV(E): Peremptory Norms of General International Law: Text of the Draft Conclusions and Legal Consequences of Peremptory Norms of General International Law (jus cogens)] A/77/10 (18 April–3 June & 4 July–5 August 2022) Conclusion 19(1).

[81] ILC Seventy-Third Session Report of the International Law Commission [Chapter IV(E): Peremptory Norms of General International Law: Text of the Draft Conclusions and Legal Consequences of Peremptory Norms of General International Law (jus cogens)] A/77/10 (18 April - 3 June & 4 July – 5 August 2022) Commentary on Conclusion 19, para 8.

through the obligations of non-recognition and non-assistance.[82] In addition, other consequences relating to the international responsibility of States not covered by the conclusions also apply within the framework of the Assembly's powers.[83]

The section to follow will apply the frameworks recognised by the ILC to the Assembly's frameworks for addressing instances of non-cooperation. This section will not look to proposing amendments to the Statute as this would require extensive negotiations and a high threshold for acceptance and ratification within the Assembly.[84] Therefore, while the Assembly's law and practice on non-cooperation could benefit from amendments to the Statute, development of these frameworks can also be achieved without resorting to amendment.[85]

6.4 Developing Remedies for Strengthening the Assembly's Responses to Non-cooperation

Looking at the provisions in the Rome Statute, as well as those developed through the Assembly of States parties for enforcing cooperation and responding to non-cooperation, one can observe that these measures have been ineffective.[86] This suggests that the Assembly is not capable of handling instances of non-cooperation in a convincing manner.[87] There is therefore the need for existing remedies for non-cooperation to be strengthened, and for further remedies to be developed should existing remedies still be ineffective.

This section will look at frameworks that can be adopted within already existing structures of the Assembly. Such possible frameworks for enforcing cooperation within the ASP could take the form of various measures or administrative sanctions against an uncooperative State. These measures could be executed through the Assembly or through a specialised committee within the Assembly.[88] Examples of responses to non-cooperation by the Assembly of States Parties include: approaching the ICJ through contentious or advisory proceedings; warnings; loss of the right to field candidates; removal of candidates; loss of voting rights; administrative fines; suspension from the Assembly; and termination of a State's membership from the

[82] Ibid., Conclusion 19(2).

[83] Ibid., Conclusion 19(4) of the Conclusions on Peremptory Norms *ibid*; see also Commentary on Conclusion 19 at pars 18 and 19; Articles on the Responsibility of States for Internationally Wrongful Acts (2001) A/RES/56/1.

[84] Clark and Heinze 2022, p. 2874.

[85] Sluiter 2018, p. 399; the author also notes that it will be difficult to attempt to amend the Statute.

[86] Ntahiraja 2017, p. 30, where the author notes that the Assembly's mechanisms for addressing non-cooperation are "legally weak and highly ineffective in practice."

[87] Sluiter 2020, p. 312.

[88] Ibid., p. 313.

ICC. This section will discuss the possibility and appropriateness of each of these proposed responses through the lens of general international law and the Rome Statute, in line with the principles entrenched within the third pillar of R2P and general international law.

6.4.1 Approaching the ICJ

As noted in a previous chapter, it was identified that issues relating to non-cooperation could also be addressed through the Rome Statute's provisions on the settlement of disputes relating to the interpretation or application of the Statute.[89] In this context, there lies the possibility that the Assembly may approach the ICJ to settle disputes relating to non-cooperation either through contentious proceedings or through advisory proceedings.[90] Under the Articles on State Responsibility, judicial settlement is envisaged as one of the tools through which the responsibility of a State can be invoked under Article 42.[91]

6.4.1.1 Contentious Proceedings

With regard to contentious proceedings, the ICJ Statute provides that the Court has jurisdiction over legal disputes concerning the interpretation of a treaty, any question of international law, the existence of any fact that would constitute a breach of an international obligation, as well as the nature or extent of the reparations to be made for such a breach.[92] A recent example of such proceedings are the disputes between Ukraine and Russia, and South Africa and Israel in the context of breaches of the Genocide convention.[93] Both of these case are still under consideration and provisional measures have been ordered by the Court in response to the activities in Ukraine and Palestine.[94] In both of these cases, the complainant States were confirmed to have standing before the ICJ on the basis that each State Party to the

---

[89] RS, above n. 53, Article 119(2)

[90] Clark and Meisenberg 2022, p. 2847.

[91] Crawford 2002, p. 258, at para 7.

[92] Article 36(2) of the Statute of the International Court of Justice 1945.

[93] ICJ, Allegations of Genocide under the Convention on the Prevention and Punishment of the Crime of Genocide [Ukraine v Russian Federation] Request for the Indication of Provisional Measures (Order of 16 March 2022) ICJ Rep 2022, 211; ICJ, Case Concerning the Application of the Convention on the Prevention and Punishment of the Crime of Genocide in the Gaza Strip [South Africa v Israel] Request for the Indication of Provisional Measures (Order of 26 January 2024) General List. No. 192.

[94] Ibid., para 86; such measures include: immediate suspension of Russian military operations in the territory of Ukraine; that Russia and any organisations and persons subject to its control or direction take no steps in the furtherance of such military operations; and that both parties refrain from taking any action which might aggravate or extend the dispute before the Court or make it more difficult to resolve; *South Africa v Israel,* Ibid., para 86, such measures include: Israel is to take all measures

Genocide Convention had a common interest to ensure the prevention, suppression and punishment of genocide, by committing themselves to fulfilling the obligations within the Convention. Such a common interest would imply that these obligations are owed to any State Party to all other States parties to ensure compliance.[95]

In this context, the Assembly of States Parties would encourage States to agree to refer a particular issue, such as non-cooperation to the ICJ. This is so that measures may be determined by the Court to address such a breach of obligations, through the application of remedies under the Articles on State Responsibility and the Conclusions on Peremptory Norms.[96]

6.4.1.2 Advisory Proceedings

Regarding advisory Proceedings, the ICJ Statute provides that the Court may give an advisory opinion on any legal question at the request of whatever body may be authorised by, or in accordance with the UN Charter to make a request.[97] In addition, the UN Charter provides that the General Assembly or the Security Council may request the ICJ to give an advisory opinion on any legal question.[98] The Charter also provides that other UN Organs and specialised agencies authorised by the General Assembly may also request advisory opinions of the Court on legal questions arising within the scope of their activities.[99]

Looking at the role of the Assembly of States Parties in the settlement of disputes, Clark and Meisenberg note that the Assembly may want to get legal advice on the scope of its activities.[100] However, there are limitations to which organizations other than the UN can make use of the advisory opinion option. This is recognised in the *Nuclear Weapons Advisory Opinion*, where the Court was tasked with determining whether it could give an advisory opinion on a question posed by the World Health

---

within its power to prevent the commission of acts of genocide, ensure that its military does not commit any acts of genocide, take measures within its power to prevent and punish the direct and public incitement to commit genocide, take immediate measures to enable the provision of urgently needed services and humanitarian assistance, take measures to prevent the destruction of evidence of genocide, and submit a report on all measures taken to give effect to the order.

[95] *Ukraine v Russian Federation,* Ibid., para 56; *South Africa v Israel,* Ibid., para 33.

[96] Clark and Meiseberg 2022, p. 2852.

[97] Article 65(1) of the ICJ Statute, above n. 93.

[98] The Charter of the United Nations (26 June 1945, 1 UNTS XVI, Entry into Force 24 October 1945) [UN Charter], Article 96(1).

[99] Ibid., Article 96(2); see also International Court of Justice *Organs and Agencies Authorized to request advisory opinions* available at: https://www.icj-cij.org/en/organs-agencies-authorized (accessed 1 September 2022) where specialised agencies authorised to request advisory opinions include the International Labour Organisation, the World Health Organisation, the International Monetary Fund and the United Nations Industrial Development Organisation.

[100] Clark and Meisenberg 2022, p. 2852.

Organisation as to whether the use of nuclear weapons by a State was a breach of its obligations under international law, including the constitution of the WHO.[101]

The Court held that three conditions must be satisfied for a body to request an advisory opinion: that the body be authorised under the Charter to request opinions; that the opinion requested must be on a legal question; and this question must be one arising within the scope of the activities of the body requesting the advisory opinion.[102] While the Court recognised that the WHO was authorised to request advisory opinions;[103] and that the question posed did constitute a legal question;[104] it found that the question did not arise within the scope of the activities of the WHO.[105] From this the Court found that it was unable to give the advisory opinion requested of it.[106]

Another difficulty is whether the Assembly or any other ICC organ can be considered as a UN Organ or one of the specialised agencies within the meaning of the UN Charter. If it cannot be regarded as one, then it cannot be authorised to ask directly for advisory opinions on its own behalf.[107] Noting that the Rome Statute proclaims the ICC as an in independent Court,[108] as well as the fact that the relationship between the UN and the ICC is regulated through a separate agreement,[109] one cannot regard the ICC as a UN Organ.[110]

While a general authorisation to request an advisory opinion may be difficult, a possible solution may be for the General Assembly to adopt a resolution that asks the ICJ a question of interest to the ICC through the Assembly's own powers to request.[111] Looking at the jurisprudence of the ICJ, it appears that the Court appears to be more willing to comply with a request for an advisory opinion that is brought forward by the General Assembly.[112] Meisenberg and Clark note that Article 96 empowers the General Assembly to ask for the ICJ's opinion on any legal question

---

[101] ICJ Legality of the Use by a State of Nuclear Weapons in Armed Conflict Advisory Opinion of 8 July 1996. ICJ Rep 1996 66 para 1.

[102] Ibid., para 10.

[103] Ibid., para 12.

[104] Ibid., para 16.

[105] Ibid., paras 18–31.

[106] Ibid., para 32.

[107] Clark and Meisenberg 2022, p. 2853.

[108] RS, above n. 53, pre para 9.

[109] Ibid., Article 2; see also the Negotiated Relationship Agreement Between the International Criminal Court and the United Nations Resolution ICC-ASP/3/Res.1 (2004).

[110] Clark and Meisenberg 2022, p. 2853; the authors also note that the ICC was created by a free-standing treaty and not through a decision or amendment to the UN Charter.

[111] See e.g. UN General Assembly Study of the Question of the Relationship of the International Atomic Energy Agency to the United Nations, Prepared by the Secretary-General in Consultation with the Advisory Committee on the Peaceful Uses of Atomic Energy at its Meetings from 27 March to 2 April 1956 A/3122, at para 15 which held that the General Assembly should take action to enable a legal question arising within the scope of the activities of the International Atomic Agency to be submitted to the ICJ for an advisory opinion.

[112] ICJ, Reservations to the Convention on the Prevention and Punishment of the Crime of Genocide Advisory Opinion of 28 May 1951 ICJ Rep 1951 15; Certain Expenses of the United Nations

and that there is no language that suggests that it may only be related to a question within the scope of that organisation's own activities.[113]

In the *Chagos Archipelago Advisory Opinion*,[114] the ICJ had to address whether the question posed by the General Assembly would assist it in the proper exercise of its functions.[115] The Court held on this specific legal issue that it could not decline to answer questions posed to it by the General Assembly on such grounds as such a determination is up to the requesting organ.[116] Such a question has also been addressed in previous advisory opinions.[117] Therefore, it may be possible for the General Assembly to ask a question which may be of little interest to it, but of crucial interest to the ICC and the Assembly of States parties as part of the UN Family.

6.4.2 Warnings

Looking at the responses to non-cooperation contained in the *Assembly Procedures Relating to Non-Cooperation* and the *Bureau Toolkit*, the various responses and templates contained in these documents place much emphasis on reminding States of their obligation to cooperate with the Court, while not really containing more coercive communications that reprimand or warn States against their actions. There is therefore a need for more coercive communications between States and the Assembly

(Article 17, Paragraph 2, of the Charter) Advisory Opinion of 20 July 1962 ICJ Rep 1962 151; Legality of the Use by a State of Nuclear Weapons in Armed Conflict Advisory Opinion of 8 July 1996. ICJ Rep 1996 226; ICJ, Legal Consequences of the Construction of a Wall in the Occupied Palestinian Territory Advisory Opinion of 9 July 2004 ICJ Rep. 2004 136; ICJ, Legal Consequences Arising from the Policies and Practices of Israel in the Occupied Palestinian Territory, including East Jerusalem, Advisory Opinion of 19 July 2024. General List No. 186.

[113] Clark and Meisenberg 2022, p. 2853.

[114] ICJ Legal Consequences of the Separation of the Chagos Archipelago from Mauritius in 1965, Advisory Opinion of 25 February 2019, ICJ Rep. 2019 95.

[115] Ibid., para 75, where the Court noted that there were differing opinions by participants to the advisory opinion as to whether the opinion requested would assist the General Assembly in the proper exercise of its functions.

[116] ICJ Legal Consequences of the Separation of the Chagos Archipelago from Mauritius in 1965, Advisory Opinion of 25 February 2019, ICJ Rep. 2019 95, paras 76–78.

[117] See e.g., Legality of the Use by a State of Nuclear Weapons in Armed Conflict, Advisory Opinion of 8 July 1996. ICJ Rep 1996 226, para 16, where the Court held that the General Assembly has the right to decide for itself on the usefulness of an opinion in light of its own needs; ICJ, Legal Consequences of the Construction of a Wall in the Occupied Palestinian Territory. Advisory Opinion of 9 July 2004 ICJ Rep. 2004 136, para 73, where the Court held that it could not substitute its assessment of the opinion requested for that of the organ seeking the opinion.

concerning issues relating to non-cooperation, in line with the obligation of non-recognition within the conclusions on peremptory norms, that convey to States that particular consequences flow from a breach of a peremptory norm.[118]

According to Akande and De Souza Dias, in the context of existing referrals of non-cooperation, the distribution of open letters or notifications may be helpful in deterring States from failing to cooperate with the Court. These communications should remind States of their cooperation obligations, as well as warn about the specific measures that the Assembly could adopt in response to the relevant instance of non-cooperation and the consequences of continued non-cooperation. These public letters should also be published on the ICC website and social media platforms to spread awareness of visits to States by ICC suspects.[119]

However, as noted above, the Assembly has not proven itself to have effectively taken up measures to address non-cooperation and has therefore failed to execute its responsibilities under the third pillar of R2P. States are therefore not deterred by the initiatives developed by the Assembly in response to their failure to cooperate. Therefore, while reminding States of their cooperation obligations towards the Court, and the consequences of failing to do, so may be helpful in strengthening their obligation to cooperate, current practice highlights that such communications may not be effective without more coercive communications that leave very little room for discretion within the Assembly's sessions where non-cooperation is being addressed.[120]

6.4.3 Administrative Fines

Another way to discourage non-cooperation is for the Assembly of States Parties to consider the appropriateness of economic sanctions against the non-cooperating State.[121] Such sanctions are covered by the rules on State responsibility where States responsible for an internationally wrongful act are required to make full reparations for the injury caused by the act.[122] While restitution and compensation may not be ideal tools for repairing the legal situation caused by the failure to cooperate with the ICC, the payment of symbolic damages through satisfaction may be a well suited potential remedy against a non-cooperating State Party.[123]

---

118 ILC Seventy-Third Session *Report of the International Law Commission [Chapter IV(E): Peremptory Norms of General International Law: Text of the Draft Conclusions and Legal Consequences of Peremptory Norms of General International Law (jus cogens)]* A/77/10 (18 April–3 June & 4 July–5 August 2022), Commentary on Conclusion 19, para 17.

119 Akande and de Souza Dias 2019, p. 12.

120 Sluiter and Talontsi 2016, p. 108, where the authors highlight that each new instance of a judicial finding of non-cooperation without a credible response, increases and confirms the impression that no consequences will come about from refusing to cooperate with the Court.

121 Kress and Prost 2022, p. 2490.

122 Article 34 of the Articles on State Responsibility.

123 Ibid., Article 37(1); Crawford 2002, p. 233 at para 6.

The Rome Statute provides that the funds of the Court and the Assembly of States Parties are retrieved through, among other sources, assessed contributions made by States Parties.[124] These contributions are assessed in accordance with an agreed scale, based on a scale adopted by the UN for its regular budget and adjusted in accordance with specific principles on which that scale is based.[125] As the Assembly of State's Parties is empowered to consider and decide the budget of the Court,[126] it may therefore be able to consider provisions that regulate payment of fines by States that have failed to cooperate with the requests of the Court. This could be done in the form of an increase in the annual contributions made by the State Party to the Court.[127] The proceeds from the additional funds retrieved from the State could then be transferred to the Trust Fund for Victims, which uses money and property collected through fines or forfeiture for the benefit of victims of crimes within the jurisdiction of the Court.[128] Alternatively, a separate trust fund could be established to manage and accept the payment of increased contributions.[129]

While this penalty may be useful in deterring States from failing to follow through with their obligations towards the Court, consideration must be made as to the limited financial resources of States Parties and the potential inability of States to pay increased contributions for the failure to cooperate with the requests of the Court. Under the Articles on State Responsibility, satisfaction shall not be out of proportion to the injury and may not take a form that humiliates the responsible State.[130] Therefore, in order to avoid the situation where States are expected to pay excessive penalties for the failure to cooperate, there would be a need to place limits on the amount that States would pay as part of their increased annual contribution that is consistent with the principle of the equality of States.[131]

6.4.4 Loss of Participation Rights in Assembly Decisions

The Assembly of States parties rely on decision-making mechanisms in order to function effectively. Such decision-making is made possible by the participation of ICC States Parties at Assembly sessions. This section will evaluate whether remedies that affect a State's participation or membership in an international organisation may

[124] RS, above n. 53, Article 115(a).

[125] Ibid., Article 117; see also Halff et al. 2022, pp. 2840–2841, where the authors highlight that the capacity of States to pay contributions to the Court is measured by means of estimates of a State's gross domestic product, adjusted in consideration of other financial matters within that State.

[126] RS, above n. 53, Article 112(2)(d)

[127] Sluiter 2020, p. 313.

[128] RS, above n. 53, Article 79.

[129] Crawford 2002, p. 233 at para 5.

[130] Article 37(3) of the Articles on State Responsibility.

[131] Crawford 2002, p. 234 at para 8, which highlights that excessive demands in the past have identified the need to impose limits on the measures that can be implemented within this remedy.

be effective consequences for responding to non-cooperation. Such remedies include the loss of a State's right to vote, the suspension of the right to nominate candidates for election to the Court, and the suspension or expulsion of States as members of the Assembly.

In the commentaries to the conclusions on peremptory norms, the ILC highlights that there are numerous examples of decisions by international organisations that illustrate the duty to cooperate to bring serious breaches to an end that are widely recognised as arising from peremptory norms. Such decisions include resolutions that establish accountability mechanisms to address such breaches that take form of suspension of a State's membership rights to an international organisation.[132] This can be illustrated by the UN General Assembly's decision in 2022 to suspend Russia's membership to the Human Rights Council as a consequence of its military activities in Ukraine.[133]

6.4.4.1 Loss of the Right to Vote

The Rome Statute provides that each State Party shall have one vote and emphasises that every effort shall be made to reach decisions by consensus in the Assembly and in the Bureau.[134] Where consensus cannot be reached, decisions on matters of substance must be approved by a two thirds majority of those present and voting; [135] while decisions on matters of procedure shall be taken by a simple majority of States Parties present and voting.[136] Like the ICC, many other international organisations rely on the cooperation of its members in order to function effectively and have developed various mechanisms to respond to and sanction Member States that do not fulfil the obligations expected of them. This includes the imposition of various administrative sanctions that effect the influence and participation of States in the decisions of the organisation.

For example, the UN Charter provides that where a UN Member State is in arrears of its payment of its contribution to the organisation, that State loses its right to vote in the UN General Assembly for a certain period of time.[137] The Rome Statute also contains a similar provision which suspends the voting rights of a State Party if they have been found to be in arrears in the payment of its financial contributions towards the costs of the Court.[138] According to Sluiter, a similar measure could be introduced

---

[132] ILC Seventy-Third Session *Report of the International Law Commission [Chapter IV(E): Peremptory Norms of General International Law: Text of the Draft Conclusions and Legal Consequences of Peremptory Norms of General International Law (jus cogens)]* A/77/10 (18 April–3 June and 4 July–5 August 2022), Commentary on Conclusion 19, pp. 73–74, para 9.

[133] UNGA 2022, para 1, "...decides to suspend the rights of membership in the Human Rights Council of the Russian Federation".

[134] RS, above, n. 53, Article 112(7).

[135] Ibid., Article 112(7)(a).

[136] Ibid., Article 112(7)(b).

[137] UN Charter, above, n. 99, Article 19.

[138] RS, above, n. 53, Article 112(8).

and applied in the case of instances of non-cooperation, where a State Party loses the right to vote within the Assembly for a specified period of time.[139]

6.4.4.2 Suspension of the Right to Nominate Candidates for Election to the Court

The Rome Statute provides that nominations of candidates for election to the Court may be made by any State Party.[140] Each State Party may put forward one candidate for any given election who is a national of any State Party to the Statute.[141] As the ICC is reliant on States to function effectively, non-cooperation therefore has a negative effect on the international reputation of the Court as an effective international tribunal. Therefore, a State's failure to cooperate with a request of the Court has a negative effect on its reputation among the Court and other States Parties.[142]

As the Statute provides that judges shall be chosen from among persons of high moral character, impartiality, and integrity,[143] a State Party with an unfavourable reputation within the Court would be assumed to be less influential in decision-making processes such as the election of judges. As a consequence of a State's failure to cooperate, there may lie the possibility that a non-cooperating State's right to nominate a candidate for an ICC elected position may be suspended or removed as a result of its conduct.[144] While the Assembly's voting history appears to have chosen candidates for election from States that are in a favourable position with the Court, a candidate from the Democratic Republic of the Congo was elected successfully as a judge in December 2014,[145] the same year of the DRC's non-cooperation decision.[146]

6.4.4.3 Suspension of Expulsion of a State Party

A more serious response against non-cooperation could take the form of the non-cooperating State having its membership to the Court suspended or completely terminated. Apart from the provisions relating to non-cooperation, the Rome Statute does not prescribe a procedure that should be followed in response to its breach. Therefore, the general rules relating to the law of treaties may provide a solution. As the ICC

[139] Sluiter 2018, p. 400.

[140] RS, above, n. 53, Article 36(4)(a)

[141] RS, above, n. 53, Article 36(4)(b)

[142] Jones 2016, p. 194.

[143] RS, above, n. 53, Article 36(3)(a).

[144] Sluiter 2020, p. 313.

[145] Assembly of States Parties 2014—Election of Six Judges—Results (16 December 2014) available at: https://asp.icc-cpi.int/elections/judges/2014/Nominations/2014-JE-results (accessed 15 September 2022).

[146] ICC, Prosecutor v Omar Hassan Ahmad Al Bashir [Decision on the Cooperation of the Democratic Republic of the Congo Regarding Omar Al Bashir's Arrest and Surrender to the Court] 9 April 2014, ICC-02/05-01/09 195.

is an institution created by a treaty, non-cooperation by States is a material breach of a treaty as it is the violation of a provision essential to the accomplishment of the object or purpose of the treaty.[147] As a consequence of a material breach of a multilateral treaty by one of the parties, the other parties may unanimously agree to suspend or terminate the operation of the treaty in the relations between them and the non-cooperating State.[148] Any State Party may invoke the breach of a treaty obligation as a ground for suspension or expulsion if the treaty is of a character that a material breach of its provisions by one party has a radical effect on the position of every party with respect to the further performance of their treaty obligations.[149]

According to Bekou, the suspension or expulsion of a non-cooperating State Party to the Rome Statute would therefore be an expected course of action.[150] However, Kress and Prost hold the opinion that resort to suspension or expulsion of a non-cooperating State should not be an option, considering the nature and overall humanitarian goal of the Rome Statute.[151] Therefore, it is in the best interests of both the ICC and its States Parties to compel a non-cooperating State to fulfil its obligations under the treaty, which cannot be achieved by suspending or expelling that State from the treaty.[152]

6.4.4.4 Implications for Decision-making Processes within the Assembly

While measures for restricting or suspending the participation of a State Party in the decision-making processes of the Assembly may be a useful consequence against the failure to cooperate, consideration should be made as to the effect that such a remedy may have in decision-making processes. There therefore lies the risk that in suspending the right to vote in Assembly sessions, the Assembly may not be able to obtain the necessary majority required from States in important decisions before it. There also lies the risk that any decision made to limit the participation rights of States within the Assembly may cause discontent among States Parties, which may therefore have the effect of alienating the Court from its members.[153]

---

[147] Vienna Convention on the Law of Treaties (23 May 1969 UN Doc A/CONF.39/11/Add.2, Entry into force, 27 January 1980), Article 60(3)(b).

[148] Ibid., Article 60(2)(a)(i).

[149] Ibid., Article 60(2)(c).

[150] Bekou 2019, p. 926.

[151] Kress and Prost 2022, p. 2490.

[152] Bekou 2019, p. 926.

[153] Sarkin 2020, p. 44.

6.4.5 *Analysing the Adoption of Additional Remedies for Addressing Non-cooperation*

According to Bekou, the consideration of new methods on how to support, strengthen and improve the ICC and the Rome Statute system as a whole is key to the success of the Court. The author emphasises that there should be a focus on the possible combined effect that the Rome Statute's frameworks and the workings of the Assembly of States Parties has on tackling instances of non-cooperation and ensuring better cooperation in future situations.[154]

In determining whether the development of additional remedies are appropriate, various factors should be considered including issues relating to fairness and proportionality, as well as various political considerations. One important factor to consider is the degree to which the non-cooperation has undermined the functioning of the Court, and whether there lies the possibility that non-cooperation can be achieved.[155] Another relevant factor includes the cooperation history of the State that has failed to cooperate with the requests of the Court. Chad and Djibouti are examples of States that have failed to cooperate with the Court on more than one occasion and have been the subject of multiple decisions of non-cooperation.[156] Therefore a more severe response would be needed in response to the actions, or lack thereof, of those States compared to those States who are "first-time offenders",[157] such as Nigeria or South Africa.[158]

---

[154] Bekou 2019, p. 937.

[155] Sluiter 2020, p. 313; the author also notes that the failure to execute an arrest warrant, with the knowledge that there is probably no possibility of cooperation being provided at a later opportunity, should rank as a serious instance of non-cooperation which substantially undermines the functioning of the Court, therefore justifying a more severe reaction compared to other forms of non-cooperation.

[156] ICC, Prosecutor v Omar Hassan Ahmad Al Bashir [Decision pursuant to article 87(7) of the Rome Statute on the Refusal of the Republic of Chad to comply with the cooperation requests issued by the Court with respect to the arrest and surrender of Omar Hassan Ahmad Al Bashir]. 13 December 2011, ICC-02/05-01/09-140; Prosecutor v Omar Hassan Ahmad Al Bashir [Decision informing the United Nations Security Council and the Assembly of the States Parties to the Rome Statute about Omar Al-Bashir's recent visit to Djibouti], 12 May 2011, ICC-02/05-01/09; Prosecutor v Omar Hassan Ahmad Al Bashir [Decision on the Non-compliance of the Republic of Chad with the cooperation requests issued by the Court regarding the Arrest and Surrender of Omar Hassan Ahmad Al Bashir], 26 March 2013, ICC-02/05-01/09-151; Prosecutor v Omar Hassan Ahmad Al Bashir [Decision on the Non-compliance by the Republic of Djibouti with the Request to Arrest and Surrender Omar Al-Bashir to the Court and Referring the matter to the United Nations Security Council and the Assembly of States Parties to the Rome Statute], 11 July 2016, ICC-02/05-01/09-266.

[157] Sluiter 2020, p. 313.

[158] Prosecutor v Omar Hassan Ahmad Al-Bashir [Decision on the Cooperation of the Federal Republic of Nigeria Regarding Omar Al-Bashir's Arrest and Surrender to the Court, 5 September 2013. ICC-02/05-01/09-159, para 13, where the Pre-trial Chamber determined that it was not necessary to refer Nigeria's non-cooperation further and merely reminded it of its obligations towards the Court; Prosecutor v Omar Hassan Ahmad Al Bashir [Decision Under Article 87(7) of the Rome Statute on the non-compliance by South Africa with the request by the Court for the arrest and surrender of Omar Al-Bashir] (6 July 2017), ICC-02/05-01/09-302 para 136.

In addition, consideration of remedies for addressing non-cooperation should also be in line with principles entrenched within the third pillar of R2P. While it has been established that this pillar is associated with the use of force, a previous chapter identified that the third pillar can also be implemented through the application of less coercive measures aimed at discouraging and deterring non-compliance with international obligations.[159] However, an issue that may face the Court and the Assembly in the establishment of mandates and tools is the potential effect that these developments will have on the relationship between States and the Court. A lenient approach to non-cooperation may have the effect of failing to encourage States to cooperate with the Court, while also undermining the image of the ICC as a strong institution that can effectively respond to instances of non-cooperation.[160] On the other hand, non-cooperation mandates and frameworks that are too strong may have the effect of further alienating the Court from the international community, especially considering the strained relationship between the Court and its African States Parties.[161] Therefore, the Assembly of States Parties should balance its mandate for addressing non-cooperation along a duty not to discourage States Parties from reconsidering their membership to the Court.[162]

6.5 Conclusion

This present chapter has identified that the Assembly of States Parties, as the political organ of the ICC, shares some links with the responsibility to protect doctrine. As R2P-based language is included within resolutions at the Assembly's annual sessions, it is clear that this doctrine is accepted by the ICC and its States Parties. In the implementation of R2P within the Rome Statute system, the assembly's efforts at promoting ratification of the Statute, State cooperation, capacity building and responding to instances of non-cooperation all constitute R2P action within the scope of the three-pillar framework. In addition, additional frameworks outside the scope of the Rome Statute system, aimed at addressing the international responsibility of States and putting an end to impunity, can all assist the Assembly in implementing the responsibility to protect.

This chapter has also identified that the Assembly, as an organ of the ICC, is reliant on the efforts of States and the international community for promoting cooperation and deterring possible instances of non-cooperation. Finally, this chapter has also identified the potential routes that can be taken to develop the Assembly's

159 UNGA 2012, para 29.

160 Jones 2016, p. 198; the author also notes that tolerance or ignorance of non-cooperation may be more damaging to the Court than the actual responses to non-cooperation.

161 Barnes 2011, p. 1617; see also Sluiter 2020, p. 312, where the author recognises that a more robust approach enforcement within the Assembly may create tensions and problems.

162 Sluiter 2018, p. 400; however, the author is also of the view that the current rate of non-cooperation is far more of a threat to the Court than the potential loss of States Parties.

responses to non-cooperation and has put forward a range of potential responses to non-cooperation that the Assembly could adopt that may strengthen its non-cooperation arsenal. One can therefore determine that the application of R2P, as well as principles entrenched in general international law, within the frameworks of the Assembly of States Parties, could assist in strengthening its procedures for addressing and remedying instances of non-cooperation that have been referred to it.

In an attempt to strengthen the institutions tasked with responding to instances of non-cooperation, this book now turns to analyse whether the UN Security Council, as the body holding the primary responsibility for the maintenance of international peace and security,[163] can benefit from the application of R2P and general international law frameworks in strengthening the interactions between the Security Council and the ICC in responding to non-cooperation. The next chapter aims to investigate how the Security Council can be better equipped to address and remedy instances of non-cooperation that have been communicated to it. In particular, the chapter will investigate how R2P can be applied to assist in strengthening the Security Council within the ICC's own cooperation frameworks, as well as within its own mechanisms under the UN Charter for responding to non-cooperation.

References

Akande D, de Souza Dias T (2019) Cooperation with the ICC: What the Security Council and ASP Must Do. ISS Africa Report 1–15, available at: https://issafrica.s3.amazonaws.com/site/uploads/ar15.pdf (accessed 12 October 2024).

Ambach P (2022) Article 112, Assembly of States Parties. In: Ambos K (ed) Rome Statute of the International Criminal Court: Article-by-Article Commentary. Beck/Nomos/Hart, Munich, pp 2767e2811.

Assembly of States Parties (ASP) (2002) First Session Official Records Part III C Rules of Procedure of the Assembly of States Parties ICC-ASP/1/3.

Assembly of States Parties (ASP) (2003) Second Session Resolution on Establishment of the Permanent Secretariat of the Assembly of States Parties to the International Criminal Court ICC-ASP/2/Res.3.

Assembly of States Parties (ASP) (2005) Fourth Session [Strengthening the International Criminal Court and the Assembly of States Parties] Resolution ICC-ASP/4/Res.4.

Assembly of States Parties (ASP) (2010a) Resumed Eighth Session Report of the Bureau on stock-taking: Complementarity [Taking Stock of the Principle of Complementarity: Bridging the Impunity Gap] ICC-ASP/8/51.

Assembly of States Parties (ASP) (2010b) Ninth Session Report of the Bureau on Complementarity ICC-ASP/9/26

Assembly of States Parties (ASP) (2014) Thirteenth Session Report of the Bureau on Complementarity ICC-ASP/13/30.

Assembly of States Parties (ASP) (2018a) Seventeenth Session Strengthening the International Criminal Court and the Assembly of States Parties Resolution ICC-ASP/17/Res.5 [Annex II Assembly Procedures Relating to Non-Cooperation]

---

163 UN Charter, above, n. 99, Article 24.; ICISS 2001, para 6.7.
Ibid., para 1.10.

Assembly of States Parties (ASP) (2018b) Seventeenth Session Report of the Bureau on non-cooperation [Annex: Toolkit for the Implementation of the Informal dimension of the Assembly procedures relating to non-cooperation] ICC-ASP/17/31. Annex III.
Babaian S (2018) The International Criminal Court—An International Criminal World Court. Springer International Publishing AG, Cham.
Barnes GP (2011) The International Criminal Courts Ineffective Enforcements Mechanisms: The Indictment of President Omar Al Bashir. Fordham International Law Journal 34(6): 1584–1619.
Behrmann C (2016) Strengthening the International Criminal Court Cooperation Regime from the European Union's Perspective. In: Bekou O, Birkett DJ (eds) Cooperation and the International Criminal Court: Perspectives from Theory and Practice. Brill, Leiden, pp 297–317.
Bekou O (2019) Dealing with Non-cooperation at the ICC: Towards a More Holistic Approach. International Criminal Law Review 19(6): 911–937.
Burke-White WW (2016) Maximising the ICC's Crime Prevention Impact through Positive Complementarity and Hard-nosed Diplomacy. In: Steinberg RH (ed) Contemporary Issues Facing the International Criminal Court. Koninklijke Brill NV, Leiden, pp. 202–212.
Burke-White WW, Slaughter A (2006) The Future of International Law is Domestic. Harvard International Law Journal 47, 327–352.
Clark RS, Heinze A (2022) Article 121, Amendments. In: Ambos K (ed) Rome Statute of the International Criminal Court: Article-by-Article Commentary. Beck/Nomos/Hart, Munich, pp. 2871–2891.
Clark RS, Meisenberg SM (2022) Article 119, Settlement of Disputes. In: Ambos K (ed) Rome Statute of the International Criminal Court: Article-by-Article Commentary. Beck/Nomos/Hart, Munich, pp 2846–2855.
Crawford J (2002) The International Law Commission's Articles on State Responsibility: Introduction, Text and Commentaries. Cambridge University Press, Cambridge.
Halff M, Torbert D, Villacis R (2022) Article 117: Assessment of Contribution. In: Ambos K (ed) Rome Statute of the International Criminal Court: Article-by-Article Commentary. Beck/Nomos/Hart, Munich, pp. 2837–2842.
Hunter E (2016) Using 'Managerial Compliance' to Strengthen ICC Cooperation. In: Bekou O, Birkett DJ (eds) Cooperation and the International Criminal Court: Perspectives from Theory and Practice. Brill, Leiden, pp. 366–395.
ICISS (2001) The Responsibility to Protect: Report of the International Commission on Intervention and State Sovereignty, available at: https://www.globalr2p.org/resources/the-responsibility-to-protect-report-of-the-international-commission-on-intervention-and-state-sovereignty-2001/ (accessed 15 July 2020).
Jones A (2016) Non-cooperation and the Efficiency of the International Criminal Court. In: Bekou O, Birkett DJ (eds) Cooperation and the International Criminal Court: Perspectives from Theory and Practice. Brill, Leiden, pp. 185–209.
Kress C, Prost K (2022) International Cooperation and Judicial Assistance. In: Ambos K (ed) Rome Statute of the International Criminal Court: Article-by-Article Commentary. Beck/Nomos/Hart, Munich, pp 2452–2701.
Marshall KA (2010) Prevention and Complementarity in the International Criminal Court: A Positive Approach. Human Rights Brief 17(2), 21–26.
Ntahiraja B (2017) Enforcing Cooperation Differently: Time to Criminalise Active Non-cooperation in the Rome Statute. In: Van der Merwe HJ, Kemp G (eds) International Justice in Africa, 2016. Strathmore University Press, Nairobi, pp. 21–49.
Owuor MO (2017) The International Criminal Court and Positive Complementarity: Legal and Institutional Framework, unpublished LLD thesis, University of Pretoria, available at: https://repository.up.ac.za/handle/2263/67865 (accessed 12 September 2022).
Phillipe X (2006) The Principles of Universal Jurisdiction and Complementarity: How do the Two Principles Intermesh? International Review of the Red Cross 88(862), 375–398.
Saba A, Akbarzadeh S (2020) The ICC and R2P: Complementary or Contradictory? International Peacekeeping 28(1), 84–109.

Sarkin J (2020) Reforming the International Criminal Court (ICC) to Achieve Increased State Cooperation in Investigations and Prosecutions of International Crimes. International Human Rights Law Review 9(1), 27–61.
Saxon D (2015) The International Criminal Court and the Prevention of Crimes. In: Sharma SK, Welsh JM (eds) The Responsibility to Prevent: Overcoming the Challenges of Atrocity Prevention. Oxford University Press, Oxford, pp. 119–159.
Sluiter G (2018) Enforcing Cooperation: Did the Drafters Approach It the Wrong Way? Journal of International Criminal Justice 16(2): 383–402.
Sluiter G (2020) Reforms to Enhance State Cooperation and Address Witness Interference. In: Steinberg RH (ed) The International Criminal Court: Contemporary Challenges and Reform Proposals. Koninklijke Brill NV, Leiden, pp. 303–313.
Sluiter G, Talontsi S (2016) Credible and Authoritative Enforcement of State Cooperation with the International Criminal Court. In: Bekou O, Birkett DJ (eds) Cooperation and the International Criminal Court: Perspectives from Theory and Practice. Brill, Leiden, pp. 80–113.
Tillier J (2013) The ICC Prosecutor and Positive Complementarity: Strengthening the Rule of Law? International Criminal Law Review, 13(3), 507–591.
UN General Assembly (UNGA) (2005) Sixtieth Session. World Summit Outcome Document. Resolution A/RES/60/1.
UN General Assembly (UNGA) (2006a) Sixty-first Session Request for the Inclusion of an Item in the provisional agenda of the Sixty-first session [The rule of law at the national and international levels] A/61/142.
UN General Assembly (UNGA) (2006b) Sixty-first Session Resolution 61/39 [The Rule of Law at the National and International Levels] A/RES/61/39.
UN General Assembly (UNGA) (2009) Sixty-Third Session Report of the Secretary-General: [Implementing the Responsibility to Protect] A/63/677.
UN General Assembly (UNGA) (2012) Sixty-sixth Session Report of the Secretary General [Responsibility to protect timely and decisive response] A/66/874.
UN General Assembly (UNGA) (2014) Sixty-eighth Session Report of the Secretary General [Fulfilling our collective responsibility: international assistance and the responsibility to protect] A/68/947.
UN General Assembly (UNGA) (2022) Eleventh Emergency Session Resolution ES-11/3 [Suspension of the Rights of Membership of the Russian Federation in the Human Rights Council] A/RES/ES-11/3.

Chapter 7
Strengthening the Security Council's Responses to Non-cooperation Through the Lens of R2P and General International Law

Contents

7.1 Introduction 184
7.2 The Security Council's Role in Protecting Peremptory Norms 185
7.2.1 The Duty to Protect Peremptory Norms 185
7.2.2 The Responsibility Not to Veto 187
7.3 Peacekeeping Operations as a Tool under R2P for Strengthening the Security Council's Role in Following up on ICC Situations 192
7.3.1 Peacekeeping Operations as Tools under the Pillars of R2P 192
7.3.2 Peacekeeping Operations and the ICC 193
7.3.3 Obstacles to Cooperation between the ICC and Peacekeeping Operations 194
7.4 Analysing the Role of the General Assembly in Strengthening the Security Council's ICC Mandate 197
7.4.1 Analysing the Application of the Uniting for Peace Resolution in the Scope of the Security Council's ICC Mandate 197
7.4.2 Analysing General Assembly Action in Reforming the Veto Powers of the Security Council 198
7.4.3 What Role for the General Assembly for Addressing Security Council Inaction? 200
7.5 Conclusion 201
References 202

Abstract This chapter seeks to examine how R2P, as well as the principles entrenched in general international law can enhance the United Nations Security Council's responses to non-cooperation referred to it by the ICC. As the body tasked with the maintenance of international peace and security under the UN Charter, the Security Council has a critical role to play in the implementation of R2P, particularly in addressing atrocity crimes. This includes its mandate towards the ICC in referring situations to the Court and respond to referrals of non-cooperation. However, the Security Council's efforts in this context have been less than ideal, with the Council failing to meet its obligations towards the Court and R2P.

This chapter focuses on the Security Council's role in the implementation of the third pillar of R2P, as well as in the protection of peremptory norms of general international law. This includes an examination of the veto power granted to the permanent members of the Council, as well as international efforts at encouraging more mindful and responsible use of this power. The chapter also considers whether

M. L. Jacobs, *The Consequences of Non-cooperation with the International Criminal Court*, International Criminal Justice Series 37,
https://doi.org/10.1007/978-94-6265-675-8_7

peacekeeping operations can serve as effective follow up mechanisms for following up on situations referred to the ICC. Finally, this chapter explores the potential of the UN General assembly to address Security Council inaction and enhance responses to non-cooperation.

Keywords Responsibility to Protect · Non-cooperation · UN Charter · UN Security Council · UN General Assembly · Peacekeeping · Peremptory Norms · Veto

7.1 Introduction

Within the framework of R2P, the Security Council's primary responsibility under the UN Charter to maintain international peace and security has afforded it with the role of ensuring that the responsibility to protect is implemented effectively in the fight against atrocity crimes.[1] This role is highlighted within the Security Council's relationship with the International Criminal Court with regards to the referral of situations to the Court,[2] as well as in responding to instances of non-cooperation that have been communicated to it.[3] However, as has been noted throughout this book, the Security Council has been unable to properly fulfil this relationship with the Court and has therefore not effectively met the duties required of it under R2P.

Seeing that the application of R2P and frameworks under general international law can assist in the improved operation of the ICC, as well as the Assembly of States Parties, in responding to and remedying instances of non-cooperation; this chapter will investigate how R2P, through the application of principles entrenched in general international law, can contribute to developing more effective frameworks within the Security Council to better realise its protection obligations, as well as contribute to more effective responses to instances of non-cooperation.

In conducting this investigation, this chapter will be structured as follows:

Firstly, this chapter will begin by analysing the Security Council's relationship with the ICC through the lens of R2P and General International Law. This section will explore the Security Council's role in protecting peremptory norms of general international law as a subset of its obligations under the third pillar of R2P. In conducting this analysis, this chapter will refer to the Security Council's veto power in the context of its relationship with R2P and General International Law, and discuss measures developed by the international community aimed at ensuring more responsible use of the veto. In the next section, the investigation will turn to establishing whether the Security Council's follow up mechanisms in situations it referred to the ICC can be

---

[1] The Charter of the United Nations (26 June 1945, 1 UNTS XVI, Entry into Force 24 October 1945) (UN Charter), Article 24; ICISS 2001, para 6.7.

[2] The Rome Statute of the International Criminal Court (17 July 1998, 2187, UNTS 3, Entry into Force, 1 July 2002) [hereinafter RS], Article 13(b); UNSC 2005, para 1; UNSC 2011a, para 4.

[3] Ibid., Articles 87(5)(b) and 87(7).

enhanced through peacekeeping operations as a tool within the arsenal of the third pillar of R2P. Finally, this chapter will look to further analyse the role of the General Assembly in addressing Security Council inaction with regard to its potential for strengthening responses to non-cooperation.

7.2 The Security Council's Role in Protecting Peremptory Norms

In evaluating the relationship between the Security Council and the ICC, particularly in the context of responses to non-cooperation, the Security Council has specific roles and responsibilities attached to it by virtue of the responsibility to protect, as well as through various principles entrenched within general international law. This section will analyse these roles and responsibilities, as well as the challenges faced by the Security Council in their proper execution.

This section will specifically focus on the role played by the Security Council in protecting peremptory norms of general international law through the lens of R2P. This role will be analysed in contrast with the veto right held by the permanent members of the Security Council, which has been resorted to in a manner that has had a negative effect upon the Council's ability to act in in the face of threats to international peace and security in an appropriate manner.

7.2.1 The Duty to Protect Peremptory Norms

In establishing the role played by international organisations such as the Security Council in protecting peremptory norms, the ILC recognises that resolutions, decisions or acts of an international organisation that would otherwise have a binding effect do not create obligations under international law if, and to the extent that they conflict with a peremptory norm of general international law.[4]

At the 73rd Session of the ILC, this provision was debated heavily, especially with regard to the potential inclusion of Security Council resolutions in the text. While a clear majority of States supported the applicability of this conclusion to decisions and resolutions of the Security Council, some States held the view that its inclusion would undermine the authority of the Security Council and open up precedent for States to ignore requests made by the Council.[5] In addition, those States who were against the

[4] ILC Seventy-Third Session Report of the International Law Commission [Chapter IV(E): Peremptory Norms of General International Law: Text of the Draft Conclusions and Legal Consequences of Peremptory Norms of General International Law (jus cogens)] A/77/10 (18 April–3 June & 4 July–5 August 2022), Conclusion 16.

[5] International Law Commission Seventy-third Session *Fifth Report on Peremptory Norms of General International Law (jus cogens) by Dire Tladi, Special Rapporteur* (24 January 2022) A/CN.4/747 (24 January 2022) para 158.

inclusion of the Security Council also cited that there was little practice in support of the resolutions of the Security Council being subject to peremptory norms.[6] It is noted that while decisions of the Security Council were not included in the text of the Conclusions, they are provided for in the commentaries as a compromise.[7] Commentary also notes that it is highly unlikely that the Security Council would adopt a resolution that would be in conflict with a peremptory norm.[8]

Linked with the duty of the Security Council not to pass resolutions or perform other binding actions that may constitute a breach of peremptory norms, is the obligation not to recognise a situation caused by a breach as lawful, nor assist in maintaining such a situation.[9] Under such a duty, the permanent members of the Security Council are required not to make decisions that may facilitate the ongoing violation of peremptory norms. Neither should they act in a manner that affects or otherwise undermines the duty of other members of the Security Council to cooperate in responding to or ending the serious breach of peremptory norms.[10]

The obligations of the permanent members to not use the veto in circumstances where atrocity crimes are being committed are also present in various international treaties. For example, the Genocide Convention places States Parties under an obligation to prevent genocide,[11] while the Geneva Conventions place an obligation upon States to ensure respect for the conventions in all circumstances.[12] In the *Bosnia Genocide* case, the ICJ held that a State must do what it can within its power to prevent genocide, depending on its ability to influence.[13]

Therefore, in the context of the actions of the permanent members of the Security Council, such a responsibility is particularly strong, taking into account the impact their actions may have on a situation as a result of the power and influence they

---

[6] Ibid., para 155.

[7] ILC Seventy-Third Session Report of the International Law Commission [Chapter IV(E): Peremptory Norms of General International Law: Text of the Draft Conclusions and Legal Consequences of Peremptory Norms of General International Law (jus cogens)] A/77/10 (18 April–3 June & 4 July–5 August 2022 Commentary on Conclusion 16, para 4 "... draft conclusion 16 applies equally to binding resolutions, decisions and acts of the Security Council; see also Herbert F "Disobeying the Security Council or a Disobedient Security Council? The effects of jus cogens on Security Council resolutions in recent debates of the ILC in the views of States" EJIL:Talk! (12 August 2022) available at: https://www.ejiltalk.org/disobeying-the-security-council-or-a-disobedient-security-council-the-effects-of-jus-cogens-on-security-council-resolutions-in-recent-debates-of-the-ilc-and-in-the-views-of-states/ (accessed 15 August 2022).

[8] Ibid., Commentary on Conclusion 16, para 5

[9] Ibid., Conclusion 19(2).

[10] Trahan 2020a, pp. 94–95, the actions of the permanent members must also be consistent with the peremptory norms under threat.

[11] Convention on the Prevention and Punishment of the Crime of Genocide (9 December 1948, UNTS 78-277, Entry into force 12 January 1951) Article 1.

[12] Common Article 1 of the Geneva Conventions of 12 August 1949.

[13] ICJ, Application of the Convention on the Prevention and Punishment of the Crime of Genocide (Bosnia and Herzegovina v Serbia and Montenegro) Judgment of 26 February 2007 ICJ Rep 2007 43 p. 221.

have over the international field.[14] Trahan argues in this regard that the permanent members, in using their veto the context of the Genocide Convention, violations of the Geneva Conventions, and other general obligations to cooperate in the prevention of specific international crimes, are violating their individual treaty obligations.[15] Therefore, the use of the veto by the Security Council's permanent members should not be applied in a manner that could be construed as a failure to recognise a situation as illegal, nor one that maintains such a situation.

7.2.2 The Responsibility Not to Veto

Within the context of R2P, concerns have been raised with regards to the use of the veto in atrocity situations. According to Illingworth, the responsibility to react to mass atrocity crimes under the third pillar of R2P lies primarily in the hands of the Security Council, therefore creating an inseparable link with the principles entrenched within R2P and the responsible use of the veto.[16] As a result of the use of the veto, the Security Council has on occasion failed to live up to its obligations under R2P, which is particularly notable in the case of intervention by the ICC aa a tool under the third pillar.[17] In assessing the right of veto afforded to the Security Council's permanent members, there lies the question whether existing rules of international law place a duty upon the permanent members of the Security Council not to use their veto powers in the case where a peremptory norm is breached.

The Security Council's failure to respond to appropriately to specific situations as a result of the veto has revived the debate on the Responsibility Not to Veto, which refers to the duty of the permanent five to refrain from using their veto powers in cases of mass atrocity situations.[18] In the *ICISS Report,* it was proposed that the permanent five should agree not to apply their veto powers in decisions relating to human protection.[19] In the UN Secretary-General's Report of the High-level Panel on Threats, Challenges and Change, voluntary restraint of the veto in cases of genocide and large-scale human rights abuses was called for. This report also declared that the veto is unsuitable in its current form in an increasingly democratic age and that it be limited to matters where vital interests are genuinely at stake.[20] However, reference

---

[14] Trahan 2020a, pp. 97–98.

[15] Ibid., pp. 98–99, the author also notes that these obligations do not cease by virtue of a State having a seat on the Security Council.

[16] Illingworth 2020, p. 386.

[17] Genser 2018 p. 500, "the use or abuse of the veto is responsible for some of the Council's most conspicuous failures...".

[18] Essawy 2020, p. 300.

[19] ICISS 2001, para 8.29.

[20] UNGA 2004, para 256.

to the responsibility not to veto was removed from the *World Summit Outcome Document* due to pressure by one of the permanent members.[21]

The responsibility not to veto was also discussed in the Secretary-General's *Implementing R2P* Report. This report described the permanent members' veto as a privilege and urged them to not use or threaten to use the veto in situations where there was a clear failure to meet obligations relating to the responsibility to protect.[22] States expressed their support for the doctrine during the plenary debate held by the General Assembly in 2009. Member States argued that the veto should not obstruct measures aimed at ending ongoing situations where atrocity crimes were occurring. Member States also expressed concern that the veto would affect the functioning of actions taken under the R2P frameworks if a major power were unable or expressed their unwillingness to prevent or halt the commission of atrocity crimes.[23]

Reference to the responsibility not to veto was also made in the 2015 Report of the Secretary General, where permanent members were encouraged to exercise restraint on the use of the veto in atrocity situations. The Report also noted that where States employed the veto in such situations, they should explain publicly any alternative strategies aimed at protecting populations at risk.[24] Although there have been these attempts at blocking veto restraint, the responsibility not to veto has been advanced as a mechanism for operationalising R2P.[25] However, although the responsibility not to veto appears to be part of R2P, commitment to it has been inconsistent, considering its omission from the *World Summit Outcome Document*.[26]

7.2.2.1 The Responsibility Not to Veto Analysed through the Lens of General International Law

In assessing the right of veto afforded to the Security Council's permanent members, there lies the question whether existing rules of international law place a duty upon the permanent members of the Security Council not to use their veto powers in the case where a peremptory norm is breached. Under the UN Charter, the Security

---

[21] UNGA 2005, para 119, "We invite the permanent members of the Security Council to refrain from using the veto in cases of genocide, war crimes, ethnic cleansing and crimes against humanity"; see also Blätter and Williams 2011, pp. 315–316.

[22] UNGA 2009a, para 61.

[23] UNGA 2009b; Statement by the Republic of Korea at the 97th Plenary Meeting "... we support the recommendation in the Secretary-General's report for the five permanent members to refrain from employing the veto, or the threat of veto, in situations of manifest failure to meet R2P obligations"; Statement by Switzerland at the 98th Plenary Meeting, "One important way to remedy this problem would be for the permanent members of the Security Council to refrain from using their veto in cases of genocide, crimes against humanity, ethnic cleansing and war crimes"; Statement by Slovenia at the 99th Plenary Meeting "We join those who call upon the permanent members of the Security Council to refrain from using their vetoes...".

[24] UNGA 2015a, para 63.

[25] Essawy 2020, p. 300.

[26] Trahan 2020b, p. 107.

Council has some limitations on the exercise in its power, in that it is required to act in accordance with the purposes and principles of the United Nations.[27] These include respect for principles of justice and international law; promoting and encouraging respect for human rights and achieving cooperation in solving international issues.[28]

Article 27(3) of the UN Charter, the legal basis for the veto power, contains a largely ignored provision which proclaims that a permanent member shall abstain from voting in a decision where that member is a party to the dispute under discussion.[29] In analysing the link between these provisions and the responsibility of the Security Council not to exercise the veto in situations where human protection is at Stake, the rules relating to State responsibility and peremptory norms of international law are important tools for concretising the Security Council's role in ensuring the responsible use of the veto in decision-making.

7.2.2.2 Veto Restraint Initiatives

Talks of veto reform is a sensitive issue within the Security Council, as it challenges the vital interests of the permanent members who wish to preserve their veto power, maintain their position of authority within the international community and further their interests by blocking potentially harmful Security Council. As a result, it is highly unlikely that the permanent members would be willing to relinquish this power through reforming the veto.[30] However, the manner in which the veto has been used within the Security Council has identified the need for more responsible use of the veto in situations where the maintenance of international peace and security is at risk.

In order to achieve more conscientious decision-making and participation within the Security Council, various UN Member States have proposed initiatives aimed at promoting restraint of the veto. Two initiatives that have gained massive amounts of support by UN Member States include the "Political Declaration on Suspension of the Veto" to UN Member States, which aims to secure a voluntary restraint on the use of the veto in R2P situations;[31] and the "Code of Conduct regarding Security Council action against genocide, crimes against humanity and war crimes", which calls upon all members of the Security Council not to vote against any credible

---

[27] UN Charter, above n.1, Article 24(2).

[28] Ibid., Article 1; see also Trahan 2020a, p. 95, where the author recognises that the current use of the veto is inconsistent with the UN's Purposes and Principles.

[29] Ibid., Article 27(3) of the UN Charter; however, see also Milano 2015, p. 222, where the author notes that recent practice of the Security Council indicates that this provision has been prominent for its non-application.

[30] Illingworth 2020, p. 388, where the author emphasizes that the idea of abolishing the veto is impossible under the current political climate and should therefore not be pursued.

[31] UN General Assembly Seventieth Session Political Statement on the suspension of the veto in cases of mass atrocities (1 August 2015) available at https://www.globalr2p.org/resources/political-declaration-on-suspension-of-veto-powers-in-cases-of-mass-atrocities/ (accessed 15 December 2020).

draft resolutions aimed at preventing or halting mass atrocities.[32] Over 100 States have signed onto these declarations,[33] which highlights the political willingness of the larger international community to hold the Security Council accountable in its decision-making processes.[34]

While these initiatives show that the international community is dedicated to hold the Security Council accountable for the use of the veto, the content of these initiatives do however identify several practical issues in the implementation and promotion of veto restraint. In general, an informal code of conduct for veto restraint does not offer better prospects for reform than any formal measures as informal measures would still require the support of the permanent members of the Security Council to be effective.[35]

A deep analysis of the text of the Code of Conduct and the Political Declaration, highlights further issues that may affect the implementation of these attempts at veto reform. Both the Code of Conduct and the Political declaration contain clauses which would allow the use of the veto would still be permitted in certain circumstances. The Code of Conduct allows for veto where the requirement of a "credible draft resolution" is not met.[36] This concept of "credible" is subjective and vague,[37] and such a clause leaves the risk of a Permanent Member to simply declare a resolution as not credible and exercise their veto.[38] In addition the development of a code of conduct for the use of the veto may hold the additional risk of undermining the

---

[32] UN General Assembly Seventieth Session Letter dated 14 December 2015 from the Permanent Representative of Liechtenstein to the United Nations addressed to the Secretary-General [Annex 1 Code of conduct regarding security council action against genocide, crimes against humanity or war crimes] A/70/621 (14 December 2015) para 2.

[33] Global Centre for the Responsibility to Protect List of Supporters of the Political Declaration on Suspension of the Veto (13 July 2022) available at: https://www.globalr2p.org/resources/list-of-supporters-of-the-political-declaration-on-suspension-of-veto/ (accessed 25 October 2024) where it is reported that 104 UN Member States and 2 UN observer missions have signed the declaration; Global Centre for the Responsibility to Protect List of Signatories to the ACT Code of Conduct (8 June 2022) available at: https://www.globalr2p.org/resources/list-of-signatories-to-the-act-code-of-conduct/ (accessed 25 October 2024) where it is reported that 121 Member States, including France, and the United Kingdom, have signed the Code of Conduct.

[34] Illingworth 2020, p. 397, where the author notes that advocacy for veto restraint appears to be putting increased pressure on the permanent members as they understand that veto restraint is an important issue for UN Members.

[35] Adediran 2018, p. 476; however, the author does note that the development of an informal code of conduct easier may be easier to enact since it does not require the amendment of the UN Charter; see also Article 108 of the UN Charter (above n. 1), which provides that amendment of the UN Charter comes into force when it has been adopted by a vote of two thirds of the members of the General Assembly.

[36] Code of conduct regarding Security Council action against genocide, crimes against humanity or war crimes, above n. 32, para 2.

[37] Illingworth 2020, p. 396

[38] Trahan 2020a, p. 89; see also Vilmer 2018, p. 339, "... what is credible to a state that supports a resolution is not credible to a state that does not...".

contributions and participation of the other members of the Security Council in decision-making in that their votes would automatically become pre-determined.[39]

The original proposal for the Political Declaration suggested that such a restraint would not apply where vital national interests were at stake.[40] The inclusion of such a clause, although not expressly included in the final document, would have made implementing veto restraint very difficult in practice as there may be different interpretations of what vital interests may be, considering the conflicting value systems among the permanent members and the influence of political considerations.[41] According to Illingworth and Trahan, the inclusion of such get-out clauses are intended to make the proposals more politically feasible by reassuring permanent members that they still have the option to protect their interests.[42] However, these clauses may also have an effect on the effectiveness of these initiatives as they continue to maintain a situation where the Security Council is deadlocked as a result of consensus among its members.[43] According to Morris and Wheeler, the recognition of a permanent member's right to protect their vital interests when restricting the veto may have the effect of rendering the responsibility not to veto completely useless.[44] Another concern with these veto restraint mechanisms is that they may risk passing resolutions that are too strong and which could damage atrocity prevention initiatives by proposing more coercive interventions as a first resort.[45]

Therefore, while veto restraint aims to promote more accountability within the Security Council through the spirit of R2P, these initiatives in their current state appear to maintain the hierarchy of the members of the Security Council because of the weak language contained therein. This highlights the need for more institutionalised reform of the veto power carried out through the structures and procedures of the UN Charter System.

---

[39] Adediran 2018, p. 477; see also Illingworth 2020, p. 404, where the author identifies that the ACT Code would compel all Members of the Security Council to vote in favour of a given resolution.

[40] Security Council Report "The Veto" (19 October 2015) 3 *Research Report* https://www.securitycouncilreport.org/atf/cf/%7B65BFCF9B-6D27-4E9C-8CD3-CF6E4FF96FF9%7D/research_report_3_the_veto_2015.pdf (accessed 25 January 2021).

[41] Morris and Wheeler 2016, p. 237.

[42] Illingworth 2020, pp. 397–398; see also Trahan 2020b, p. 128, where the author notes that the inclusion of language about vital national or State interests was most likely included to make veto restraint in the face of atrocity crimes more acceptable to the permanent members who might otherwise view these initiatives as attacks on the powers granted to them by the UN Charter.

[43] Ibid., pp. 397–398; see also Trahan 2020b, p. 129, where the author does not support the use of these carve-out clauses.

[44] Morris and Wheeler 2016, p. 238.

[45] Vilmer 2018 p. 343; see also Illingworth 2020, p. 399, where the author notes that there is a connection between veto restraint and the increased possibility of military force exercised under the third pillar of R2P.

7.3 Peacekeeping Operations as a Tool under R2P for Strengthening the Security Council's Role in Following up on ICC Situations

The Security Council's specific role in the implementation of R2P primarily lies within the context of the third pillar, namely the facilitation of collective responses by the international community following the failure of a State to meet its responsibilities under the first pillar.[46] As noted in a previous chapter, such responses include the referral of atrocity situations to the ICC for investigation. While the Security Council has referred situations to the ICC, and thus has assisted in contributing to the prevention and prosecution of serious international crimes, it has not effectively followed up on these situations, particularly where instances of non-cooperation have been referred to it.[47] This failure to follow up is detrimental to the credibility of the Security Council in its role in maintaining international peace and security.[48]

While a previous chapter has identified that follow-up mechanisms could possibly be developed to strengthen the Security Council's ability to monitor developments in the situations that have been referred to the ICC by the Security Council, this section aims to establish whether peacekeeping operations mandated by the Security Council to operate in situations under investigation by the ICC can assist the Security Council in ensuring more effective follow up mechanisms. This investigation will be conducted in the context of the relationship between peacekeeping operations and the pillars of R2P.

7.3.1 Peacekeeping Operations as Tools under the Pillars of R2P

In the situation where a State has failed to comply with an obligation to cooperate in the arrest and surrender of a suspect to the ICC where such cooperation is also mandated by a Security Council referral, such a failure amounts to a threat to international peace and security to which swift action should be taken by the Security Council. Under the Rome Statute, provision is made for the cooperation of any intergovernmental organisation to assist in the execution of the Court's mandate.[49] The

---

46 Genser 2018, p. 432; UNGA 2012, para 59.

47 Twenty-Eighth Report of the Prosecutor of the International Criminal Court to the United Nations Security Council Pursuant to UNSCR 1593 (14 December 2018) available at https://www.icc-cpi.int/itemsDocuments/181214-rep-otp-UNSC-1593_ENG.pdf (accessed 4 April 2020) para 16, "… none of the decisions finding compliance and/or referring the matter to the ASP and UNSC have been responded to by the Council."

48 Sluiter and Talontsi 2016, p. 105; see also UNSC 2012, Statement by Colombia p. 10, "… when the Court issues arrest warrants and they are not carried out, what is at stake is the credibility of the Council's decisions and authority."

49 RS, above, n. 2, Article 87(6).

result for the Court is that it may ask the Security Council for other forms of cooperation, which could entail the cooperation of peacekeeping forces in the arrest and surrender of suspects.[50]

Peacekeeping operations mandated by the Security Council have a particularly important role in supporting the implementation of R2P. The effective operationalisation of a Peacekeeping mandate has the effect of supporting the host State in fulfilling its responsibility to protect through all the pillars of R2P. In particular, such peacekeeping mandates can assist the State in developing its capacities to protect under the second pillar, as well as in assisting in the physical protection of populations where the State is unable to do so under the third pillar.[51] In the context of the ICC, peacekeeping missions can use their protection capacities under the third pillar to assist the ICC with investigations and ensuring that suspects are arrested and surrendered to the Court. Therefore, the direct cooperation of a peacekeeping mission may be helpful in securing suspects where the requested State is unwilling or unable to cooperate with the requests of the Court.[52]

7.3.2 *Peacekeeping Operations and the ICC*

Since the establishment of the ICC, peacekeeping missions have been mandated to support international justice processes by assisting the situation State in cooperating with the Court through the development of cooperation frameworks.[53] This relationship is regulated by Article 54(3) of the Rome Statute, which mandates the ICC Prosecutor to seek the assistance of intergovernmental organisations and arrangements in investigations and arrests. While explicit reference to the ICC has not always been forthcoming in earlier resolutions,[54] such peacekeeping operations, such as MONUC were mandated to cooperate with efforts to ensure that those responsible for serious violations of human rights and international humanitarian law were brought to justice.[55] Later peacekeeping mandates contain explicit reference to the ICC, calling on authorities in these situation States, together with the peacekeeping operations to hold perpetrators of atrocity crimes accountable and cooperate with the Court in accordance with State obligations under the Rome Statute.[56] In order to further cooperation between peacekeeping operations and the ICC, memoranda of

---

[50] Babaian 2018, p. 101.

[51] Hunt and Sharland 2020, p. 226.

[52] Kress and Prost 2022, p. 2474.

[53] Venigandla 2021, p. 5, where the author notes that these frameworks allow peacekeeping missions to play an important intermediary role in assisting the situation State to fulfil their obligations to the Court.

[54] Ibid., p. 6, where the author notes that hesitancy to give explicit reference to the ICC in such resolutions can be attributed to political dynamics within the Security Council.

[55] UNSC 2004, para 5(g).

[56] UNSC 2011b, para 19; see also UNSC 2013, para 27; UNSC 2014, para 38.

understanding have been concluded by the Court and some of these operations with a view to establishing frameworks for specific forms of assistance.[57] The language in these memoranda of understanding mirrors that of the relationship agreement between the ICC and the UN, and has the effect of formalising cooperation between the peacekeeping operations and the ICC.[58] Among the various levels of support that peacekeeping missions can provide to ICC situations and investigations include assisting States to build up their capacities to pursue justice and accountability as well as in enforcing arrest warrants and summonses, therefore addressing the ICC's lack of enforcement authority and a State's potential lack of enforcement capability.[59]

7.3.3 Obstacles to Cooperation between the ICC and Peacekeeping Operations

Cooperation between peacekeeping operations and ICC faces various obstacles, mostly associated with political considerations by host States who appear to have priorities that are contrary to the work of the Court and the peacekeeping operation.[60] Cooperation with the ICC and peacekeeping missions also may have the effect of doing more harm than good in the region.[61] Therefore, extending the mandates of peacekeeping operations in these situation States to include cooperation between the ICC and the peacekeeping mission would be met with considerable backlash.[62] A particular issue lies with how a mandate with the ICC and peacekeeping operations in these situations may constitute a breach of the basic principles that govern peacekeeping: consent, impartiality and the prohibition of the use of force.[63]

[57] See e.g. Memorandum of Understanding Between the United Nations and the International Criminal Court concerning cooperation between the United Nations Organization Mission in the Democratic Republic of the Congo and the International Criminal Court (8 November 2005) UNTS 2363 II-1292; Memorandum of Understanding between the United Nations and the International Criminal Court concerning cooperation between the United Nations Operation in Cote d'Ivoire (UNOCI) and the Prosecutor of the International Criminal Court (23 January 2012) UNTS 2803-II-1358.

[58] Venigandla 2021, p. 6.

[59] Ibid., p. 7.

[60] Ibid., p. 8.

[61] Ibid., p. 10.

[62] Hamilton 2016, p. 356.

[63] United Nations Peacekeeping *Principles of Peacekeeping* available at: https://peacekeeping.un.org/en/principles-of-peacekeeping (accessed 12 May 2022).

7.3.3.1 Consent

With regards to the principle of consent, the UN General Assembly has emphasised that the consent of the government is fundamental for the deployment of a peacekeeping mission.[64] Current practice has highlighted in this regard that the Security Council has been reluctant to interfere where there is an absence of host State consent to ICC Jurisdiction, despite being the body through which situation States like Libya and Sudan were referred to the ICC.[65] While the Security Council can in theory deploy such missions without consent under Chapter VII of the Charter, such an action would be impractical and dangerous, with the risk that a peacekeeping operation becomes a party to the conflict and being drawn away from its role in keeping the peace.[66] Therefore, State consent to both the presence of the peacekeeping mission and to the jurisdiction of the ICC is crucial to enable effective cooperation. An additional concern lies with the lengths to which a peacekeeping force would have to resort when conducting arrests, which raises further concerns about the potential use of force in such a situation.[67]

7.3.3.2 Impartiality

In the context of impartiality, one should take into consideration how such a principle may not be easily practiced where high-profile arrests are to be executed. Under the principle of impartiality, peacekeeping operations should be impartial in their dealings with parties to the conflict, but not neutral in the execution of their protective mandate. Therefore, where parties to the conflict commit serious breaches of international law which negatively affect the outcomes of the peace process, a peacekeeping operation should not condone such action. In addition, these operations must avoid activities which may compromise its impartiality in a situation, as doing so may undermine the credibility and legitimacy of the peacekeeping operation and may lead to a situation where consent from the parties to the conflict is withdrawn.[68] Looking at this principle through the lens of ICC cooperation, Security Council referrals to the ICC are politically motivated as they involve situations where securing the arrest of an accused has been deemed so crucial that their freedom

---

[64] UNGA 2015b, para 127.

[65] Venigandla 2021, p. 8, where the author highlights that obstruction to peacekeeping operations has been an ongoing challenge for the UN.

[66] Hamilton 2016, p. 358; see also Kress and Prost 2022, p. 2474, where the authors note that Article 87(6) empowers the Court to seek the cooperation of peacekeeping forces in cases of failed States or States hostile to the Court.

[67] Ibid., p. 359.

[68] United Nations Peacekeeping *Principles of Peacekeeping* available at: https://peacekeeping.un.org/en/principles-of-peacekeeping (accessed 12 May 2022); see also UNGA 2015b para 118, which highlights that decisions about deploying a peacekeeping operation into situations of sustained armed conflict must be taken in full knowledge of the limits of a United Nations force and the potential that those limits may be exposed.

constitutes an ongoing threat to peace and security. Therefore, any attempt to arrest persons that have played such a role in the conflict would in theory be incompatible with the principle of impartiality.[69]

7.3.3.3 The Use of Force

The final principle, the prohibition of the use of force, has some consequences for cooperation between the Security Council and the ICC. When pursuing and capturing ICC suspects that are often in positions of power and influence, there lies the situation where peacekeeping operations will need to be granted permission to use all necessary means to fulfil their mandates.[70] In this regard, while UN peacekeeping operations are not an enforcement tool through which force can be used to achieve their goal, force may be used at a tactical level, with Security Council authorisation, in order to protect the implementation of the mandate. The use of force should only be relied on as a measure of last resort, taking into consideration the basic principles of fairness, proportionality and with the least amount of force necessary to achieve the desired effect.

Therefore, a decision concerning the use of force in such situations must be made in consideration of a number of factors such as the mission capability; public perceptions; humanitarian impact; force protection; the safety and security of personnel; and the effect of such action on national and local consent for the mission.[71] In addition, the use of force in such situations has political implications for all parties involved and can often give rise to unforeseen and unwanted circumstances, which may include a full-scale conflict between peacekeepers and State forces still loyal to high-profile suspects.[72] In this regard, one should take into consideration how changes in the political climate in a situation State can have an influence on a host State's cooperation with the ICC, such as the removal of Al-Bashir as the leader of Sudan.[73]

---

[69] Hamilton 2016, p. 361.

[70] Ibid., pp. 359–360.

[71] United Nations Peacekeeping *Principles of Peacekeeping* available at: https://peacekeeping.un.org/en/principles-of-peacekeeping (accessed 12 May 2022).

[72] Hamilton 2016, p. 360; see also UNGA 2015b, para 122, which highlights that such operations may make peacekeeping forces a party to the conflict, requiring attention to the various consequences that flow from the sustained use of force.

[73] Venigandla 2021, p. 10.

7.4 Analysing the Role of the General Assembly in Strengthening the Security Council's ICC Mandate

As noted in Chap. 3 , the UN General Assembly is granted with the power to make recommendations to the Security Council. Such recommendations may include the General Assembly exerting pressure on the Security Council to refer situations to the ICC,[74] as was attempted with regards to the situation in North Korea.[75] As an important purpose of the UN Charter is to maintain international peace and security through collective measures,[76] all UN Organs are required to engage in collective measures and not just the Security Council.

7.4.1 Analysing the Application of the Uniting for Peace Resolution in the Scope of the Security Council's ICC Mandate

In the instance that the Security Council fails to act on situations relating to the maintenance of international peace and security, the application of the Uniting for Peace Resolution presents an opportunity for the General Assembly to step in and address such inaction. International practice indicates that the General Assembly is competent to determine on its own initiative that the Security Council has failed to execute its protection mandate in the face of threats to international peace and security. This is supported by the text of the Uniting for Peace Resolution,[77] and the practice of the General Assembly in convening emergency special sessions both with and without referral from the Security Council.[78]

In the *Certain Expenses of the United Nations* case, the ICJ observed that the UN Charter makes it clear that the UN General Assembly is also concerned with international peace and security. The Court also observed that the Assembly's power to recommend measures for the peaceful adjustment of a situation itself implies

[74] Ramsden and Hamilton 2017, p. 896, where the authors also observe that the Security Council and the General Assembly have increasingly formed habits of cooperation and dialogue with one another on other human rights and security issues.

[75] UNGA 2015c, para 8, "... consideration of referral of the situation in the Democratic People's Republic of Korea to the International Criminal Court and consideration of the scope for effective targeted sanctions against those who appear to be most responsible...".

[76] UN Charter, above n. 1, Article 1(1).

[77] UNGA 1950.

[78] UN General Assembly *Emergency Special Sessions* available at: https://www.un.org/en/ga/sessions/emergency.shtml (accessed 15 September 2022) where it is identified that emergency special sessions have been requested by the Security Council as well as by members of the UN General Assembly.

that some kind of action should be taken.[79] Therefore, the purpose of the UN in the maintenance of international peace and security provides the General Assembly with the power to recommend enforcement measures in the event of Security Council deadlock.[80] The competence of the General Assembly to assess the performance of the Security Council is also implicitly accepted in the *Wall Advisory Opinion*. Here the ICJ found that the emergency special session in question had been convened as per the Uniting for Peace Resolution, despite the matter not having been referred by the Security Council.[81] In addition, while resolutions of the General Assembly are non-binding to the Security Council, the application of the Uniting for Peace Resolution provides a forum through which support can be generated for actions taken in the spirit of the principles entrenched in R2P without approval of a deadlocked Security Council.[82]

7.4.2 Analysing General Assembly Action in Reforming the Veto Powers of the Security Council

While the previous section identified that informal veto restraint mechanisms such as the France/Mexico initiative and the ACT Code of Conduct highlight the enthusiasm among UN Member States to develop appropriate guidelines for the proper and responsible use of the veto, they are highly unlikely to result in concrete change within the decision-making functions of the Security Council. This has highlighted the need to develop more formal mechanisms for controlling the Security Council's use of the veto. In Chap. 3, the General Assembly's efforts at restraining the veto power through the passing on Resolution 76/262 was identified,[83] together with an analysis of the reception of the resolution by Member States.

The adoption of Resolution 76/262 opens the floor to many potential changes to decision-making within the Security Council. In particular, it has the potential to enhance the participation of all UN Member States in situations where the Security Council is unable to carry out its mandate. In addition, this resolution has the potential to enhance the accountability of the permanent members of the Security Council in situations where the maintenance of international peace and security is

---

[79] ICJ, Certain Expenses of the United Nations (Advisory Opinion of 20 July 1962) ICJ Rep 151, p. 163.

[80] Ramsden 2016, p. 283.

[81] ICJ, Legal Consequences of the Construction of a Wall in the Occupied Palestinian Territory (Advisory Opinion of 9 July 2004) ICJ Rep 136 p. 151.

[82] Koester 2015, p. 396.

[83] UNGA 2022.

at risk.[84] Although the resolution is a highly needed tool for enhancing accountability and decision-making within the Security Council,[85] the concerns raised by those States resistant to the resolution cannot be ignored. In particular the claim by India that there was a lack of inclusivity highlights that there appears to be a lack of transparency among decision-makers within the General Assembly.[86] In addition, taking into account China's fears of procedural confusion and inconsistency, one will only see the outcomes of this resolution once the opportunity arises in practice.[87] Another concern lies with the efficacy of such a resolution, considering that mechanisms for discussing and acting on the Security Council's failure to act are already in place.[88] Finally, the impact of the resolution on decision-making has the potential to be minimal at best, considering that Member States already offer public explanations of their votes in Council sessions. Therefore, having the Permanent Members explain their reasons to a larger group of States within the setting of the General Assembly may not act as a deterrent.[89]

As of November 2024, there have been thirteen instances of veto use within the Security Council since the passing of Resolution 76/262,[90] with the president of the General Assembly emphasising in the 2024 debate on the veto, that the Security Council "remains unable to collectively address critical peace and security situations" in Gaza, Mali, Syria, and Ukraine.[91]

---

[84] Thompson SK, Landgren K and Romita P "The United Nations in Hindsight: Challenging the Power of the Security Council Veto" (28 April 2022) *Just Security* available at: https://www.justsecurity.org/81294/the-united-nations-in-hindsight-challenging-the-power-of-the-security-council-veto/ (accessed 1 May 2022).

[85] Ibid.

[86] Business Standard *India expresses concern over UNGA draft resolution on 'veto power use'* (27 April 2022) available at https://www.business-standard.com/article/international/india-expresses-concern-over-unga-draft-resolution-on-veto-power-use-122042700040_1.html (accessed 1 May 2022) "The UNGA resolution was eventually adopted without consensus, without the conduct of the voting procedure."

[87] United Nations Meetings Coverage General Assembly Adopts Landmark Resolution Aimed at Holding Five Permanent Security Council Members Accountable for Use of Veto GA/12417 (26 April 2022) available at: https://www.un.org/press/en/2022/ga12417.doc.htm Statement by China.

[88] Business Standard *India expresses concern over UNGA draft resolution on 'veto power use'* (27 April 2022) available at https://www.business-standard.com/article/international/india-expresses-concern-over-unga-draft-resolution-on-veto-power-use-122042700040_1.html (accessed 1 May 2022).

[89] See above n. 84.

[90] See draft resolutions S/2022/431, 538, and 720; S/2023/506, 638, 773, 792, 970; S/2024/173, 239, 255, 312 and 302, at United Nations, *Security Council Meetings & Outcomes Tables [Security Council Veto List]* available at: https://research.un.org/en/docs/sc/quick (accessed 1 November 2024).

[91] United Nations "General Assembly debates Security Council's rising veto use" (23 April 2024) *UN News* available at: https://news.un.org/en/story/2024/04/1148896 (accessed 12 September 2024).

7.4.3 *What Role for the General Assembly for Addressing Security Council Inaction?*

In determining the proper role for the General Assembly for responding to instances of non-cooperation with the ICC not handled appropriately by the Security Council, consideration must be made as to the role that the Security Council may play in triggering General Assembly action. As noted in the Uniting for Peace Resolution, the General Assembly may act where the Security Council has failed in its primary responsibility. However, the resolution also specifies that the Security Council may request that the General Assembly convene an emergency special session.[92]

While either the General Assembly or the Security Council may trigger the Uniting for Peace Resolution, it is preferrable that the Security Council makes such a determination.[93] This is due to the fact that the Security Council's request, with respect to the language of the Charter conferring primary responsibility upon the Council, would constitute a certification that it is no longer exercising its functions on a particular situation.[94] In addition, by respecting the right of the Council to trigger such a resolution, harmony will be maintained between the Security Council and the General Assembly.[95] It is also important to note that while the Security Council does not have the legal authority to control acts of the General Assembly, members of the Security Council may seek to pass a resolution that objects to any assertion of legal power made by the Assembly.[96]

Therefore, while the General Assembly has the power to address Security Council inaction in the face of ICC non-cooperation through the passing of resolutions and recommendations, in tandem with the Security Council as per *The Wall Advisory* opinion, and through the adoption of the Uniting for Peace Resolution in an emergency special session; the application of this power is subject to the varied political will of Member States.

---

[92] UNGA 1950.

[93] Ramsden 2016, p. 298.

[94] Carswell 2013, pp. 469–470; the author notes that the Security Council's certification that it is no longer exercising its functions on a particular situation entails that the veto right has been exercised by the Permanent Members of the Security Council and as a consequence, the Security Council has failed to effectively exercise its responsibilities in the maintenance of international peace and security.

[95] Ramsden 2016, p. 298.

[96] Ibid., p. 289; the author also notes that the Assembly is only likely to recommend enforcement action under Uniting for Peace with the support of at least one Permanent Member of the Security Council.

7.5 Conclusion

This chapter has confirmed that the UN Security Council has an important role to play in the implementation of the Responsibility to Protect, as well as an important role in providing the International Criminal Court with the additional capacity to obtain the cooperation of States in order to function effectively.[97] In particular, the Security Council, together with its members, has a considerable influence on the effectiveness of the ICC as a promoter of R2P.[98] In this context, Mills holds that the Security Council must provide better support to the ICC through material and mandatory means.[99]

This present chapter has also identified that should the Security Council be unable to fulfil its responsibilities under R2P there should be mechanisms in place to better respond to atrocity situations, including the failure to cooperate with the ICC. Such mechanisms include the development of more effective frameworks under international law for addressing and restraining the use of the Security Council veto in decisions involving the maintenance of international peace and security and involving the General Assembly in peace and security decision-making processes.

At an aria-formula meeting commemorating the 20th Anniversary of the entry into force of the Rome Statute, States considered how to support existing Security Council referrals to the ICC through follow up on situations and instances of non-cooperation; strengthening the role of peacekeeping missions operating in ICC situations; and the imposition of sanctions. This meeting identified various obstacles to Security Council referrals and considered alternative measures in instances where the Security Council is unable to reach consensus because of the veto. Such alternative measures included the application of the informal veto restraint initiatives, as well as the recent work of the UN General Assembly in responding to Security Council inaction through its emergency powers and its adoption of a resolution calling for Permanent Members to give reasons for their decision to veto.[100] This meeting highlighted the continued commitment of the international community to strengthen the relationship between the ICC and the Security Council in the fight against impunity for serious international crimes.

---

[97] Contarino and Negron-Gonzales 2013, p. 424, "The relationship between the ICC and the UNSC is direct, important, and complex."

[98] Ibid., p. 435.

[99] Mills 2015, p. 98, where the author emphasises that the Security Council should involve all UN Member States within the framework of the Rome Statute.

[100] UN Web TV Arria Formula Meeting: 20th anniversary of the entry into force of the Rome Statute: reflections on the relationship between the International Criminal Court and the Security Council (24 June 2022) available at: https://media.un.org/en/asset/k16/k16jhghpke (accessed 25 June 2022).

References

Adediran B (2018) Reforming the Security Council through a Code of Conduct: A Sisyphean Task? Ethics & International Affairs 32(4), 463–482.

Babaian S (2018) The International Criminal Court—An International Criminal World Court. Springer International Publishing AG, Cham.

Blätter A, Williams PD (2011) The Responsibility Not To Veto. Global Responsibility to Protect 3(3), 301–322.

Carswell AJ (2013) Unblocking the UN Security Council: The Uniting for Peace Resolution. Journal of Conflict and Security Law 18(3), 453–480.

Contarino M, Negron-Gonzales M (2013) The International Criminal Court. In: Zyberi G (ed) An Institutional Approach to the Responsibility to Protect. Cambridge University Press, Cambridge, pp 411–436.

Essawy RM (2020) The Responsibility Not to Veto Revisited under the Theory of 'Consequential Jus Cogens'. Global Responsibility to Protect 12(3), 299–335

Genser J (2018) The United Nations Security Council's Implementation of the Responsibility to Protect: A Review of Past interventions and Recommendations for Improvement. Chicago Journal of International Law 18(2), 419–500.

Hamilton K (2016) The Role of Peacekeeping Operations in International Criminal Justice: Obstacles to Assistance Following Security Council Referrals to the ICC. Journal of International Peacekeeping 20(3–4), 342–362.

Hunt T, Sharland L (2020) Implementing R2P through United Nations Peacekeeping Operations: Opportunities and Challenges. In: Jacob C, Mennecke M (eds) Implementing the Responsibility to Protect: A Future Agenda. Routledge, Abingdon, pp 215–235.

Illingworth R (2020) Responsible Veto Restraint: a Transitional Cosmopolitan Reform Measure for the Responsibility to Protect. Global Responsibility to Protect 12(4), 385–414.

ICISS (2001) The Responsibility to Protect: Report of the International Commission on Intervention and State Sovereignty, available at: https://www.globalr2p.org/resources/the-responsibility-to-protect-report-of-the-international-commission-on-intervention-and-state-sovereignty-2001/ (accessed 15 July 2020).

Koester C (2015) Looking Beyond R2P for an Answer to Inaction in the Security Council. Florida Journal of International Law 27(3), 377–398.

Kress C, Prost K (2022) International Cooperation and Judicial Assistance. In: Ambos K (ed) Rome Statute of the International Criminal Court: Article-by-Article Commentary. Beck/Nomos/Hart, Munich, pp 2452–2701.

Milano E (2015) Russia's Veto in the Security Council: Whither the Duty to Abstain under Article 27(3) of the UN Charter? Zeitschrift fur auslandisches offentliches Recht und Völkerrecht 75(1), 215–231.

Mills K (2015) R2P and the ICC: At Odds or in Sync? Criminal Law Forum 26, 73–99.

Morris J, Wheeler N (2016) The Responsibility Not to Veto: A Responsibility Too Far? In: Bellamy AJ, Dunne T (eds) The Oxford Handbook on the Responsibility to Protect, 1st edn. Oxford University Press, Oxford, pp 227–246.

Ramsden M (2016) Uniting for Peace and Humanitarian Intervention: The Authorising Function of the U.N. General Assembly. Washington International Law Journal 25(2), 267–305.

Ramsden M, Hamilton T (2017) Uniting Against Impunity: The Un General Assembly as A Catalyst for Action at the ICC. International and Comparative Law Quarterly 66(4), 893–921.

Sluiter G, Talontsi S (2016) Credible and Authoritative Enforcement of State Cooperation with the International Criminal Court. In: Bekou O, Birkett DJ (eds) Cooperation and the International Criminal Court: Perspectives from Theory and Practice. Brill, Leiden, pp 80–113.

Trahan J (2020a) Questioning Unlimited Veto Use in Face of Atrocity Crimes. Case Western Reserve Journal of International Law 52(1), 73e100.

Trahan J (2020b) Existing Legal Limits to Security Council Veto Power in the Face of Atrocity Crimes. Cambridge University Press, New York.

UN General Assembly (UNGA) (1950) Fifth Session Resolution 377 A [Uniting for Peace] A/RES/377.
UN General Assembly (UNGA) (2004) Fifty-Ninth Session Report of the High-level Panel on Threats, Challenges and Change [A more secure world: our shared responsibility] A/59/565 (2 December 2004).
UN General Assembly (UNGA) (2005) Revised draft outcome document of the high-level plenary meeting of the General Assembly of September 2005 submitted by the President of the General Assembly UN Doc. A.59/HLPM/CRP.1/Rev.2 (10 August 2005).
UN General Assembly (UNGA) (2009a) Sixty-Third Session Report of the Secretary-General: [Implementing the Responsibility to Protect] A/63/677.
UN General Assembly (UNGA) (2009b) Sixty-third Session. 97th-101st Plenary Meetings A/63/PV.97; A/63/PV.98; A/63/PV.99; A/63/PV.100; A/63/PV.101.
UN General Assembly (UNGA) (2012) Sixty-sixth Session Report of the Secretary General [Responsibility to protect timely and decisive response] A/66/874.
UN General Assembly (UNGA) (2015a) Sixty-Ninth Session Report of the Secretary-General [A Vital and Enduring Commitment: Implementing the Responsibility to Protect] A/69/981 (13 July 2015).
UN General Assembly (UNGA) (2015b) Seventieth Session Report of the High-Level Independent Panel on Peace Operations on uniting our strengths for peace: politics, partnership, and people A/70/95 (17 June 2015).
UN General Assembly (UNGA) (2015c) Sixty-ninth Session Resolution 69/188 [Situation of human rights in the Democratic People's Republic of Korea] A/RES/69/188.
UN General Assembly (UNGA) (2022) Seventy-sixth Session Resolution 76/262 [Standing Mandate for a General Assembly debate when a veto is cast in the Security Council] A/76/L.52.
UN Security Council (UNSC) (2004) Resolution 1564, [on extension and strengthening of the mandate of the UN Organization Mission in the Democratic Republic of the Congo (MONUC)] S/RES/1565.
UN Security Council (UNSC) (2005) Resolution 1593 [Sudan] S/RES/1593.
UN Security Council (UNSC) (2011a) Resolution 1970 [Peace and Security in Africa] S/RES/1970.
UN Security Council (UNSC) (2011b) Resolution 1991 [Democratic Republic of the Congo] S/RES/1991
UN Security Council (UNSC) (2012) 6849th Meeting of the UN Security Council S/PV.6849.
UN Security Council (UNSC) (2013) Resolution 2100 Resolution [on establishment of the UN Multidimensional Integrated Stabilization Mission in Mali (MINUSMA)] S/RES/2100.
UN Security Council (UNSC) (2014) Resolution 2149 [Central African Republic] S/RES/2149.
Venigandla SA (2021) Protection Justice and Accountability: Cooperation between the International Criminal Court and UN Peacekeeping Operations. International Peace Institute available at: https://www.ipinst.org/2021/05/cooperation-between-icc-and-un-security-council (accessed 15 May 2022).
Vilmer JJ (2018) The Responsibility Not to Veto: A Genealogy. Global Governance: A Review of Multilateralism and International Organizations 24(3), 331–349.

Chapter 8
Conclusions and Recommendations

Contents

8.1 Conclusions 206
8.1.1 Enforcing the Obligation to Cooperate 206
8.1.2 R2P and General International Law as Additional Tools for Strengthening Responses to Non-cooperation 208
8.1.3 The Role of R2P and General International Law in Strengthening Responses to Non-cooperation 209
8.2 Recommendations 212
8.2.1 Strengthening the ICC's Responses to Non-cooperation 213
8.3 Final Recommendations and Conclusions 214
References 216

Abstract This chapter seeks to summarise the various conclusions reached in previous chapters of this monograph. This chapter will identify that the International Criminal Court's frameworks for non-cooperation, along with the remedies at the disposal of the ICC Assembly of States Parties and the UN Security Council have been ineffective in responding to and remedying instances of non-cooperation in an effective manner. This chapter will also highlight that frameworks other than those contained in the Rome Statute may be suitable for addressing these instances of non-cooperation or otherwise complementing existing responses to non-cooperation. This includes frameworks present within the responsibility to protect, as well as various sources of general international law. This chapter will then conclude the study by proposing several recommendations for strengthening and complementing the ICC's responses to non-cooperation through the application of frameworks identified throughout this book.

Keywords International Criminal Court · Non-cooperation · Assembly of States Parties · UN Security Council · Responsibility to Protect · General International Law · Conclusions and Recommendations

M. L. Jacobs, *The Consequences of Non-cooperation with the International Criminal Court*, International Criminal Justice Series 37,
https://doi.org/10.1007/978-94-6265-675-8_8

8.1 Conclusions

In its more than twenty years of operation, the ICC has established itself as an important mechanism for the adjudication of serious international crimes. However, international criminal tribunals like the ICC are very much "giants without arms or legs" which require artificial limbs, namely States, to function effectively, If the ICC is unable to receive cooperation from States, it is unable to fulfil its mandate.[1] Notwithstanding the instances of non-cooperation identified in Chap. 2 of this book, States have generally been willing to cooperate with the Court in the investigation and prosecution of crimes in its jurisdiction. Even though non-cooperation has not become commonplace, any instance of non-cooperation has the effect of seriously damaging the reputation of the Court, as well its ability to function effectively as per its mandate.

In this book, the ICC's frameworks for responding to non-cooperation by States was analysed, with a view to establishing more effective responses and remedies. In the search for more effective remedies, this book looked to develop frameworks through the lens of the responsibility to protect doctrine, and principles developed under the rules of general international law. In conducting this analysis, this book was able to reach the following conclusions with regards to the current structures available for responding to and remedying the non-cooperation of States.

8.1.1 Enforcing the Obligation to Cooperate

Since the establishment of the ICC, the enforcement and implementation of obligations under the Rome Statute has been an important topic of debate. In an article written in 1999, Penrose highlights the importance of enforcement in international criminal law by identifying that appropriate mechanisms need to be in place that are capable of enforcing the law, since law without enforcement is reliant on States acting selflessly in order to peacefully coexist with each other in an international environment that is influenced by economic and political factors.[2] In such a case, law without effective enforcement measures is likely to fail.[3] This book has highlighted a number of issues in the effective enforcement and implementation of the ICC's cooperation frameworks with regards to responses to non-cooperation.

---

[1] Cassese 1998, p. 13.

[2] Penrose 1999, pp. 350–351.

[3] Ibid., p. 351.

8.1.1.1 Inconsistent Decisions on Non-cooperation

In Chap. 2 it was confirmed that the Pre-Trial Chambers of the ICC have heard many non-cooperation cases. While these cases have assisted in developing the law on non-cooperation, they have identified a myriad of issues within the Court's frameworks for enforcing and addressing cooperation. An analysis of the existing case law highlights that the Court's wide powers granted to it in the exercise of discretion in these cases has not been helpful in establishing uniform responses to non-cooperation. There appears to be confusion surrounding what guides the Pre-Trial Chamber's in its exercise of discretion, which has led to inconsistent decisions in cases with similar facts and circumstances.[4]

An additional concern lies with the negative attitude of the Pre-Trial Chambers towards the procedures and remedies that follow a finding and referral of non-cooperation. The decision on South Africa's non-cooperation in the Al-Bashir case illustrates this frustration as a referral of non-cooperation was not called for, as previous instances of non-cooperation had not resulted in effective measures against States following a referral.[5] Such a negative attitude towards non-cooperation by the Court's own chambers is dangerous for the effective enforcement of State obligations owed to the Court, as it sends a message to States that they do not face any substantial consequences for refusing or failing to cooperate with the Court's requests.[6]

The negative attitude expressed by the Pre-Trial Chamber in the decision on South Africa's non-cooperation in the Al-Bashir case is due to the fact that the Assembly of States Parties and the UN Security Council, as the bodies tasked with remedying instances of non-cooperation following a referral, have not responded to such referrals in an effective manner. While the Assembly has developed procedures and a toolkit to assist in responding to non-cooperation, these measures lack any coercive weight to them and consist mainly of soft political and diplomatic tools aimed at reminding States of their obligation to cooperate with the Court.[7]

While the Security Council has a wide variety of tools at its disposal to respond to threats to international peace and security, it has failed to effectively address issues relating to cooperation in situations it has referred to the Court. The lack of follow up on these situations and the failure to respond to non-cooperation cases that have been referred to it by the ICC Pre-Trial Chambers gives off the impression that the Security Council does not see non-cooperation as a priority within its protective mandate, which has negative implications for the effective functioning of international criminal justice.[8]

---

[4] Sluiter 2020, p. 311.

[5] Prosecutor v Omar Hassan Ahmad Al Bashir [Decision Under Article 87(7) of the Rome Statute on the non-compliance by South Africa with the request by the Court for the arrest and surrender of Omar Al-Bashir] ICC-02/05-01/09-302 (6 July 2017) paras 137–138.

[6] Sluiter 2020, p. 311.

[7] Bekou 2019, p. 927; Sluiter 2020, p. 312.

[8] Aloisi 2013, p. 167.

8.1.1.2 Identifying the Need for More Effective Responses to Non-cooperation

This book has identified that the frameworks developed and executed by the ICC and associated bodies for responding to instances of non-cooperation have been largely ineffective. This highlights the need for these frameworks to be strengthened for there to be real consequences that actually deter States from choosing not to cooperate with the requests of the Court.

Should the measures developed by the ICC and its associated bodies be ineffective in preventing and addressing instances of non-cooperation, alternative measures aimed at strengthening the mandate of the Court and encouraging States to cooperate with its requests should be considered. This is recognised by the ICC itself where case law has recognised that the non-cooperation provisions within Article 87(7) of the Statute are but one of many tools that can be used to secure cooperation.[9] In this context, this book has identified the need to divert from the black letter of the Rome Statute and consider the application of principles and frameworks within the context of the responsibility to protect principle and the rules of general international law.

8.1.2 R2P and General International Law as Additional Tools for Strengthening Responses to Non-cooperation

Chapter 3 of this book identified that that the ICC and R2P, as recent developments in international law, are complementary to each other as tools in the fight against serious atrocity crimes. This is since they are tasked with addressing the similar situations where atrocity crimes are occurring, and that they are reliant on the cooperation of States in order to function effectively. The complementary nature of the ICC and R2P is reflected within the three pillars of the doctrine.

This chapter has also highlighted that R2P can assist in strengthening the ICC's mandate and increase its legitimacy within the international legal structure. A strong R2P agenda within the ICC may assist in creating ideal conditions needed to ensure the effective functioning of international criminal justice. R2P also has the added effect of increasing the involvement of the international community in the work of the ICC, which has the effect of encouraging States to join and cooperate with the Court's requests, especially requests relating to the arrest and surrender of suspects.

---

[9] ICC, Prosecutor v Saif Al-Islam Gaddafi [Decision on the non-compliance by Libya with requests for cooperation by the Court and referring the matter to the United Nations Security Council] (10 December 2014), ICC-01/11-01/11-577, para 23; ICC, Prosecutor v Uhuru Muigai Kenyatta [Judgment on the Prosecutor's appeal against Trial Chamber V(B)'s "Decision on Prosecution's application for a finding of non-compliance under Article 87(7) of the Statute"] (10 December 2014), ICC-01/09-02/11-1032, para 52.

8.1.2.1 Frameworks for Strengthening Non-cooperation Remedies under General International Law

The obligations and principles within R2P are recognised within frameworks entrenched in general international law that promote cooperation and the protection of populations from international atrocity crimes, as well as a general obligation to cooperate in response to such breaches is recognised within the framework of the rules of State responsibility for internationally wrongful acts. This obligation is further strengthened through the recognition that breaches peremptory norms of general international law require more effective and stricter responses than other internationally wrongful acts. The protection of peremptory norms is further highlighted within the framework of the Genocide Convention and the Geneva Conventions, as well as within the continued development of international law by the ILC. This book has highlighted that closer interactions with these frameworks and the Rome Statute may be handy in strengthening the Court's cooperation structures.

In this context, attention should be brought to structures developed through the lens of general international law, particularly in the context of the rules of State responsibility, as well as the rules surrounding peremptory norms. These include obligations of cessation and non-repetition of the internationally wrongful act, as well as obligations to compensate or otherwise repair the damage caused by the wrongful act. Noting that the prevention and prosecution of crimes under the Rome Statute and R2P are classified as peremptory norms of general international law, as per the ILC's Conclusions on Peremptory Norms, there is a collective obligation upon the international community to cooperate to lawfully bring to an end the breach of such norms, as well as neither recognise such situations as lawful nor assist in maintaining such a continued breach.

In addition, this book identified the potential for States to react individually to such breaches through the use of collective countermeasures and resort to judicial settlement through the International Court of Justice. While measures for responding to instances of non-cooperation were possible, it was also emphasised that collective measures recognised in institutionalised frameworks were the preferred method for responding to such breaches.

8.1.3 The Role of R2P and General International Law in Strengthening Responses to Non-cooperation

In this book, it has been highlighted that R2P and General International Law have a crucial role in strengthening the Structures within the assembly of States Parties and the UN Security Council for promoting cooperation and addressing the failure to cooperation. The application of these frameworks has specific implications for the proper execution of the mandates of these bodies

8.1.3.1 R2P and the Assembly of States Parties

As the political and diplomatic arm of the ICC, the Assembly requires the full participation of States in order to function effectively. This highlights the need for there to be effective capacity building structures in place as per the second pillar of R2P,[10] which places an obligation upon the international community to assist States in building up their capacities to effectively execute their primary responsibility to protect. In this regard, the Assembly is required to monitor ratification of the Statute, work with the international community to promote universal ratification, and develop measures aimed at strengthening cooperation. One way in which this can be achieved is through effective promotion of the complementarity principle. The Assembly is granted with the power to assist in strengthening domestic jurisdictions to allow them to be better equipped to respond to and address serious international crimes.[11] This study has emphasised that the Assembly has a special role in promoting positive complementarity but is held back in this regard by a lack of resources and human capacity. This has highlighted the need to give the Assembly Secretariat additional powers to assist it in the effective coordination of positive complementarity activities.

Regarding responses to non-cooperation, this book has highlighted that the Assembly's current frameworks for addressing the failure to cooperate need to be strengthened as they are not coercive enough. Such responses can be strengthened and complemented through several measures. This includes the application of the Assembly's general powers under Article 112(2)(g) of the Rome Statute, the adoption of resolutions that attempt to clarify issues in interpretation of the Statutes provisions on cooperation or resort to judicial settlement. Additionally, there lies the possibility that the application of frameworks within other sources of international law can be utilised to strengthen the Assembly's responses to non-cooperation. These include judicial settlement through the International Court of Justice; more emphasis on warning and reminding States of their obligation to cooperate; the implementation of administrative fines as a form of reparation as per the Articles on State Responsibility; removing the right to vote or nominate candidates for election, and suspension or expulsion of a State Party from the Assembly. While these proposals may be useful, this book has identified that they may not be effective without the proper exercise of political will by States. In addition, care must be made not to develop remedies that may alienate the Court from State Parties.

---

[10] Saba and Akbarzadeh 2020, p. 97, where the authors highlight the need for closer interactions between the ICC and the second pillar of R2P to ensure more effective capacity building structures.

[11] Review Conference of the International Criminal Court *Resolution on Complementarity* RC/Res.1 (8 June 2010) para 9; Goldston (2011) *Complementarity and the ASP: Opportunities for Impact [Presentation to the Hague Working Group on the Rule of Law]* available at https://www.justiceinitiative.org/publications/complementarity-and-assembly-state-parties-opportunities-impact (accessed 5 January 2021).

8.1.3.2 R2P and the Security Council

In this book, it was emphasized that the Security Council's track record in responding to ICC non-cooperation has been less than effective. This highlights the need for the Security Council to fully realise its obligations towards the ICC in the spirit of the principles entrenched in the UN Charter and the Responsibility to Protect. In particular, it has been highlighted that the Security Council requires structures in place to ensure better follow up of situations that it has referred to the Court. This may be done through the application of a working group tasked with monitoring the implementation and enforcement obligations towards the Court, and in responding to the failure to cooperate. Alternatively, the expansion of the Security Council's informal working groups on international tribunals to include the ICC may also be effective in this context, as well as expanding peacekeeping mandates in situation States to assist the Security Council in following up and executing the requests of the Court in executing arrest warrants.

It is also stressed that the Security Council's decision-making processes are constrained by a lack of consensus and political will among its members. This study has identified the need to reform or otherwise restrict the use of the veto power granted to its permanent members through the lens of the responsibility not to veto, in which the Permanent Members of the Security Council are under a duty to refrain from using their veto powers in situations where atrocity situations are occurring. This duty is reinforced within the frameworks on State responsibility and the protection of peremptory norms, where States and the international organisations they represent are under an obligation to cooperate to bring to an end any serious breach of such obligations, and not to recognise such breaches as lawful, nor render aid or assistance in maintaining an unlawful situation.

To fully recognise the responsibility not to veto, this book has also analysed the development of veto restraint initiatives that have been developed by the international community aimed at promoting more responsible use of the veto in situations where the maintenance of international peace and security is at stake. While these initiatives are supported by many States, there are however concerns with the proper implementation of such initiatives as they contain weak language that appears to maintain the hierarchy of the permanent members of the Security Council. This has highlighted the need to apply institutionalised frameworks aimed at encouraging more responsible decision-making within the Security Council.

8.1.3.3 The Role of the General Assembly in Strengthening Security Council Responses to Non-cooperation

This book has also identified that the General Assembly has a role to play in assisting in securing cooperation with the ICC and strengthening responses to non-cooperation by recommending measures in situations where the Security Council has been deadlocked by a lack of consensus among its members. Such measures include the power to make recommendations to the Security Council;[12] the convening of an Emergency Special Session under the Uniting for Peace Resolution which aims to set up measures designed to mirror the structure of Chapter VII of the UN Charter;[13] and recent efforts at implementing formal mechanisms for restraining the veto.[14] These frameworks are handy tools for enhancing the participation of all UN Member States in situations where the Security Council is deadlocked and enhancing the accountability of the Permanent members in decisions where consensus is important for the maintenance of international peace and security.

This book has highlighted however, that the application of the General Assembly's powers to address Security Council inaction is subject to some constraints. Most notably is the recognition that the Assembly's powers, although authoritative, are merely recommendatory and therefore not binding upon the Security Council.[15] In addition, there are concerns relating to the appropriateness of the Uniting for Peace Resolution as it has an effect on the powers and hierarchy of UN bodies.[16] The application of the Assembly's powers is further constrained by the political will and selectivity of UN Member States in addressing specific situations where international peace and security are at risk.

8.2 Recommendations

In light of the findings and conclusions presented in this book, it is recommended that the frameworks developed to address and punish non-cooperation be strengthened further in line with the responsibility to protect, as well as principles entrenched in general international law. The development of more effective responses to non-cooperation will have the effect of showing States that are real consequences for failing to execute the requests of the Court, as well as showing the international community that the ICC is dedicated to the fight against impunity for serious international crimes. In addition, the Assembly of States Parties, the UN Security Council, and alternative institutional structures tasked with atrocity prevention and the maintenance of international peace and security can be better equipped to develop and implement frameworks aimed at promoting cooperation and following up on instances of non-cooperation. Therefore, the following recommendations can be made with regards to the development of effective structures for enforcing cooperation and responding to non-cooperation:

---

[12] The Charter of the United Nations (26 June 1945, 1 UNTS XVI, Entry into Force 24 October 1945), Article 12(1).

[13] Carswell 2013, p. 459.

[14] UNGA 2022, which mandates the convening of a formal meeting within 10 working days of the casting of the veto by one or more of the Permanent Members of the Security Council and hold a debate on the situation as to which the veto was cast.

[15] UNGA 2009, para 63; Ryngaert and Cuyckens 2013, p. 114.

[16] Melling and Dennett 2017, pp. 300–304.

8.2.1 Strengthening the ICC's Responses to Non-cooperation

With regard to the ICC's structures for making judicial findings of non-cooperation, the referral of decisions to the Assembly of States Parties and the UN Security Council should be an automatic response to a finding of non-cooperation serious enough to initiate non-cooperation proceedings.[17] This would have the result of ensuring that the procedure under Article 87(7) is used in a consistent manner, resulting in well-reasoned and high quality decisions that are in conformity with the requirements of natural justice.[18]

8.2.1.1 Developing Effective Remedies within the Assembly of States Parties

Noting that the Court, as well as the Assembly of States Parties, have recognised that current frameworks currently in place for responding to non-cooperation have been less than effective, it is identified that more coercive measures should be in place that do not replace existing diplomatic responses, but instead complement and strengthen these responses in a manner that encourages States to cooperate with the Court. These remedies may be strengthened through the application of remedies and principles within the rules on State responsibility and peremptory norms of general international law to already-existing frameworks within the Rome Statute and the Assembly's non-cooperation toolkit. Looking at the Assembly's non-cooperation frameworks, such remedies proposed include judicial settlement through the international court of justice through contentious or advisory proceedings; warning States of the consequences they face for failing to cooperate with the Court; the imposition of economic sanctions, namely an increase in contributions to the Court; suspending State participation in important decisions of the assembly, such as the loss of the right to vote and nominate candidates for election to the Court; and suspension or expulsion of a State from the Court.

8.2.1.2 Strengthening the Security Council's ICC Mandate

This book has emphasised that efforts should be made to encourage the Council to provide more effective follow up on situations it has referred to the Court, through the establishment of a working group tasked with monitoring the Security Council's work with the ICC or expand the mandate of the already existing working group on international tribunals to include the ICC. The potential role of peacekeeping missions in such situations may also assist in encouraging better follow up, as well as in securing the arrest of ICC suspects.

---

[17] Sluiter 2020, p. 313.

[18] Sluiter and Talontsi 2016, p. 108.

With regard to the Security Council's voting system, efforts should be made to encourage the permanent members of the Council to exercise their veto right in a responsible manner in decisions involving serious international crimes. This can be done through application of informal veto restraint mechanisms developed by States, as well as through the involvement and recommendations of the General Assembly following the failure of the Security Council to reach consensus. Finally, the Security Council should be encouraged to respond to instances of non-cooperation in a timely and decisive manner through the application of its powers under Chapter VII of the UN Charter, in the spirit of principles and obligations entrenched within general international law.

8.2.1.3 Emphasis on Collective Responses to Non-cooperation

While this book has identified that States can potentially respond to instances of non-cooperation through the application of individual measures outside the framework of the Rome Statute, it is advised that such measures are to be used with caution. It is therefore recommended that remedies for non-cooperation should rather be implemented through the collective frameworks entrenched within the Rome Statute and the UN Charter, considering the principles recognised within the three pillars of R2P. In doing so, the responses to non-cooperation can be implemented in a manner that is legitimate, internationally recognised and accepted not subject to potential abuse by States acting on their own volition. Therefore, the frameworks developed by the Rome Statute and the UN legal order should be implemented in a manner that encourages States to cooperate, strengthens the capacities of States to follow through with their obligations to these bodies, and discourages or otherwise deters States from choosing not to execute their cooperation obligations.

8.3 Final Recommendations and Conclusions

This book has investigated how the International Criminal Court's frameworks for responding to instances of non-cooperation by States Parties to the Rome Statute can be developed and strengthened through the application of the responsibility to protect and through principles entrenched in general international law. As the Court is reliant on the cooperation of States in order to function effectively, particularly in arresting and surrendering suspects to the Court for prosecution, it is crucial that State capacities are strengthened to ensure that the obligation to cooperate is effectively enforced.

It is also crucial for States to be aware that there are serious consequences for failing to cooperate in situations where there are serious atrocity crimes being committed. Firstly, there are serious consequences for the victims of these crimes as non-cooperation has the effect on the administration of justice as a result of perpetrators not being held legally accountable for their actions. Secondly, the failure to secure perpetrators of serious international crimes has implications for the international reputation of the ICC in that its legitimacy and effectiveness as an international criminal tribunal is questions. Lastly, the failure to cooperate with the Court has an effect on the reputation of States within the international community, leading to a loss of political and financial assistance from States.

Therefore, in determining effective remedies for addressing non-cooperation, consideration should be made to strengthening existing responses to the failure to cooperate or developing additional remedies that recognise the implications of a State's failure to assist in ensuring that the perpetrators of serious international crimes are brought to justice. In addition, the Assembly of States Parties and the UN Security Council should be encouraged to use their powers in responding to non-cooperation in a manner that illustrates their dedication and political will to assist the ICC in the justice system and ending impunity for serious international crimes. This highlights the need for effective enforcement measures within these bodies that are implemented consistently in all non-cooperation decisions communicated to them for consideration.[19]

In this book, it was identified that the responsibility to protect is an important tool in the arsenal of the ICC for strengthening its mandate and the obligations of States in cooperating with the Court. The three-pillar system has the effect of strengthening frameworks for enhancing State cooperation with the Court within all the bodies tasked with assisting in ensuring States comply with their obligations to the Court and responding to non-cooperation. It is however highlighted that all these mechanisms, once developed and strengthened to the appropriate standard, will only be effective with the proper exercise of political will by States within these organisations. States should therefore be active in public forums, demonstrating their political commitment for protecting populations from serious international crimes, promoting the development of effective prevention measures, and developing timely and decisive responses to the proliferation of serious international crimes.

While this book has identified the need for more effective tools for strengthening cooperation in matters relating to the to the prosecution of international crimes and the maintenance of international peace and security, it has also identified that there is a continued commitment among the international community to ensure that these tools are readily available. However, as it currently stands, the International Criminal Court, the Assembly of States Parties and the UN Security Council have much work to do to ensure that States are held accountable for failures to comply with their obligations under the Rome Statute.

[19] Sluiter and Talontsi 2016, p. 108.

References

Aloisi R (2013) A Tale of Two Institutions: The United Nations Security Council and the International Criminal Court. International Criminal Law Review 13(1) 147–168.

Bekou O (2019) Dealing with Non-cooperation at the ICC: Towards a More Holistic Approach. International Criminal Law Review 19(6): 911–937.

Carswell AJ (2013) Unblocking the UN Security Council: The Uniting for Peace Resolution. Journal of Conflict and Security Law 18(3) 453–480.

Cassese A (1998) On the Current Trends towards Criminal Prosecution and Punishment of Breaches of International Humanitarian Law. European Journal of International Law 9(1): 2–17.

Melling G, Dennett A (2017) The Security Council veto and Syria: responding to mass atrocities through the "Uniting for Peace" Resolution. Indian Journal of International Law 57, 285–307

Penrose MM (1999) Lest We Fail: The Importance of Enforcement in International Criminal Law. American University International Law Review 15(2), 321–394

Ryngaert C, Cuyckens H (2013) The General Assembly. In: Zyberi G (ed) An Institutional Approach to the Responsibility to Protect. Cambridge University Press, Cambridge, pp. 109–129.

Saba A, Akbarzadeh S (2020) The ICC and R2P: Complementary or Contradictory? International Peacekeeping, 28(1), 84–109.

Sluiter G (2020) Reforms to Enhance State Cooperation and Address Witness Interference. In: Steinberg RH (ed) The International Criminal Court: Contemporary Challenges and Reform Proposals. Koninklijke Brill NV. Leiden, pp. 303–313.

Sluiter G, Talontsi S (2016) Credible and Authoritative Enforcement of State Cooperation with the International Criminal Court. In: Bekou O, Birkett DJ (eds) Cooperation and the International Criminal Court: Perspectives from Theory and Practice. Brill, Leiden, pp. 80–113.

UN General Assembly (UNGA) (2009) Sixty-Third Session. Report of the Secretary-General: [Implementing the Responsibility to Protect] A/63/677.

UN General Assembly (UNGA) (2022) Seventy-sixth Session Resolution 76/262 [Standing Mandate for a General Assembly debate when a veto is cast in the Security Council] A/76/L.52.

Index

A
Ad-hoc tribunals, 66, 94
Administrative fines, 153, 168, 173, 210
Administrative sanctions, 168, 175
Advisory opinion, 115, 138, 139, 143, 170–172
Advisory proceedings, 168–170, 213
African Charter on Human and Peoples' Rights, 140
African Court of Justice, 12, 13
Any other function, 57
Appeals Chamber, 4, 10, 31, 33, 39, 40, 42, 58, 62, 67, 134, 149
Article 112. *See* Assembly of States Parties
Article 13(b). *See* UN Security Council
Article 2(4), 82
Article 87(7). *See* Non-cooperation
Article 97. *See* Consultation Procedures
Article 97 consultations. *See* Consultation procedures
Article 98(1), 34
Articles on State Responsibility for Internationally Wrongful Acts, 8
ASP. *See* Assembly of States Parties
Assembly Bureau. *See* Assembly of States Parties
Assembly of States Parties, 3, 6, 14, 15, 22, 23, 25–28, 30, 31, 33, 34, 38–40, 42, 44, 48, 49, 51, 56, 59, 71, 72, 75, 101, 127, 137, 141, 149–151, 154–156, 159–164, 166, 170, 173, 174, 179, 180, 184, 207, 209, 212, 213, 215
Assembly Procedures Relating to Non-cooperation, 49, 167, 172
Atrocities, 67, 80, 92, 95, 99, 111, 118, 141, 159
Atrocity prevention, 90, 92, 94, 97, 101, 191, 212
AU, 12, 26–29

B
Barcelona Traction, 133, 143
Benjamin Netanyahu, 43
Bensouda. *See* ICC Prosecutor
Blaskic, 67, 134
BRICS, 36
Bureau, 26, 51, 56, 69, 159, 163, 175

C
Canadian Government, 83
Capacity building, 90, 100, 142, 156, 161, 179, 210
Case law, 10, 12, 23, 24, 41, 42, 44, 127, 138, 144, 207, 208
Case law on non-cooperation, 14, 18, 23, 43
Cessation and Assurances of Non-repetition, 128
Chad, 24, 33, 34, 73, 178
Chagos Archipelago. *See* Advisory opinion
Chapter VII. *See* UN Charter
China, 117
Civil society, 18, 53, 161, 163
Code of conduct, 190, 198
Collective obligation, 131, 141, 209
Compensation, 129, 173
Complementarity, 95, 99, 100, 155–166, 210
Compliance mechanisms, 166, 167

M. L. Jacobs, *The Consequences of Non-cooperation with the International Criminal Court*, International Criminal Justice Series 37,
https://doi.org/10.1007/978-94-6265-675-8

Consensus, 7, 18, 83, 107, 114, 175, 201, 212, 214
Consent, 62, 194–196
Consultation procedures, 21, 41
Contentious proceedings, 169
Convention on the Prevention and Punishment of the Crime of Genocide, 133
Cooperation regime, 2, 6, 19, 43, 44, 48, 75, 150
Countermeasures, 142, 145–149, 209
Court of Appeal at Nairobi, 25
Crimes against humanity, 2, 5, 24, 43, 80, 90, 95, 135, 189
Customary international law, 10, 33, 62, 82, 106, 132, 138, 150

D
Decision-making Processes. *See* Discretion
Deferral, 61, 64
Democratic Republic of the Congo, 176
Discretion, 4, 33, 40, 42, 43, 136, 173, 207
Discretionary power, 24, 27, 32, 38, 43
Djibouti, 24, 33, 34, 41, 178
Domestic legislation. *See* Complementarity
DRC. *See* Democratic Republic of the Congo

E
Emergency special session, 113, 114, 116, 197, 198, 200, 212
Enforcement mechanisms, 44, 60, 61, 73, 135
Ethnic cleansing, 5, 80, 90
Expulsion, 175, 177, 210, 213

F
Fairness and proportionality, 178
Finding of non-compliance, 28, 38
Follow up, 7, 31, 48, 55, 56, 66, 70, 71, 73, 74, 184, 192, 201, 211, 213
Former Yugoslavia, 66, 83

G
Gambia v Myanmar, 134
General Assembly. *See* UN General Assembly
General international law, 6, 7, 9, 15, 75, 119, 126, 131–133, 136, 141, 146, 151, 155, 167, 169, 180, 183–185, 208, 209, 213, 214
General power, 57, 210
Geneva Conventions, 150, 159, 187, 209
Genocide, 2, 5, 24, 95, 118, 134, 135, 144, 146, 170, 186, 189
Genocide Convention, 134, 140, 144, 159, 169, 170, 187, 209
Government of Canada, 37
Greentree process, 160

H
Humanitarian intervention, 14, 81–84, 91, 103
Human Rights Council, 175
Hungary, 43

I
ICC Prosecutor, 29, 35, 40, 62, 68, 97, 98, 101, 158, 193
ICISS. *See* International Commission on Intervention and State Sovereignty
ICISS Report, 8, 84, 93, 104, 107, 113
ICJ. *See* International Court of Justice
ICTY, 62, 67, 68, 134, 149
ILC. *See* International Law Commission
Immunities. *See* Immunity
Immunity, 10, 26, 32, 34, 37, 64
Impartiality, 176, 194, 195
Implementing R2P Report, 8, 88, 89, 91, 94, 99, 108, 188
Individual Responses to Breaches. *See* Peremptory Norms
Institut de Droit International, 133, 147
International community, 4, 5, 15, 18, 36, 75, 80, 83, 86, 87, 89, 90, 92, 94, 96, 99, 100, 103, 105, 106, 112, 127, 128, 130–133, 141–143, 147–149, 151, 162, 179, 184, 189, 190, 192, 201, 208–212, 215
International Court of Justice, 86, 142, 209, 210, 213
International Covenant on Civil and Political Rights, 140
International criminal justice, 93, 94, 96, 99, 102, 103, 162, 207, 208
International criminal law, 69, 70, 74, 96, 101, 163, 206
International criminal tribunal, 10, 18, 33, 36, 37, 62, 66, 69, 74, 93, 206, 215
International human rights treaties, 140

International law, 4, 6, 8, 15, 37, 53, 57, 67, 71, 75, 80, 86, 103, 105, 106, 118, 126, 127, 131, 132, 134–136, 141, 144, 147, 149–151, 155, 169, 184, 185, 187, 189, 195, 201, 209, 210
International Law Commission, 15, 126, 134
Internationally Wrongful Act, 15, 127, 129, 143, 145, 150, 155, 167, 173, 209
International organisations, 118, 132, 135, 136, 139, 164, 167, 175, 211
International peace and security, 7, 15, 28, 60, 61, 63–65, 67, 69, 73, 81, 104, 105, 111–113, 115, 127, 180, 184, 185, 189, 192, 197, 198, 207, 212, 215
Investigations and prosecutions, 3, 20, 21, 68, 96, 101
Israel, 144, 169

J

Jordan, 4, 32–34, 40, 41, 58
Judicial responses, 23, 41
Judicial settlement, 7, 59, 91, 143, 209, 210, 213

K

Kampala Review Conference, 157, 160, 163
Kenya, 24–26, 40, 42
Kosovo, 83, 148

L

Law of Treaties, 58, 176
Legal Consequences of the Construction of a Wall in the Occupied Palestinian Territory, 112, 133
Libya, 38, 39, 62, 63, 68, 71, 72, 91, 96, 97, 195
Liechtenstein, 106, 116
Loss of Participation Rights, 174
Loss of the Right to Vote, 213

M

Malabo Protocol, 12, 13
Malawi, 24, 26, 33
Material breach, 177
Minister of Justice and Constitutional Development v The Southern African Litigation Centre, 30, 31
Mongolia, 2, 23, 36–38
Multilateral treaty, 62, 177

N

Nairobi High Court, 25
NATO, 83
Nigeria, 24, 26, 27, 178
Non-cooperation, 2–15, 18, 20, 22–24, 26, 27, 30, 31, 33, 34, 36, 38–44, 48–58, 61, 65–72, 74, 75, 80, 101, 103, 126, 127, 131, 137, 141–143, 148–151, 154, 155, 157, 166–169, 172, 173, 176, 178–180, 184, 185, 192, 201, 206–215
Non-cooperation focal points, 51, 53
Non-intervention, 81–83
Non-State armed groups, 92
Nuclear weapons, 171

O

Obligation *erga omnes*, 14, 133
Obligations *erga omnes partes*, 133, 134, 144, 151
Obligations of non-recognition and non-assistance, 137, 168
Obligation to arrest and surrender, 9, 20, 27–29, 43
Obligation to cooperate, 3, 9, 12, 18, 19, 22, 24, 31, 32, 56, 62, 68, 72, 135, 136, 140, 166, 172, 192, 207, 210, 214
Occupied Palestinian territories, 139
Omar Al-Bashir, 3, 24
Omar Hassan Ahmad Al-Bashir. *See* Omar Al Bashir

P

Pacta tertiis, 62
Peacekeeping operations, 73, 104, 185, 192–196
Peremptory norms, 7, 8, 15, 127, 131, 132, 134–137, 139–142, 151, 155, 167, 173, 183–186, 209
Peremptory norms of general international law, 7, 8, 15, 126, 127, 132, 133, 142, 151, 155, 183, 184, 209, 213
Permanent members, 7, 69, 70, 105, 114, 116, 183, 186–191, 199, 211, 214
Pillar One, 90, 98, 99
Pillar Three, 91, 100, 101, 131, 166, 167
Pillar Two, 90, 99, 100, 156
Political declaration, 190, 191

Political norm, 5, 95
Political will, 60, 69, 71, 75, 95, 118, 146, 156, 161, 165, 200, 210–212, 215
Pre-trial Chamber, 3, 4, 26–34, 37, 38, 40–42, 60, 65, 73, 207
Preventing non-cooperation, 41, 126
Primary responsibility, 5, 15, 60, 80, 85, 95, 98, 104, 111, 112, 142, 157, 162, 180, 184, 200, 210
Promoting cooperation, 5, 15, 38, 41, 49, 179, 209, 212
Prosecutor v Dusko Tadic, 62
Prosecutor v Tihomir Blaskic, 67, 149
Putin, Vladimir Vladimirovich, 35

R

Recommendations, 50, 51, 55, 59, 65, 67, 113, 114, 149, 160, 197, 200, 212, 214
Referral, 24, 30, 31, 38–40, 42, 44, 48, 54, 57, 61, 63, 68, 70–72, 101, 107, 184, 192, 197, 207, 213
Referrals of non-cooperation, 4, 44, 173
Regulations of the International Criminal Court, 23
Reparations, 128–130, 143, 169, 173
Report of the Bureau on Non-cooperation, 28, 52
Report of the Court on Non-cooperation, 69
Report of the High-Level Panel on Threats, Challenges and Change, 85, 187
Resolution 119, 114
Resolution 1265, 104
Resolution 1593, 33, 64
Resolution 76/262, 116, 198, 199
Resolutions, 48, 54, 58, 62, 66, 68, 72, 86, 107, 112, 114, 132, 154, 175, 185, 186, 191, 193, 198, 210
Responding to non-cooperation, 7, 12, 15, 24, 44, 48, 49, 75, 155, 168, 175, 180, 212, 215
Responses to non-cooperation. *See* Non-cooperation
Responsibility Not to Veto, 187, 188, 191, 211
Responsibility to Protect (R2P), 5, 7, 9, 15, 75, 80, 81, 85, 89, 93, 101, 105, 109, 112, 118, 126, 127, 151, 155, 179, 184, 188, 193, 201, 206, 208, 211, 212, 214, 215
Restitution, 129, 130, 173
Rome Statute, 2–6, 8, 9, 11, 12, 14, 15, 18–22, 25, 27–31, 34–37, 44, 48, 54, 57, 61–64, 68, 72, 75, 90, 94, 98, 99, 101, 112, 127, 135, 136, 141, 143, 149–151, 156–158, 162, 165, 169, 174–179, 192, 193, 201, 206, 208–210, 214, 215
Rule of law, 53, 98, 156, 157, 161
Rules of Procedure, 57, 163
Russia, 35, 37, 70, 71, 114, 117, 148
Russian annexation of Crimea, 139
Rwanda, 66, 74, 83

S

Satisfaction, 129, 173, 174
Secretariat, 162–165, 210
Security Council. *See* UN Security Council
Self-defence, 14, 81
Separate legal personality, 62
Settlement of disputes, 58, 59, 169, 170
South Africa, 24, 29–31, 36, 40, 44, 48, 60, 138, 144, 160, 169, 207
Southern African Litigation Centre, 29
Sovereignty, 18, 71, 82, 83, 85
State not Party to the Statute, 19
State Responsibility. *See* Articles on State Responsibility for Internationally Wrongful Acts
State sovereignty, 62, 63, 71, 82, 83
Sudan, 33, 34, 69, 195
Supreme Court of Appeal, 30, 31
Suspension, 168, 175, 177, 210, 213
Suspension of the right to nominate candidates, 175, 176
Symbolic damages. *See* Administrative Fines
Syria, 70, 111, 112, 199

T

Tadic. *See* Prosecutor v Dusko Tadic
The Greentree. *See* Greentree process
The Informal Working Group on International Tribunals, 74
The International Commission on Intervention and State Sovereignty, 83
The Prosecutor v Saif Al Islam Gaddafi, 38
The Prosecutor v Uhuru Muigai Kenyatta, 39
The Situation in Sudan. *See* Omar Al-Bashir
The UN General Assembly, 7, 92, 104, 105, 112, 113, 116, 136, 175, 184, 195, 197, 201

The Wall advisory opinion, 115, 138, 148, 198, 200
Third-party countermeasures. *See* Countermeasures
Timely and Decisive Response, 91–92, 142, 215
Travel of ICC suspects, 53
Trial Chamber, 39, 40, 42, 138
Trust Fund for Victims, 174

U
Uganda, 28
Ukraine, 34, 35, 116, 139, 169, 175, 199
United Nations, 60, 61, 63, 80, 82, 84, 117, 136, 150, 189
Uniting for Peace Resolution, 108, 113–116, 197, 198, 200, 212
UN Member States, 19, 63, 65, 68, 70, 72, 73, 83, 103, 106, 108, 112, 115, 189, 198, 212
UN resolutions, 61, 106, 138
UN Secretary-General, 8, 83, 86, 91, 93, 98–100, 106, 156, 187
UN Security Council, 6, 7, 14, 15, 19–21, 23, 25–28, 30–34, 38, 40, 42, 44, 48, 60, 66, 75, 86, 91, 93, 95, 101, 104, 127, 141, 143, 150, 151, 159, 201, 207, 209, 212, 215
Use of force, 14, 65, 80–82, 85, 91, 102, 107, 114, 137, 179, 194–196

V
Veto, 7, 70, 108, 114, 116, 117, 183, 184, 186–191, 198, 201, 211, 214
Vienna Convention on the Law of Treaties, 58

W
War crimes, 2, 5, 24, 35, 43, 80, 90, 94, 189
Warnings, 168, 172
Whaling in the Antarctic, 144
Working group, 74, 211, 213
World Summit, 108, 154
World Summit Outcome Document, 87, 108, 135, 154, 188

GPSR Compliance

The European Union's (EU) General Product Safety Regulation (GPSR) is a set of rules that requires consumer products to be safe and our obligations to ensure this.

If you have any concerns about our products, you can contact us on ProductSafety@springernature.com

In case Publisher is established outside the EU, the EU authorized representative is:

Springer Nature Customer Service Center GmbH
Europaplatz 3
69115 Heidelberg, Germany

Batch number: 10755292

Printed by Printforce, the Netherlands